The Plural Event

'Although philosophy is obliged from the start by the tradition that provides it with all the terms for understanding and meaning, it is also true that philosophy must refuse tradition's gift. How to remain faithful to the task of philosophy while preventing thinking from accepting and returning the gift, this is the question Andrew Benjamin pursues in *The Plural Event*. In a set of illuminating and provocative readings of Descartes, Hegel, and Heidegger, Benjamin demonstrates that to think philosophically means to *rework* philosophy, to deploy it anew, each time as if for the first time, in the abeyance of tradition. Through multifaceted and profound analyses, this book explores the ontological and temporal consequences of such an approach to thinking for philosophy, and seeks to reconceive it in terms of singularity and an ontology of the event.'

Professor Rodolphe Gasché

Andrew Benjamin teaches philosophy at the University of Warwick. His publications include *Translation and the Nature of Philosophy* and *Art, Mimesis and the Avant-Garde*, both Routledge.

The Plural Event

Descartes, Hegel, Heidegger

Andrew Benjamin

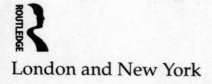

London and New York

First published 1993 by
Routledge
11 New Fetter Lane, London EC4P 4EE

Simultaneously published in the USA and Canada
by Routledge
29 West 35th Street, New York, NY 10001

Typeset in 10/12pt Palatino by
Ponting–Green Publishing Services, Chesham, Bucks
Printed and bound in Great Britain by
Clays Ltd, St Ives plc
Printed on acid-free paper

British Library Cataloguing in Publication Data
Benjamin, Andrew
  Plural Event: Descartes, Hegel, Heidegger
  I. Title
  190

Library of Congress Cataloging in Publication Data
Benjamin, Andrew E.
  The plural event : Descartes, Hegel, Heidegger /
  Andrew Benjamin.
      p.   cm.
  Includes bibliographical references and index.
    1. Events (Philosophy)   2. Ontology.
    3. Descartes, René, 1596–1650.
  4. Hegel, Georg Wilhelm Friedrich, 1770–1831.
  5. Heidegger, Martin, 1889–1976   I. Title.
  B105.E7B45   1993
  111–dc20   93–16570

ISBN 0–415–09528–X
    0–415–09529–8 (pbk)

. . . as always, for Jennifer

εἰδέναι χρὴ τὸν πόλεμον ἐόντα ξυνόν καὶ
δίκην ἔριν καὶ γίνομενα πάντα κατ' ἔριν
καὶ χρεώμενα

Heraclitus, 80

(It must be recognised that war is common to
all and conflict is justice and that the all comes to
be in accordance with conflict and is necessitated
by it.)

Contents

With this table of contents, as with the title, the occasional addition of proper names is intended to act as no more than a guide. Each section and the relation between sections raises the question of continuity and with it the philosophical question of the relationship between philosophy and its presentation. The problem of presenting philosophy beyond the hold of system will entail avoiding the paradoxical hold of the explanatory preface.

Acknowledgements	ix
Beginning	1
Opening presentation	5
The new again	15
Furthering beginning	22
Beginning again: naming beginning	30
Descartes' body of forgetting	34
Descartes' 'thing'	53
Intermezzo: conflict naming	61
Hegel's 'need'	83
Hegel's fruit	97
After fruit	106
Intermezzo: necessary relations	112
Opening gifts	129
In Heidegger's gift – sacrifice	134
Giving again	140
From here to eternity	157
Approaching events again	165

Working through   169
Translating repeating   178
Repeating – the open ended   183

Notes   193
Bibliography   205
Index   208

Beginning

Again an essay, a beginning, here marking out an attempt to reconsider, perhaps even to rework philosophy and a related critical philosophical practice in terms of events and their enjoined judgement.[1] Here the attempt – the work which is the process of its effectuation – forms an integral part of the result itself. The recognition of the difficulty of any easy separation of work and content can be taken as marking, in part, the contemporary within philosophy. Within the process of reconsidering and reworking it will be argued that relation and repetition are two components central to the envisaged task. (It goes without saying that the content of these two 'terms', as is the case with the above 'components', will be clarified in the work to come, thereby both forming and informing it.) Consequently rather than taking what is designated or denoted by *event*, *judgement*, *repetition* and *relation* as given and thereby admitting of an unproblematic repetition – a repetition articulated within the Same – they will come to be (re)formulated via an engagement with a number of philosophical texts in which the effect of their work can be traced.

In the engagement, in working through it, a point of departure is provided. Its being provided means that the task at hand will consist of working in relation to the presentation of these tracings, constructing thereby a relation. What is constructed will, at the same time, involve an inevitable reworking of relation; a rethinking of relation itself. The problematic question of relation's own 'relation' to its repetition and thus, in a sense, to its history cannot be avoided. What will remain as a possibility therefore, and this will be true for all the 'terms', 'concepts', etc. under discussion here, is a possible relation of non-relation to their given, thus pregiven, determinations. (The latter is the work of tradition.) This is a possibility brought about by the abeyance of these determinations. The realisation of this potential – a realisation whose need will always be strategic – indicates the way in which it is possible to think of the abeyance of tradition rather than its destruction. Working through the already given will form an integral part of the work's project. It will be the procedure for developing a renewed formulation of the event. Renewal in this instance will amount to a presentation of an ontology of events. It is a task that will sustain the proceeding. As will emerge – afterwards, within it as the afterwards – it is a task that will have already been begun.

Here, taking up the event will be marked by the incorporation of repetition; a repetition which will, of course, resist the necessity to repeat that construal of repetition handed down by tradition in order to be repeated. (Working with the procedure of distancing inherent in resistance forms a fundamental component of the present task.) Contemporaneous with formulating a conception of repetition and event in relation to a differential ontology is the related undertaking of being able to indicate how such an ontology works in order that the effect of its presence, its being present, incorporates the distancing of the aspirations of classical epistemology with the ensuing consequence that what emerges in its place – though still keeping the possibility of knowledge in site – is judgement. The effective dominance of epistemology, and its necessary incorporation of what will be termed the 'structure representation', will cede their place to judgement. It will be in terms of this emergence that the project of epistemology will itself be recast repeating knowledge by distancing the centrality of representation. In other words it is by resisting the necessary reciprocity between classical epistemology and representation that the possibility for a reworking of the stakes of knowledge will be opened up. Again as will be suggested the presence of movement and work, hence distancing, reworking, resisting, renewal, holding in abeyance, rethinking, etc., affirms the effective presence of repetition.

With a task of this complexity the initial problem may appear to be beginning. How, for example, would the distancing of dominance, the sundering of continuity, begin? The history of philosophy in its continual referral to beginning reflects its own preoccupation with establishing for itself its own point of departure; the gesture of foundationalism. Presenting the beginning as a problem is therefore a philosophical manoeuvre that already has a long history. As a consequence of the existence of that history, beginning with beginning will consist of an operation which, it can be argued, will have already begun. Even though this means that a procedure has already been identified, more will still be at stake here in this particular beginning than what would amount to nothing other than an assessment of the viability of a procedure which was itself advanced in terms of a beginning that did no more than concern itself with beginnings. In this instance there will be a different point of departure involving a substitution of that which is taken to be central. What this will mean at this stage is that the strategy that comes to be articulated within the terms set by the posited centrality of beginnings will itself be taken as central. The move away from the straightforward instantiation of beginning, beginning's problem – its being as given – will take place in relation to an opening that occurs within it – an opening occurring simultaneously with the identification of the difficulties encountered once the status of the beginning has become problematic and thus when the question of how to begin has itself been advanced; in other words once the problem of beginning has been advanced in its own terms. Moreover, though as a consequence, the difficulties in question bring with them their own set of preconditions, ones which generate and sustain the beginning problem as a problem.[2]

In general these conditions pertain to that specific conception of identity – here that particular construal of philosophical identity – in which identity is both established and secured as a result of an initial differentiation. Within the confines of such a philosophical approach the positing of beginning as being that which is in itself problematic forms part of the attempt to differentiate philosophy, or the locus of the philosophical, from, on the one hand, other activities of a similiar type or, on the other hand, sites mistakenly identified as the philosophical. It is only because of an initial, posited similarity – a similarity that will result in an inevitable difference – that the problem of where or how to begin does itself begin. The recognition of this state of affairs works to open up beginning.

The beginning once it is connected to that concern with beginnings, as would be evidenced in a more detailed account of the above example, now returns in terms of the necessity to take into consideration that which generates and sustains the 'problem'. Beginning again is a reworking signalled, at least initially, by the importance to be attached to conditions of existence. What these conditions amount to here is that which is at work within and thus which generates the specific beginning and with it the ubiquitous beginning problem. It is not as though the problematic nature of beginning exists in itself. Consequently it is the presence of an ineliminable link – a connection with structuring force – between preconditions and presentation that allows for an opening to be situated with greater precision. Here conditions, even though they cannot be reduced to it, are nonetheless still connected to that which is inscribed within and thus which structures not the emergence of philosophy *per se* (as if there were such an entity as philosophy *per se*) but that conception of the philosophical in which the identity of philosophy – the conception's identity – could only be established by a process of differentiation (the differentiation from the non-philosophical). In sum, therefore, the present pertinence of these conditions is connected to this particular formulation of the emergence of the philosophical.

While this may seem to amount to no more than the rehearsal of an uncritical acceptance of the structuring force within transcendental philosophy, such a semblance would in the end be misleading. What is involved is a different form of argument, one involving a different type of recognition. The guiding argument is neither foundational nor anti-foundational but rather stems from the recognition that philosophical arguments form part of philosophy's history and as such they are already related to the tradition of which they form a part. They are constituted as arguments by their historicity. It is this relation – be it implicit or explicit – that figures as providing in part the conditions of possibility for a given philosophical position. What will emerge in the following is a continual reworking of this claim such that its apparent affinity to essentialism – an essence given through the name, the name philosophy as in some way naming the essential – becomes a distancing that occasions the possibility of a thinking, a philosophical inauguration, that itself is enacted in the distancing of the either/or of sameness and novelty (the latter marking the ontology and temporality of fashion). There will be a reworking that marks the abeyance rather than the redemption of the essence. It will be suggested throughout the work to come that the impossibility of any standard philosophy of destruction (Descartes, Heidegger) demands that strategies marked out by terms such as abeyance, displacing, distancing, etc. be given central consideration.

Opening presentation

Establishing identity, the identity of the philosophical through the work of differentiation, takes place, for example, in Hegel's argument that while philosophy may involve thought it needs to be distinguished from what he describes as 'thought in general'. The force of this distinction lies first in the possibility, once it is formulated, of presenting philosophy as escaping any reduction to common sense. In general terms – i.e. in terms not simply Hegelian – this would amount to trying to overcome the reduction of a prevailing identity to a constituent part. It must be noted that here this presentation has to take place, and can only take place, in terms of this formulation. The importance of avoiding this type of reduction is found in the resulting argument of Hegel's that what is described as 'common sense' is out of step with consciousness itself. Again in broader terms this means that the constituent part is not in accord with the prevailing identity or universal. Second, it gives philosophy specificity while maintaining its connection to consciousness. It is therefore simultaneously associated and dis-associated. Third, the consequence of this mutual association and disassociation is that it allows philosophy to contain the truth of consciousness – a truth that is inevitably betrayed by common sense, even though common sense is presented as itself already comprising an aspect of consciousness. The identity of philosophy arises out of this differentiation. Establishing identity as a result of the process of differentiation is only possible because of the nature of the initial association. (The necessary presence of this reciprocity of dependence must be noted.) This movement, rehearsing the problem of identity as linked to the relationship between associa-tion and disassociation, will be examined in greater detail at a later stage. What is here identified as association and disassociation, it will be argued, forms an integral part of what can be called after Hegel, though not following him, the logic of diremption. The interplay of association and disassociation will be redefined in terms of the problem of the chance or contingent occurrence, a problem that is itself articulated within – thus articulating – the logic of diremption. (It is therefore unthinkable outside of it. The mere positing of diremption is no more than a naive gesture, gesturing towards the philosophical.) Logic in this context means the structured presentation and strategic use of diremption; diremption as discursive. The use here is its work. With diremption there remains the difficulty of what it names and thus to what extent it can be understood as naming diremptively. The turning backwards and forwards of terms on themselves attests, it will be argued, to the anoriginal presence of a differential ontology. (In the end it may be that diremption names the event.) It will be further suggested that this is an ontological claim and not simply one that is concerned with semantics and thus polysemy.

Elements of the above presentation of the emergence of phil- osophy – a presentation as adumbration – shadows the position advanced by Hegel in the 'Introduction' to the *Shorter Logic*. Its location in the 'Introduction', and therefore as comprising part of the introductory strategy – the strategy of introduction as begin- ning – is central. As a result, therefore, it is a formulation that gives rise both to a specific presentation of philosophy and a particular way in which philosophy comes to be presented. In each instance what is involved is an attuning; a related accord; one which can be provisionally described as being constrained to mark out and sustain the relationship, the tune, between the conception of philosophy that is being presented and the presentation itself. Here the constraint marks out a homology. Homology emerges, therefore, as an already present necessity. The unavoidability of its presence is linked to the role it has to play. Homology is present – effectively present – in its having provided, in terms of either its presence or absence, an absence always to be overcome, a con- stitutive element of the formulation of the problem of beginnings. It is thus that what is figured here is a particular orchestration of the philosophical; in other words the presentation of an envisaged harmonic reciprocity between the conception of the task and its enactment. It is expressed by Hegel in the following.

> As it is only in form that philosophy is distinguished from other modes of attaining an acquaintance with this same sum of being, it must necessarily be in harmony/in accord/in tune (*übereinstimmung*) with actuality and experience.
>
> (SL 8, 47)[3]

Within the terms advanced here the consequences that are of immediate interest are those that pertain both to this 'harmony' and then its subsequent enactment. (Subsequent must have a correlative rather than a purely sequential force.) The relation between 'harmony' (this construal of harmony and thus this instance of its naming) and its enactment will be articulated in terms of its own intrinsic, even though implicit, conception of time. The temporality of this relation identifies a process within the subject/object distinction. It is thereby taken as figuring in how a given disunity comes to be unified. These consequences can be developed in terms of their implict temporality and as such it will become clear that time, initially here presented by the work of tenses, is inseparable from specific modes of being and styles of recognition.

The time in question will include at least two interrelated components. The first is that the 'harmony' to which Hegel refers is not just already established – it must be recognised as such. In other words it is not the existence of the harmony taken on its own that is essential, it is also, and equally, the recognition of its existence as harmony and therefore the recognition of its already having been established that is central. Precluded, therefore, is the temporal dimension of experimentation. The recognition will come to articulate the already present harmony as itself and in so doing maintain as precluded the possible presence of the alterity of ad-venture: the advent of an event. The second component also involves presuppositions and consequences. Even though it is clear that the recognition and the articulation cannot be out of accord with the harmony, they must also, and more emphatically, comprise part of the formation of the harmony. Furthermore while it is true to argue that actual philosophy within the frame of this argument is – i.e. is philosophy – only in so far as it is in tune with itself, there is an additional point that must be made. It is simply that were philosophy to be viewed as discordant – as in itself discordant and thereby as being in essence conflictual – then such a recognition would have to have misrecognised the nature of a philosophical accord and therefore of the actuality of philosophy. As a consequence it would have had to fail to recognise the fundamental identity within difference and thus of the whole within the singular; moreover it would also be constrained to have failed to recognise the actualised possibility of avoiding such misrecognitions. Within the latter purview and thus only within it the history of philosophy would become the history of a series of particular and idiosyncratic positions. In broad terms it is the possibility of this form of singularity that Hegel opposes in the *Difference Essay* in his critique of Reinhold.[4] The opposition is repeated throughout his writings in terms of the general problem of the *'eigentümlich'*.[5] Here propriety and the particular engage and are engaged in the formation of that which, in part, generates and accounts for what for Hegel is the 'need' for philosophy, The 'need', this 'craving', will be examined in greater detail at a later stage.

Hegel's argument in the *Shorter Logic* proceeds with the implicit assertion that philosophy has always been potentially in accord with itself. Its having 'always been' thus allows for philosophy to have a history. However, it is only with its own actuality that this accord can be presented as such. What this means is that its own actuality is the necessary precondition for its being presented as a complete and self-completing harmony. It comes to be actualised as itself within itself. Writing such a score is therefore a writing up – after the event – of a self-enclosing and enclosed totality. Hegel's own image of circles within circles creates this picture. It spatialises the dynamic harmony within philosophy by framing what for Hegel is the necessary interarticulation of philosophy and presentation. The image is the intended self-presentation of the work of homology.

> Each of the parts of philosophy is a philosophical whole, a circle rounded and complete in itself. In each of these parts, however, a philosphical Idea is found in a particular specificality or medium. The single circle, because it is a real totality, bursts through the limits imposed by its special medium, and gives rise to a wider circle. The whole of philosophy in this way resembles a circle of circles. The Idea appears in each single circle, but, at, the same time the whole idea is constituted by the system of these peculiar phases, and each is a necessary member of the organisation.
>
> (32)

The writing of philosophy – the writing and the philosophy at work in Hegel's text – is, as a result of this harmonic organisation, inextricably linked to a type of mirroring which is itself only possible within and as the process of reflection. The consequential action of the interplay of circles, its work, is presented at work and thereby enacted in a representation that aspires, of necessity, to be a pure presentation. This is the presentational result of the intended centrality of reflection which necessitates that what could be described as the work of the work must neither intrude into nor alter the presentation itself. This obligation is written into philosophy. Philosophy, in order to be philosophy, is obliged from the start. It is thus that the *Encyclopedia* is written and with it that all philosophical writing is thereby constrained and obliged. Philosophy here functions with its own form of the imperative.

As has already been indicated, what is under consideration at this stage is not the viability of this particular construal of philosophy, but rather the interconnection between the conception of philosophy within it and the mode of presentation (i.e. philosophical writing) that such a construal entails. This interplay, marking an interdependence between philosophy and presentation, gives rise to another question. With it the place of opposition, a counter positing, yields its place to distance; the question of distance and with it of abeyance. Its most straightforward formulation is: how, given the inherent reciprocity between task and presentation, can a philosophy that resists the reduction to the systemic – the work of systems – be presented? Maintaining the semblance of a Hegelian frame means that there are two possible responses to this question. The first would be to argue that such a construal of philosophy misconstrues and that therefore it should always be denied the name philosophy (an obligation of philosophical propriety). The second would be to respond by arguing that as a presentation of philosophy it is inadequate because it is an incomplete expression of the philosophical. Again what is of interest here is the basis of such responses. This can be elucidated by recognising that the larger area of inquiry – albeit philosophical inquiry – to which the first element of this twofold response gives rise is the problem of naming since both involve the denial of the right to use the name or to take it over. Here what is generated by this specific state of affairs is the question: what is named by the name philosophy?

In regard to the second response it is clear that the formulation of incompleteness is itself dependent, while again demanding a reciprocity of dependence, on a particular construal of completion. (Within the purview of naming, completion can be understood as that state of affairs in which the name names, or will name, absolutely; a type of coextensivity between name and named.) In general terms while such responses to the possibility of distancing the dominance of system – its re-placement – may appear to be straightforward and unproblematic since they appear simply to counter the activity (here philosophy) by denying it the name that it seeks to have or take over, this appearance is belied in two distinct ways.

The first is by the presence in each response of their own sets of preconditions and entailments all of which work to locate the responses within a set of already identified philosophical practices (identified *as* philosophical). It would follow, therefore, that any attempt to justify (or counter) these practices would simply rehearse the problem that the response to the attempt to distance system was intended to overcome. The second is that once expressed – perhaps reformulated – in terms of naming, it then emerges that what remains unthought within these responses is the very conflict that the manipulation of the name is intended to obviate. The attribution and use of names involves a dimension of power that only overcomes the presence of conflict to the extent that the effective presence of both – power and conflict – is forgotten. In other words what is forgotten is at the same time the original conflict as well as the ensuing one. Forgetting is of course never a simple happening; indeed, as will be suggested, the interarticulation of conflict and naming can be taken as harbouring the structure of the event. (As will emerge because of the effective presence of the anoriginal plurality of the event, its structure will be harboured in a number of sites.)

The complexity at work in the practice of any attempt to formulate philosophy beyond the range of system provides, for the most part, the content of the work to come. This does not mean that the arbitrary has replaced the necessary. What is involved, however, is the necessity to replace the systematically arbitrary use of such oppositions. Replacing consists of working through places that have already been given. Countering and distancing mean that the counter move cannot be a simple op-position. There is more to be considered here than that which is framed either by the logic of the either/or or the strategy of counter positing. Acknowledging the already given – the presented as gift – demands that the presence of tradition be taken into consideration and therefore that the process of giving no longer remain unquestioned and thus simply accepted. Taking over tradition will involve having to admit its complexity.

No matter what conception of tradition is in play it can never preclude the play of negativity, namely that gesture which attempts to enact tradition's refusal. The gift of tradition – here understood formally as the already given – allows for a formulation of refusal which takes the form of the attempt to deny the gift; to return it by turning it back. What is intended is a denial, one with the specific consequence of casting the gift from sight/site. Refusal would become the project for a projected complete disassociation, actual op-position. While refusal fails in its attempt to counter, its position – the project of refusal – must nonetheless still be considered. The importance of this consideration is that it will open up the possibility of a different way of construing the temporality of the gift and with it the ontology of the given. Rather than taking the present as the site of an intended refusal – albeit a purported and in the end failed refusal – it will be reworked such that it will come to be given as that site given in and for repetition.

One way in which the project of refusal could be enacted would be in terms of a singularity that was presented as an occurrence that no longer played a role in and thus which formed no part of an economy of exchange – exchange here marking the presence of meaning, its being given and taken, thereby forming part of what would amount to a hermeneutic economy. What refusal entails in this instance would be the intended complete disassociation from the workings of an economy generated and guaranteed by the logic of the gift. In regards to tradition the gift comprises the present provision of the terms for understanding, meaning, etc. Refusal and disassociation would envisage as possible an occurrence presented as a singularity precluding the possibility of any relation. With this formulation there emerges what could be described as the structure of singularity.

It is precisely this structure of singularity that, it will be suggested, provides in certain instances the effective force of Heidegger's formulation of the possibility of thinking Being (*Sein*) independently of its relation to entities (*Seinden*). Due to its work, therefore, it is this structure that will be questioned by attempting to show that it is itself only possible because of the retained presence – albeit a necessary presence – of varying movements of exclusion; i.e. sacrifice, blinding, forgetting and the obliteration of relation. Each of these movements is related and the work of one compounds that of another. The structure of singularity is not limited to the project of thinking Being. Even though it demands another orientation, it can be seen as figuring in the structured possibility of the 'new' and thus also of a certain presentation of the temporality of the new. This occurs to the extent that the new is conceived as being the consequence of an intention to establish that which is both original and absolutely singular.

In the argument developed throughout the essay to come the singular and the new will cede their place not to the affirmation of continuity but to the rearticulation of repetition; its becoming subject to the process that it, itself, names. Singularity and continuity form part of an opposition that will be displaced in being reworked such that both continuity and the singular – even the aspirations of the absolutely singular – reappear beyond the constraints of their founding opposition. It is in precisely this way that the logic of oppositions can be seen to founder. The role/rule of intention now sustains its own collapse. It remains, of course, maintained as found(er)ing; maintaining with it the ineliminable presence of relation.

The interplay of maintaining and found(er)ing means that what is envisaged here – in part comprising the task at hand – is the attempt to allow for the occurrence of the event by taking up, opening, the language of tradition via a reworking and repetition of both concepts and the form of their presentation. The procedure, as has been noted, will involve working through a number of texts. The work in question and the works questioned give rise to the realised possibility of a philosophical presentation that will stem from this reworking precisely because it enacts it. It must be added that despite the presence of enactment, its taking place, the philosophical presentation is not reducible to it (again an irreducibility that marks the contemporary). What comes to be enacted defies the law of system by opening up philosophy as an event that precludes, while not occluding, the possibility of self-enclosure. The presentational and philosophical necessity of homology will have been supplanted. The enactment involves the inscription of spacing as the mark of, and as marking, the irreducibility of philosophy and presentation. This irreducibility brings with it its own construal of methodological time, for with the writing out of presentational prediction, the necessary teleology of style, what comes to be opened up is a writing responding to the need to trace – i.e. neither copying nor imitating – the consequences to which this irreducibility gives rise.

As has already been indicated, central to this reworking is the plural event and its necessary relation to judgement. Their articulation and involvement while fundamental are yet to be clarified. They will come to be deployed, however, within and as part of the activity they delimit. Working through texts both philosophical and literary does not serve to place philosophy in the space occupied by commentary, as though one were replacing the other. The logic of the either/or will not form the frame within which a re-enactment of the relationship between philosophy and presentation takes place. As a beginning it can be suggested that what is designated here as 'working through' involves and deploys a particular stance and understanding of tradition.[6] The designation attests to its site and with it the already present instantiation of tradition as providing an eliminable locus of relation. And yet this still leaves open the question of the precise nature of tradition.

A possible even though provisional answer to the question 'what is tradition?' could always start with the relatively unproblematic linkage between tradition and communication on the one hand and tradition and community on the other. Tradition in this sense becomes the work of history whose articulation is understood – hence the need to incorporate communication – in so far as there already exists a group to understand it; hence the presence of community conceived as the locus of understanding. Despite its encompassing nature it is because this answer leaves open the inevitable question of how these links and movements are themselves to be understood that, even in its own terms, it is far from satisfactory. In other words merely positing community and communication only compounds the problem, for the conception of identity and semantics presupposed in any formulation that community and communication are given must themselves be clarified in advance. At the very least, therefore, this move will have to take up and respond to the question: in terms of what will this clarification take place? An answer to this type of question cannot be provided by either 'community' or 'communication'. If, however, the nature of the question is changed and a shift of emphasis takes place then a preliminary response is possible. It will arise from the identification within the process of linking tradition, community and communication of the specific conception of time at work within the process itself.

The links between tradition, community and communication are in general, thus traditionally, envisaged as establishing and thereby as being established within temporal continuity. However here, rather than accepting continuity as given and therefore accepting it as that which provides history's temporality, a different tack will be taken. In the place of the closing of time, tradition's time must be opened, reopened. One consequence of this opening will be that instead of locating tradition within time, where time is central and present as historical continuity, there will not just be a different approach and thus a change in direction, the temporality of changing – i.e. the temporality proper to a shift within philosophical orientations – will have to be taken into consideration. As a point of departure this will mean that the relations within which tradition is given will appear as being of greatest significance. In being given they provide the site of reworking. These relations come to be given while coming to be established through the process of interpretation. This interplay of giving and receiving, of working and reworking, of presentation and repetition, signals the presence of a more complex temporality and at the same time of a conception of giving and receiving in which what is given is reworked beyond the given and therefore potentially beyond its given designation or meaning. It is this reworking that becomes the reception; a becoming incorporating the twofold of existence and propriety. Opening up interpretation, as with the opening up of the semantic, can only be accounted for by reference to the ontology of the event. As linkage opens itself up to being rethought, time is repeated anew and with it the present will only ever be able to be constructed as the site of repetition; an intense present. In sum what this allows for is the possibility of breaking the complacency of tradition, where tradition is understood as necessitating the sedimentation of 'past' occurrences and thus the increasingly regimented and rigidified determinations of meaning and understanding.[7] Distancing in this instance will involve the effective presence of a form of repetition.

One of the problems that must be pursued, therefore, will be the time of tradition. What will emerge from undertaking this task is the possibility of thinking tradition within the terms set by repetition. It will be necessary to distinguish between various construals and hence presentations of repetition. In the same way it is essential to note that each one brings with it a particular temporality. Repetition, the differences between its varying formulations, involves the differences maintained by irreducible ontologico-temporal concatenations. While an obvious question to be addressed here would concern the formulation and with it the implications of this irreducibility, the more immediate task at hand is the possibility of thinking tradition beyond the interpretive purview of its own tradition. The 'beyond' here marks the presence of relation and as such attests to its ineliminable primordiality. It opens up the necessity to reformulate relation through its positioning as spacing. Relation becomes therefore more than the mere mark of spatiality, that mark in which the presence of relation is no more than the emergence of spacing. Spacing and relation involve more than that state of affairs in which one becomes a description or formulation of the other. Indeed spacing is implicated in more than spatial relations. Its presence and the consequences of its mode of being present will come to figure within the site of judgement while at the same time providing judgement's necessity, the necessity for its effective presence. Judgement is the response to irreducibility – the status of the event – itself a spacing given within and thus held by ontology. Irreducibility is not undecidability. It is thus that spacing will emerge as another possibility for ontological difference. It is the latter point that will be approached at a suitable interval in relation to Leibniz. Relation and spacing will be taken within, though in the end beyond, the confines of the Leibnizian monad.

The new again

Again, what is involved is a type of back tracking occurring by opening up – reopening – the question of tradition (forcing its re-presentation though now as an open question). Here this will be done by allowing for the possibility that the work of tradition can be suspended with the occurrence of the new; the positing of the new. Accepting this possibility as a point of departure entails, as has already been suggested, that the new take on, and take it on of necessity, the status of a singular event; the new as that which announces the presence of a unique occurrence, occurring without relation. It follows from such a formulation that its possibility is *ipso facto* also the possibility of an original and absolutely singular event. However, even in accepting the force of the supposition of actual singularity, the singular without relation, it remains the case that such a possibility has a history. The new repeats in this precise sense therefore the history of beginnings. Its relation to its own history is always already there.

Again this state of affairs must be taken as implying that it is through its own history – the history of the positing of absolute singularity – that the new needs to be worked. History, here, in addition to providing the new with a continuity such that what is designated historically as the new forms no more than a harmless self-repetition, also works to construct a specific problem, namely history's 'outside'; the abeyance of the all inclusive presence and interpretive dominance of that history. An outside which would take the form of history's other; the other of self-representation's continuity. Again it should be remembered that otherness (alterity) cannot be a simple op-position a counter positing yielding discontinuity.

The problem once posed opens up the possibility of a space beyond the continuity of the new as history and thus as the historical, a space that can be worked back. (The new in this instance would still be linked to repetition in that repetition (itself) rather than being overcome could only ever be reworked, thereby becoming always more than itself and with it indicating, retroactively, that it was never just itself. There will have never been an original itself.) Understanding what it is at stake in this reworking will emerge from the attempt to clarify this link and with it the inherent relation. The difficulty at this stage, however, concerns the consequences of redeploying the new, of using it anew. What this will mean is that the precise nature of renewal will itself have to be renewed within and as the very process that it would seek to identify. Forming this process will be more than just a presentation of interpretation as a type of redemption articulated within the temporality of *Nachträglichkeit*[8] since it will also be the case that this will occur within the process itself; in sum occurring as its result. In broad terms what is involved here is the problem of tradition and tradition's time. Accepting that this is what is at stake will mean that redeployment will amount to moving the new from the frame of history in which it functions as a chronological marker – one with the potential to periodise – to the realm of interpretation. (Interpretation here has a generality that despite its marking a process still stands in need of greater clarification e.g. what still remains is the problem of how the question of the ontology of the object of interpretation can itself come to be posed. The endurance of such problems opens up a further area for philosophical work by extending the reworking of the event's ontology.)[9]

Once the new is moved from the frame of history this has the immediate consequence of necessitating a reformulation of time. However, the reformulation cannot turn historical time (the time of historicism) and thus the time marked out by chronology and sequence into an end the departure from which constructs the reformulation – the reworking – into a singular event. What must be maintained is the possibility of dating within the impossibility of its providing the frame of thinking time..Henceforth historical time – the positing of it as given – will have given way to questions concerning meaning, thereby yielding the time of interpretation and bringing with it its own reinscription of the historical. This reformulation will concern, in addition, though not as an addition, the temporality of relation. Time, if the move from continuity to interpretation is assumed, can no longer be expressed in either historical or chronological terms, i.e. periods or dates. Time and the new – with their own envisaged relations – will form and thereby comprise ineliminable elements within the actuality of inter-pretation itself. The displacing of chronology does not mean that it has been replaced. All interpretations will bear a date. Dating, however, does not provide the temporality of interpretation; it merely allows it to bear a signature – to be signed – and thus to bring into play the attendant risk that interpretation henceforth will always be able to take place in relation to the signature. The impossibility of overcoming dating, and with it the retention of relation despite the desire for absolute singularity, inscribes the lack of determinacy within the signature into that which it signs. The stability of the signature is marked by its instability, the consequence being that it is the very absence of a singular determination – complete decidability – that allows both for the positing of decidability, the decided as singular, and then for its deconstruction.

The new must be seen as continuing to figure within a number of predetermined configurations. There is an already pre-existing language of the new involving these different configurations, e.g. the new checks continuity; the new as opposed to the old; the new breaks repetition. Within the standard presentation of these con-figurations, and because the new is only present in them as a marker providing the possibility of historical specificity, the components themselves remain unquestioned. Moreover the rela-tion which links and separates them is simply given and thus present as the consequence of positing. Still working within the move to interpretation it can be argued further that once the new is placed within that realm this will mean that attention then will have to be paid to the claim made by the designation new, i.e. the claim the new makes for itself. The constituent parts within the predetermined configurations will need to be examined in greater detail, as will the relation within which the contrast itself comes to be enacted. In the end it is the relation that is of greatest significance. Again what comes to be opened up is the general problem of how relation is to be understood. The immediate difficulty here is the priority – in both a temporal as well as an evaluative sense – that is to be given to the general. In moving from the opposition between general and particular the general loses its essential unifying force and becomes the site of irreducible particularity. As such it will open up the name. The name, working as it does within a logic similiar to the signature, will open once it is recognised that any particular specificity given to it must be understood first in relation to the ontology of the named – i.e. that which can never be represented as itself because there is no singular *itself* to represent – and second, and relatedly, as a pragmatic determination. Again what is central is ontology and time – and thus what will be designated as the ontologico-temporal that allows for plurality and irreducibility. Diversity and variety will give way to the ontology of the event. In giving way they re-emerge as continual after effects. Construed outside of strictly ontological concerns they become moments of the Same.

Returning to the specific it is within the actuality of inter-pretation that the new will always involve, either explicitly or implicitly, a claim made in relation to tradition. If the claim concerns the affirmed presence of the absolutely new then, though only on the level of intentional logic, this will both isolate and identify that moment or place at which tradition is not renewed.[10] In other words rather than its being a renewing of tradition the absolutely new will intend, in the sense that its logic will work toward, tradition's non-renewal; the refusal of the already given. There are two problems at the centre of this understanding of the new.

The first is the potential to disrupt singularity once the forgotten presence of the claim's necessary presence (either as a signature or as a name is recovered). The second and more immediate problem is that in spite of its intentional logic what is ignored by such a claim is an implicit mediation that forms part of the designation itself. The new as the absolutely other is already mediated by its being the other. Alterity involves a minimal structure of recognition and therefore something occurs in the taking over of alterity as alterity. Alterity will therefore involve relation, a relation that will inevitably be more than the connections established by recognition. (Recognition runs the risk of always staying at the level of objectivity.) What must be maintained is first that there is always something in addition to pure alterity and second that the content already present in recognition is in fact ineliminably present when recognition is constituted as interpretation. In other words, a constitution that takes place in the move away from that elemental recognition of the objectivity of the object and towards its meaning, towards that is the advent of the event. What comes into play with it – almost as marking its presence – is the necessary interplay of the hermeneutical (a term which at the very least covers both interpretation and semantics, the range of meaning) and the ontological.

The inherent presence of mediation brings to the fore the appearance of a paradox informing the new (the new now as an original determination – admitting of mediation – and thereby, and of necessity, existing in contrast to the new as the posited absolutely other). It is within the terms set by mediation and the apparent paradox that the new will initially come to be situated. It is inevitable, for example, that tradition is both renewed and not renewed. This inevitability both marks the impossibility of the absolutely new and affirms the possibility of the new. This twofold is marked by relation. Understanding that there is more at work here than a simple paradox will involve allowing for a consideration that will take place in addition to any understanding that is limited by the internal components of the predetermined configurations – old/new, continuity/new, repetition/new. The 'consideration' will not be the addition of a further element, compounding the tradition of the new, but rather it will mark the abeyance of these predetermined configurations.

How, therefore, is relation to be thought? Answering this question will lead to the displacing of paradox because of its necessary privileging of the terms given by the logic of identity. The consequence of this projected displacing will mean that the force of this logic will no longer dominate. It follows from this logic's abeyance linked to the ensuing centrality being given to the enactment of a repetition beyond the Same – provisionally the logic of the again and the anew – that the philosophical problem of identity will be repeated anew. It will be therefore in being given again. Returning to the question of relation, a start can be made with the new's claim, one made for the absolutely new – a claim which it claims for itself and is thereby acclaimed by itself, though always within the terms provided by its own intentional logic.

The claim of the new – a claim that must incorporate the claim to be the new – announces a relation. However, within the claim, either of or for the absolutely new, a claim it must be added that has the same status as unmediated desire, the relation has to be cancelled. The necessity is binding. The absolutely new, in order that it be absolutely new, must appear as the singular event, one both isolated and isolable, an occurrence whose time – whose now – must be thought in terms of a singular and unmediated present. Again the necessity is binding. Given the emergence of this necessity there is a necessary counter. Against the former necessity it must be recognised that the relation that is in fact announced – announced of necessity – is the one enacted within the denial of relation. There is thus a limit to this movement. While the interplay of denial and/as affirmation may yield paradox, paradox does not exist in itself. It is rather that paradox marks, by marking out, the difficulties encountered at the borders of the logic of identity. Nonetheless the work of paradox – the appearance of the co-present affirmation and denial of identity – needs to be retained, thereby introducing a further necessity. The presence of another form of necessity has to be acknowledged for it is also the case that the singularity of the event must be sustained though no longer as an element within paradox. What will be sustained, however, is neither the absolutely singular nor its presence as an addition. Paradox will give way to repetition which in turn reclaims the stakes of identity by staking out the claim for identities within difference. Such an identity will henceforth be designated as the pragma, a being within a generalised becoming. It should be clear that the use of this term is to designate a formal state of affairs. What is yet to be clarified is a more exact description of the nature of the relation between its formal existence and any specific content.

The singular occurrence cannot be denied, it insists. Its singularity works within the relation that denies absolute singularity but in which singularity comes to be enacted and maintained. (It will be seen that singularity when expressed in an absolute way involves the twofold presence of destruction and forgetting as integral to the realisation of that which is entailed by its intentional logic.) Once again it is essential to note that were this described as no more than a paradox then that would be to construe singularity – its impossible possibility – within the terms given by the logic of identity. The singular event comes to be singular only in its not being the absolutely singular. It is therefore the work of relation that generates and sustains singularity. Furthermore, the precise nature of the relation will always be determined by the event, as an event. The event's relations, accepting all the complexity that this possessive entails, are themselves the site where tradition is enacted. Enacting here designates a presencing. What is presented and the force of the presentation will always be specific. It is thus that the specific form taken by its presence resists automatic generalisation. The result of the impossible possibility of universality is that, because the claim of the new will always involve a particular relation to tradition, the relation cannot itself be separated from the presence of tradition. Relation is, in this precise sense, always already present; its primordiality is thereby affirmed. With that affirmation comes the necessity to recognise that primordiality entails actualised particularity. There are two problems, however, that stem from this formulation. Both will admit of an attempted resolution via the introduction of naming.

The first problem involves how this inevitable link to tradition is to be understood. The second is opened up by the first as it pertains to the possibility that despite the inevitability of the link it is still not the case that the work of tradition is enacted in the same way and thus with the same force in each instance. The work of tradition may itself be a complex marked by irreducibility; it would thus no longer have either a straightforward referent or designate a unified place in which the unity of its content is handed down. The lack of unity or a determined referent means that to some extent the problematic element identified here re-enacts the source of semantic confusion that theories of naming attempt to resolve. Despite a tenuous beginning the link between naming and tradition can be taken a step further if what is taken as central to approaching tradition can be formulated within the confines of the question 'what is named by tradition?' It is in terms of naming and thus, in the end, the name as event that will provide a way of taking up the presentation of philosophy in texts by Descartes and Hegel, philosophy here understood as a response to the question, 'what is philosophy?' The name philosophy, the becoming of the name, becomes the tradition of philosophy.

The temporality of the putative absolutely singular event, i.e. the event when posed outside of the complexity marked by paradox, comprises a present devoid of mediation. It is thus that it is thought to open up a future or futural possibility without relation. In reworking the event beyond paradox and thus in terms of repetition the presence of time must itself be reposed. The repetition of time, and with it the specifically entailed mode of being, is of greatest significance to the extent that it can be argued that present with the event – though not within the event as though the event and the relation were constructed as a type of inside/outside opposition – are the relations that sustain it and which therefore mediate it. The event in becoming complex – its complexity therefore becoming it – gives rise to two related questions. Both will be addressed in detail further on. The first is how the temporality of this event will be understood. The second is the related question of what the nature is of the concepts and categories through which this understanding is to take place. The complex opens up the question of its own understanding. As such tradition is reintroduced, since tradition, its repetition within and as the Same, is that which of its accord can be taken as providing the possibility for understanding; this is the work of the already given. In pursuing this line of argument it is possible to suggest that the understanding and the rules that it provides comprise the effect of tradition. Here simple cognition gives way to history[11] (history within philosophy, marked out and named by tradition). Tradition, the time of tradition and the question of understanding work to designate a further opening.

Furthering beginning

Despite the centrality that has been given to becoming (and with it to repetition) the first move in any response to the question of time – the time of tradition – must begin by noting that neither the Bergsonian concept of *durée*[12] with its emphasis on pure becoming to which 'intuition' (*l'intuition*) provides the only access, nor a present construed as pure intensity – pure as singular – and thus constructed as a site devoid of conflicting values because difference is only ever understood as either variety or diversity rather than being of itself differential, can provide the basis for an adequate answer to this question if they are taken as ends in themselves. Nonetheless they gesture towards such a basis in that neither can account for a formulation of repetition which sanctions – beyond the range of paradox – identities within difference. Indeed they are to a certain extent constrained to exclude such a construal of repetition. Accepting repetition will allow for a connection to be established between paradox understood as the active presence of the logic of identity and time (the connection takes the form of an interarticulation). What must be avoided is the either/or in which it would be argued that, because the new cannot be reduced to the temporal moment, it thereby follows that the new can never be present, as the new, at the present.

While it is inherently problematic trying to incorporate the intention of a projection – be it artistic or interpretive – whose aim is the new, it remains the case that a type of intentionality must be maintained (maintained, that is, as the self-attribution of the work's purpose). Retaining a conception of intentionality does not mean that intention is to be ascribed to an authorial subject. On the contrary it will form part of the project and thus pertain to its intentional logic. (This logic is, as has been suggested, the complicated relationship between task and enactment as conceived in and by the work.) Displacing the centrality of projection as a simple teleology means removing the specificity that comes to be attached to the telos. Intended projection contains what, to use Walter Benjamin's expression, can be described as 'motifs of redemption'.[13] These motifs are realised once the projection is reworked such that it becomes no more than pure project and which works therefore to re-work the present as a site of differential intensity; a throwing forward whose force is internal rather than directional. And yet that internality will itself either have or come to acquire direction. The work of project – the pro-jection – will take on the character of both the provisional and the pragmatic. The presence of movement deriving from either internality or the external acquisition of direction points to an opening and thus a division between different forms of philosophical (and artistic) strategies. As such, of course, what is also necessarily implicated in any further consideration of this movement is the ontology of the object of interpretation as that which sustains and thus which provides the materiality that grounds and sanctions this particular type of strategy. What is involved here is a division between, on the one hand, a given relation to tradition that affirms the abeyance of tradition's dominance, the affirmation being the work of the work, while on the other, the abeyance only emerging as the consequence of having had to work against the object's intentional logic.

This twofold connection between internality and direction is of fundamental importance. The 'coming to acquire' introduces – or rather reintroduces – repetition since it signals the work's own repetition, its being in being repeated, within interpretation and thus as interpretation. (Interpretation becomes a type of repetition, thereby dividing repetition, turning it – 'repetition' – into a name and furthermore signalling again the necessity to take up the link between interpretation and *Nachträglichkeit*.) The repetition of the work – its being given again – cannot be adequately formulated in chronological terms. Chronology would merely account for the site of its repetition, its date. This on its own is far from sufficient. What needs to be understood is that further element that sanctions repetition, namely the work itself.

The work is a complex event. Complexity is marked out by the work's own irreducibility. The site of difference – the complex event – involves difference as differential since what is at stake here is the ontology of the work, the object of interpretation. Difference in this instance is not diversity. And yet of course difference can be said to exist. However, what is the existence of difference? What is it that exists as different? If difference exists – i.e., if it can be said to be – then irreducibility pertains to modes of existence i.e. to modes of being. As such therefore difference becomes ontological difference. It is not as though interpretations are ontologically different as such, it is rather that the presence of an irreducibility of the work (and the object in the end becomimg the event) to itself as being that which sanctions the plurality of interpretations can itself only be accounted for ontologically. Consequently the work is the site of anoriginal heterogeneity.[14] As such it sanctions its own repetition – a repetition involving difference rather than identity – within interpretation. Each interpretation will be a singular occurrence, the pragma, understood in the beginning as actuality within potentiality. The singular occurrence, however, will be marked on the one hand by the impossibility of the identity – e.g. the coextensivity – of actuality and potentiality, and on the other by the necessary presence of relation, the necessity of the latter emerging because of the necessity of the former. It is only in terms of relation that it is possible for there to be a repetition in which something can be said to have occurred for the first time. The reworking of the work is its coming to acquire a determination that is new. The movement here marks an opening. The recurrence of the work – recurring as the pragma with the event – is not the eternal recurrence of the new but a repetition in which the reworking of the work means that it comes to be presented both again and anew. Here the new figures within and as repetition. It will be addressed in terms of that which both identifies and articulates the interplay of identity and repetition, namely the pragma. Again, the pragma is an identity within difference; formally therefore a being within a general becoming. The pragma will emerge as a site where the interrelationship between being and becoming is expressed beyond the range of the logic of identity and thus falling beyond any ready rearticulation within contradiction and paradox. The identity of the pragma will need to be thought in terms of the specificity provided by the relation in which it – the pragma – is sustained. In general terms the pragma will mark the abeyance of the traditional formulation of the opposition of being and becoming demanding a rethinking of identity as the regional. What will take place therefore is a reworking via repetition that repeats and reworks the site.[15]

Within interpretation the force of the logic of the again and the anew resides, in part, in the relation that comes to be envisaged with tradition. Tradition is not a description of what has been. Despite the fact that it seems to invoke a 'past' – even though it is a past oscillating between the differing though not necessarily conflicting determinations of history and nostalgia – tradition more properly involves dominance and futurity. It is for this reason that tradition needs to be considered as a determination in advance, and thus as constituting the gift of the already given. The futurity in question is complex. There are two ways of formulating the given. What is given is given in advance and is therefore futural in the sense that it exists in the future for any particular. However, its being given has in sense already taken place and it is thus not straightforwardly futural. The future in the latter sense is already part of the present. It is the combination of these two states of affairs that forms an integral part of the constitution of the present. They are part of that which forms its complexity and intensity.

While recognising that the work of tradition, as will be argued, involves both the gift and the potential for its refusal (a potential that will to a greater or lesser degree always be at work in the mediation of its reception), there can be no pure receptivity. The practice of interpretations that work against dominance and the pre-given nature of both meaning and propriety will involve a repetition of a work in which a space is opened and a relation constructed whose determinations have not been preordained; again, with it, the event is affirmed. In other words, rather than there being an already existent relation either to be discovered or rediscovered, relation will have to come to be established. It will no longer be given. Once again what is at issue is internality, though an internality with exteriority rather than direction. These considerations will of course be played out in the attempt to formulate the event as the site of irreducible difference. The event *qua* event will always already have been determined by its irreducibility. This, however, should be understood as a claim about the ontology of the work – the object of interpretation – and therefore as incorporating the argument that any determination is parasitic upon an already given and thus primordially present irreducibility. A division between intended works or objects emerges to the extent to which this irreducibility is affirmed.[16] As always the important element here is not difference as such but that irreducibility as difference is the differential ontology that *is* the ontology of the event. It is this state of affairs that will eventually give rise to a redeemed understanding of propriety.

Even though the distinction is not absolute it is vital to construct and maintain, if only as strategy, the difference adumbrated above between works whose internality has direction – a direction determined by its relation to the already given – and those works which come to acquire it through the process of interpretation and the action of repetition. In the latter case, direction via repetition, the new – the redeemed new – involves the repetition enacted by the logic of the again and the anew. The temporality of this process of reworking and repeating is provided in part, as has been indicated, by a generalised reworking of the Freudian concept of *Nachträglichkeit*. (It is, of course, already being reworked.) The difficulty here is recognising that there is an analogue on the level of interpretation between on the one hand such an interpretive act and the tradition of interpretation, and on the other a work whose internality is such that it acquires direction and is thus moving both within and away from the determinations of the already given.

Repetition becomes the new. It becomes it. The contrast here, however, is with the singular event whose internality is such that the new no longer figures within repetition in the sense of being sustained by it. And yet even in this instance repetition has not been extruded. Repetition will figure. In this particular case it pertains to the repetition of tradition. This repetition is neither that of historical continuity nor the simple unfolding of dominance. Repetition in this instance involves the concepts and categories handed down by (and as) tradition, tradition's giving of itself, and which determine meaning and understanding prior to any one instance in which comprehension – be it semantic or interpretive – takes place. Here repetition is present as the continual giving of the already given.

The presence of this determination gives rise to the possibility of succumbing to the trap of wanting, as a consequence, to define the new in simply negative terms. The way this can be avoided – ensnaring the snare – is by refusing generality. There can be no single way in which the concepts and categories that mark out the possibility of meaning are shown by the presentation of a work, once taken up as imparted by the event, to be unable to incorporate its 'meaning' within their own terms. The limit, the moment where the question of meaning and propriety remains open, becomes a formulation of the new. The occurrence of the new – its advent arising as eventful – is inevitably pragma-tic. In being a strategy internal to specific works, it resists generalisation and prediction. The acuity of the problem such works create, works as objects, events, exists for philosophy while not being coextensive with philosophy. The events in question, for example, figure within the visual arts and literature as much as in the strictly philosophical. And yet, of course, the individual determination of art as opposed to philosophy is not a determination involving a simple opposition. It is given in and by tradition; again the logic of the gift. Consequently to the extent to which there is a questioning of the borders such an act – the questioning as a repetition though one no longer bounded by the Same – is itself only possible because of the co-operative presence of relation and repetition; questioning as a displacing self-enacting. The question of borders involves a different construal of complexity than the one provided either by addition or supplementarity; complexity is more complex than it appears. There is more than an outline. The conception of the new at work here is to be understood as no longer commensurate with an intended absolute singularity. The singular will emerge as the pragma in the place of the purely singular. The effectivity of the opposition between absolute and relative is thereby suspended.

Formulating the new in relation to tradition and to the conditions of possibility for meaning and understanding opens up the possibility of redefining the new within philosophy and in connection with philosophy's complex relation to objects of interpretation in terms of the avant-garde. In the act – the process – of redefining the new is stripped of the masquerade of fashion and the effective presence of fashion's temporality. (It is, of course, clear that this redefinition is reciprocal. It is thus that the avant-garde comes to be given philosophical content.) In both instances the specificity of the work is central. This, in part, is the reason why the project of the new is not predictive. Prediction necessitates either generality or a form of universality. In addition it is constrained to operate within that frame in which the instant becomes the exemplar. Reworking the new removes it from the domain of exemplarity. The new becomes no more than an example of itself. The challenge that is presented by the new – the new in the sense defined above – because it concerns meaning and understanding, is finding a language, incorporating style and terminology, perhaps therefore even a conceptual language, within which what delimits the newness of the new can find expression. This is the reason why there must be experimentation.[17] The new will demand to address and to be addressed in different ways. The new therefore comes to be redeemed within the terms set by the ineliminable presence of relation and thus of repetition. The task here is formulating this presence. It must be remembered that any formulation brings with it the very problems of style and presentation that have already been noted. The new will come to be rethought within repetition. Repetition in losing its deterministic sense will itself become a site that repeats the opening made possible by naming, repeating, thereby, the inherent problems presented by the name 'diremption', problems which are themselves present when diremptive naming is taken as a question. With the occurrence of these differing moves and thus with the re-presentation of repetition in terms of an anoriginal complexity – the complexity inherent in its name – the latter, repetition, will become subject to, though clearly also the subject of, a differing repetition. Furthermore it will be argued that within this subjection – the movement within repetition – representation will break with its traditional link with the image and thus be recast as another differing form of repetition. It is precisely this particular type of move that is linked to redemption; linked, that is, to the possibility of differentiating difference within repetition. Repetition comes to be more than a merely self-identical concept; its opening displays its plurality. Consequently therefore it will eschew the very unity that is denied by the process which it – repetition – even in its most elementary form names. Repetition will always involve the addition of complexity. With this addition the original complexity of the event can be returned, repeated. This origin is the existence of the event, its being. As such therefore repetition returns ontology to the centre of philosophical thinking. It is, of course, a return as repetition which will itself demand a rethinking of repetition.

Finally, the specificity of philosophy as opposed to the arts is both maintained and questioned by its formulation within an attempt to rework the new. Out of it there emerges the strategy of a philosophy – perhaps even a philosophical thinking – that in positing the centrality of tradition will also allow for its abeyance and thus its being displaced. (Tradition here will have to incorporate the homology sometimes demanded and predicted by philosophy and presentation even though the nature of the incorporation as well as its content will demand a different philosophical understanding.) The same (Same) does not have to be understood in precisely the same (Same's) way. Tradition's displacement will become the place of philosophy and thus of a certain philosophical presentation. Indeed it emerges as philosophy's place, thereby opening up the problem of incorporation and with it of the effective presence of retention, perhaps one demanding a type of denegation. In general therefore there is no attempt to turn on tradition by denying its presence.[18] Not only, as will be suggested, is this futile as argument, it is nihilistic as gesture and only possible in terms of a systematic forgetting. As will be seen, forgetting must be recalled within contemporary philosophical thinking, bringing with it a reactivation of memory.[19] With memory the philosophical task of the historical re-emerges but now thought beyond the confines of representation and in terms of a repetition held by vigilance. The latter – vigilance – will serve to introduce the political into the historical by allowing memory to be active.

Here what is essential is philosophy as continually coming to define and redefine its place in terms of its working through tradition. (In the end what will be named is precisely this conflictual working through.) In strategic terms what this will mean involves avoiding the traps of futility and nihilism by recognising that their potential forms part of the opening that has been situated here. The dialectic that incorporates truth and untruth gives way to the reworking and thus redemption of the already given – tradition as the determination in advance – in which via repetition that which is given again is given precisely because the given has taken over the quality of the name.

Problems and questions in not yielding either their automatic solutions or answers become as a consequence openings that demand work. The project that this entails is determined by the work of these openings, as well as that which comes to be at work in them. As openings, with them, the event is drawn into a general reworking of the concepts and categories of philosophical work; reciprocally it draws them with it; a reworking which sustains the specificity of the event because it is inextricably involved in the formulation and constitution of the event *qua* event. It is in terms of the specificity of the event – its being as event – that what is sustained is a reorientation of the philosophical task, a reorientation that is, of course, the work of repetition.

Beginning again: naming beginning

The problem of beginning within philosophy opens out in at least two different directions. The first posits the possibility of a new beginning. A point of departure which by its very nature fails to be included in what preceded it because the preceding is deemed to have failed in the task that it set for itself. This is, in outline, the direction taken by Descartes. It is one that eschews any self-conception of the effective presence of the historical in that its own ad-venture is that which introduces the possibility of history (even though as will be seen it is history as the end of history). The second involves the argument that far from there being a project to begin again – a projected new beginning within philosophy – there is the need to recognise that philosophy has already begun. History can be inscribed in terms of the emergence of the position of recognition: a recognition incorporating its own coming-to-emerge. It is this recognition that seems to counter, countering by both regrouping and redescribing, the posited new beginning. Not only does such a move check what is at stake in the first opening, it repositions the projected singular identity of such positions in terms of an impossible aspiration that would entail either simple particularity or the idiosyncratic. Here in the second approach, and in contradistinction to any simple particularity, there will be a different conception of the singular. It is one in which the singular is singular in so far, and only in so far, as it is a part of but apart from the whole. (The problem of what will henceforth be called the logic of the apart/a part will be examined in greater detail in relation to its work – a work situated beyond the range of intentional logic – in Hegel's actual formulation of diremption and division within the *Difference Essay*.[20] It should be noted that this formulation occurs in response to what Hegel identifies as the 'need' for philosophy. This specificity will in the end be of considerable significance.) The singular thus construed comprises an integral component of the process of diremption. This as the above suggests is in broad outline the Hegelian direction. Here the task at hand involves tracing the work – the move from the outline – enjoined by these two different philosophical directions. In both instances there is more at stake than an implicit response to the question of philosophy's identity. In moving from the response there emerges another point of departure – a differing orientation – namely the question; the question itself and thus the inherently problematic status of the 'itself'.

The question – what is philosophy? – brings to the fore, at least initially, two related sets of problems. The first concerns the status of the question and the formulation of identity within it – recognising that this formulation, as with the question, may have more than one determination – while the second pertains to how what will count as a response, as well as how the conception of identity within any given response, is to be understood. Again what will be suggested is that the assumptions and consequences, be they implicit or explicit, inhering in the relationship between question and response are shown in the problem of naming. The question will only become more than just the simple instantiation of the question form to the extent that it is not supposed to open onto, or to open up, what had been predicted by the question or presumed to be included within and as its content. This opening of the question sanctions complexity. Once it is no longer just a question, the question then overcomes the confines of its content in so far as that content is henceforth no longer contained in its singularity – as a singular determination – whether that singularity be ontological or semantic, by the question. The direct result of this breaking of containers, the shifts in confines, is that what comes to be questioned is the question itself.

The question – what is philosophy? – can always be made to appear banal, however. It is moreover a question whose banality is compounded once there has been the adoption of that approach to questioning which sees the response as in some ineluctable way clearly written into the question (an insertion of the question into prediction). The inscription would position the question in terms of an uncovering of the covered. Pursuing this line of argument does, however, give rise to an inevitable difficulty. It emerges in the following way. (It rehearses the Hegelian direction.) If the answer to the question of philosophy is not, in some way at least, already inherent in the question then, it could be argued, all answers are unconnected and disparate because the implicit possibility of there being an essence of philosophy – that which is essentially philosophical – is in some sense denied. Therefore, it would have to be concluded, the question 'what is philosophy?' may never actually get to be posed. Here the philosophical positions of both Hegel and Heidegger can to a certain extent be seen to merge.[21] Perhaps it is here that banality is unavoidable.

There is a way around this dilemma. It comes from recognising that one of the constitutive elements of this difficulty is also there in the pervasive problem of naming. Here it takes the form of what appears to be a secondary question, namely what is named by 'philosophy' in the question, what is philosophy? (The centrality of the more general but nonetheless problematic status of naming would appear by extension. One will be seen to address the other.) Noting the effective presence of this other question will allow for a shift away from the centrality of the question towards that which is at work within it i.e. the strategies of formulation within the question. The question is the locus for the problem of naming and therefore the actative within the question – the strategies of formulation – are also present in the question of the name: questioning therefore naming. The strategic importance of naming lies in what is assumed – the assumption of tradition – to provide the conditions of existence for any answer to the question of what the name names. The name marks out the work of tradition and in bringing contestation to the name – allowing the name to name it – sanctions a dis-placement of tradition's work, itself the abeyance of dominance.

In sum in asking the question of the name the attempts by both Descartes and Hegel to respond to the question of philosophy can therefore, if only as a beginning, be interpreted as responses to the question of the name and thus as attempts to identify what is named within the question 'what is philosophy?' This particular beginning will allow a link to be established between names and events via the inherent conceptions of identity they sustain, and reciprocally, which are sustained by them. The name will eventually give way to the event of naming and thereby to the name as event. These moves which will act out the process of a continual reworking are made in the proceeding. Again they take beginning as always more than a simple instantiation of the problem of beginning.

In both cases, Descartes and Hegel, the question of philosophy and its coming to be formulated will be traced in terms of its presentation. Rather than following general arguments which are constrained to make assumptions about the status of the positions under discussion in this instance attention will be paid to the detail, to what shall be described henceforth as the struggle to formulate. It will be suggested that central to the Cartesian formulation, though barely announced within the posited centrality of method – a method announcing God while implicitly denouncing his philosophical necessity – is the interplay between destruction, memory and forgetting. Furthermore the necessity of forgetting and the posited triumph of method are coupled to the problematic presence of the body. It will be argued that the body, despite the attempts to overcome it, nonetheless still intrudes. Consequently its re-emergence – bodily presence – will be the intrusion of that which had thought to have been completely extruded. The difficulty arises because of what is demanded by having to expel the body. For there to have been a complete extrusion what must also be overcome is the mark of the extrusion itself. There can be no trace of the extrusion, the scar left by bodily elimination. It is the possibility of realising this necessity that will come to be questioned.

In the case of Hegel centrality will be given first to the way in which the presence of time, and with it spacing, in the formulation of diremption in the *Difference Essay* works to undo the division it was intended to establish, and second to the presentation of difference, in terms of the possibility of different philosophical positions, in the Introduction to the *Shorter Logic* (Sections 1–18). This textual restriction is not a limitation. It is envisaged as opening up the problem of presentation, of presenting it within a presentation marked by spacing and distance. The emphasis on the textual does not occur as the exclusion of the philosophical. It occurs in terms of what comes to be presented within, and thus also as, any attempt to formulate. In other words the effectuation and the work of the textual can be taken as forming an integral part of philosophy's own activity.

Descartes' body of forgetting

The *Meditations* opens with doubt.[22] An opening stated in the subheading of the 'First Meditation', *'De iis quoe in dubium revocati possunt'* (II,177). The possible scepticism of such an opening, however, is immediately checked since the opening line of the Meditation serves to position doubt in relation to the existence of uncertainty, false opinions and that which is itself doubtful. Doubt does not exist in itself, nor, as will be suggested by the time the *Meditations* are written, is it purely epistemological. Doubt is not therefore an instance of Pyrrhonian scepticism. (Descartes suggests the same in a letter to Reneri pour Pollot, April/May 1638.[23]) It is part of the strategy that involves overcoming the totality – the 'all' (*omnia*) – that had been handed down. Once this is done it will then be possible for philosophy to 'begin all anew from the foundations' (*atque a primis fundamentis denuo inchoandum*) (II,177). Prior to broaching the philosophical inauguration stated in the *Meditations*, it will be essential to examine what is at play in a similar attempt to empty both history – the handed down – from the present as well as the present self of its history. It will serve to indicate that the presence of both these manoeuvres is necessary;

one cannot work without the other. In fact one presupposes the other.

The complexity of this situation is captured by Descartes in a letter to Pere Mesland, 2 May 1644. (The last part of the quotation refers to the *Principles of Philosophy*, a work which was also published in 1644.)

> The difficulty of learning (*d'apprendre*) the sciences which is in us and the difficulty of representing to ourselves clearly the ideas which are naturally known; it comes from the false prejudgements/prejudice of our childhood (*des faux préjugés de notre enfance*) and from other causes of our errors that I have attempted to explain in a work that I have in press.
>
> (III, 71)

The movement described here involves the identification of a restriction of self-potential by 'prejudgement' or 'prejudice'. In their most straightforward presentation the 'false prejudgements/prejudice of our childhood' are for Descartes the result of an education system run along Scholastic lines. There is more involved here, however, than would be achieved by trying to establish, or even by having established, a critical distance from certain educational practices. The same argument would have to be advanced in any attempt to set out and analyse Descartes' evaluation of his own education that takes place in the *Discourse*. Once again there would be an addition. This additional element, the one that would figure in both instances, is signalled by Descartes in the 'Abrégé' to the *Meditations*. Here doubt is presented as that which will 'deliver us from all types of prejudice/prejudgements' (*nous délivre de toutes sortes de préjugés*) (II,399). While what must be pursued is the link between doubt and 'prejudgement/prejudice', it should be noted that the removal of prejudice by doubt has the effect of preparing the 'mind' (*esprit*) to 'detach itself from the senses' in order for it then to arrive at the truth. It becomes a precondition for the attaining of truth.

The intervening presence of the necessary absence of the body, its being in being determined, also opens up an important area of inquiry. This is especially the case given that the 'Third Meditation' could be described in part as enacting a systematic elimination of the body. It is as though the body has become waste. Furthermore in the *Second Responses* the body – in terms of the senses – is linked to 'some false prejudgement' (*quelque faux préjugés*) as a cause of human error. In both the *Meditations* and the *Passions of the Soul* (Article 3) the body is doubly displaced in that its representation – the presentation of the body, the subject's own body, to the subject – must take place beyond the range of the body and thus outside of bodily vision. The body involves a double displacement. The body touches the heart of representation.

It should not be thought that doubt is restricted to only certain of Descartes' texts. Indeed the contrary is the case in that doubt can be seen to figure throughout his writings. However, what is figured changes in a fundamental way in the course of his writings. (There is no straightforward figure of doubt except as it would occur in a generalised and hence inappropriate strategy of abstraction.) In the *Rules for the Direction of the Mind* Descartes draws a distinction between doubt and ignorance. The connection is deployed in relation to Socrates. In both cases what is at stake is the absence of knowledge and the subsequent need to obtain it. In Rule 13 this move is presented in terms of an implicit affirmation of knowledge.

> Socrates posed a problem about his own ignorance, or rather doubt, when he became aware of his doubt, he began to ask whether it was true that he was in doubt about everything and his answer was affirmative.
>
> (I, 161)

Whether Socrates' ignorance – what is often discussed under the heading of Socrates' 'disavowal of knowledge' – is real ignorance or a feint whose purpose is linked to a specific conception of knowledge and thus to the rhetoric of argument proper to that conception is not the central issue here. The important point in this instance is that the presentation of doubt as epistemological doubt means that it intends to involve no more than the absence of knowledge of a particular given object. The concentration on the particularity of the object, where what is in doubt is limited to knowledge of the object, means that what is excluded from the process of doubt is the possibility of knowledge itself. If it were to be included its presence would have entailed the positing of a grounding epistemology or a grounding ontology (e.g. Fichte's strategy in *The Science of Knowledge*)[24] where the positing and that which it was intended to establish were not themselves determined by a concern exemplified by the knowledge of specific objects. Doubt delimited by the specific particularity of the object as opposed to the domain of epistemology itself is signalled slightly earlier in the *Rules for the Direction of the Mind*.

If, for example, Socrates says that he doubts everything it necessarily follows that he understood at least that he is doubting and hence that he knows that something can be true or false etc. for there is a necessary connection between these facts and the nature of doubt.

(I, 147–8)

Even though this move forms part of a twofold general argument – and it is an argument that will become central to the Cartesian method of 'clear and distinct perception' – which on the one hand concerns knowledge of the simple, and on the other the consequences that stem from the ineliminable presence of the subject of doubt, doubt here is still directly linked to the acquisition of knowledge. Doubt does not enact the attempt to create a radical divison in the time of tradition. It is not linked to repetition in that it does not form an integral element in an attempted philosophical inauguration. Finally what is absent from Descartes' early considerations is the move to the transcendental; in other words what are yet to be explicitly formulated as what are lacking and thus still to be acquired are the conditions of possibility for knowledge. The move from the specificity of objects is therefore not towards the totality of objects but to the possibility, and thus the ground of possibility, of knowledge itself.

It is precisely the latter conception of doubt, however, that occurs in the *Meditations*. Indeed it can be argued that the importance of doubt in the *Meditations* is signalled by the fact that within the wider strategy of the text there is more, as has been argued, than just the connection of doubt to narrowly epistemological concerns. Doubt is linked to the strategy of destruction and the possibility of a philosophical inauguration; the inception of the transcendental. In the 'Second Meditation' and after having advanced the supposition that all that he saw was false and that all previously held beliefs and thoughts were fictions of the mind (*chimerae*), Descartes then asks, '*Quid igitur erit verum?*' (What then shall be true?) (II,182). It should be noted immediately that Descartes' question is not, '*Quid est verum?*' (What is true?). In other words he is not asking what truth is as though either there were an already given answer at hand or the conditions in terms of which an answer could be given were themselves already established. The use of the future tense (*'erit'*) plus the presence of the term *'igitur'* – marking consequence – work to open up the question of truth. It comes to be opened not simply because there is no predetermined answer to the question but because the conditions of possibility for any answer are not given. The existence of doubt means that it is no longer possible to make use of the answers that have already been given to this question. (It should already be clear that what is figuring here is the refusal of the given and with it therefore the envisaged destruction of tradition's gift.) All such answers would have the same status as a prejudgement or a prejudice. In being the determinations of prejudice they are therefore the object of doubt. This is the force of the combination of *'igitur'* and the future tense. Moreover it is precisely this force that takes the question beyond the range of the purely epistemological. Any problems arising here occur because of what is *not given*. What is absent is exactly that which is going to count as an answer to the question *Quid erit igitur verum*. As a point of departure, therefore, it is vital to develop an understanding of what is marked out by the 'not given'. Part of this process will include the attempt to open up the temporal considerations – the differential temporality of a complex – that are at play in the 'not given', and thus in that which is 'not given'. The 'not given' as will be suggested begins to enact that which is demanded within the formulation of a philosophy of destruction. Indeed as will emerge it is precisely the link between that which is not to be given and what arises in Heidegger in terms of think Being 'without relation' either to Beings or metaphysics that establishes their differing philosophical strategies as part of a more encompassing philosophy of destruction.

In *Descartes against the Skeptics* E.M. Curley in a general description of the distinction between Descartes' early texts, e.g. *The Rules for the Direction of the Mind*, and later texts such as the *Discourse on Method* and the *Meditations* presents it in the following terms. After quoting a passage from the *Discourse* that linked doubt to the re-evaluation of opinions and beliefs he then goes on to draw the more general conclusion that it

is this project, the project of systematically reviewing one's past beliefs and casting out those which do not conform to the

highest standards of rationality, which defines Descartes'
mature work. [25]

Before commenting on this passage it should be noted that a
similar approach to the question of doubt is found in M. D.
Wilson's study *Descartes*. In this particular case it emerges with
regard to Descartes' professed doubt concerning the existence of
God. She quotes A. Kenny's question as to whether or not
Descartes really doubted God's existence and then goes on to
respond to the question in the terms in which it was posed.[26]
Rather than there being either a positive or negative response to
this question it is the question itself that lacks acuity. On one level
it is of no great importance whether or not the doubt was real
since the force of this particular instance of doubt is to be located
in how it is overcome; in other words in how God's existence is to
be established and the knowledge of that existence presented.
(Such proofs are henceforth, for Descartes, not in God's gift;
neither proof nor knowledge are God given.) The epistemological
possibilities of either faith or wisdom no longer hold sway.
Scientia will have taken the place of *sapientia* and with it
Augustine's philosophical project will have been overtaken.[27]
Even the suggestion that innate ideas may maintain God's gift is
far from adequate. The important point in relation to such ideas
is not their existence *per se* but their coming to be clearly and
distinctly perceived. This point is clarified in considerable detail
by Descartes in the first part of the *Principles of Philosophy*.
   In Section 54 Descartes states that, 'No one is able to deny that
such an idea of God is in us' (III, 124) and then goes on to argue
that such an idea can be had 'clearly and distinctly'. It is in
addition clear and distinct perception which overcomes the
existence of prejudgement/prejudice (Sections 16, 47 and 50).
Moreover Descartes' opening argument in Sections 1–11 establishes the prority of method – clear and distinct perception – as
that which will ground certainty in the wake of doubt. The overall
problem is captured in Section 43. Here Descartes' claim is that

It is certain however that we would never take the false for the
true provided we give our assent only to what we clearly and
distinctly perceive. Because God is not a deceiver the faculty of
knowledge that he gave us will not fail, nor will the faculty of
the will if they are not extended beyond that which we know.

(III, 116)

It should be added that this perception is not vision as such. Vision more properly pertains to the body. Using the language of the 'Second Meditation' what occurs is 'an inspection of the mind'. It is an inspection yielding the object – 'la chose' – as it is. It is thus that it is only once God has been clearly and distinctly perceived and is therefore no longer the object of doubt that it is possible to link God to the faculty of knowledge. This argument is not straight-forwardly circular since the link between God and knowledge is in fact philosophically unnecessary. The strategy of doubt can always be reimposed; however, such a reimposition, occurring after the event of doubt, where doubt is understood as destruction, would be limited to the epistemological in so far as it would only exist in relation to certain objects. It is this lack of necessity that is brought out in the restriction imposed on the faculties of knowledge and the will in the last lines of Section 43. The only way in which knowledge can be limited to its own proper domain is via the exercise of method, e.g. the movement from the complex to the simple and then back to the complex. (The limit is the one that is imposed by representation and therefore enacts the necessity inherent in it.) The use of method need make no reference to God. The source of the faculty of knowledge is no longer either the source or the basis of knowledge. Finally, that it is method that triumphs over doubt is argued for by Descartes in the following passage from the *Second Responses*:

> as soon as (*aussitôt que*) we can conceive clearly some truth, we are naturally taken to believe it. And if this belief is so strong that we have no reason to ever doubt what we believe, there is *nothing more* to look for (*il n'y a rien à rechercher davantage*); we have touched all the certitude for which it might be reasonable to wish.
>
> (II, 569, my emphasis)

The significant elements in this particular formulation of Descartes' position are first his use of the temporal marker '*aussitôt que*', and second the conclusion that announces epistemological fini-tude (almost a type of epistemological exhaustion), a position marked in the text by the expression 'nothing more'. 'Nothing more' gives rise to a space within the time of development, a permanent present which is itself created by the finality of the '*aussitôt que*'. The temporal dimension of this formulation is central to Descartes' overall philosophical position. The time of simultaneity is at work in the structure of representation – the coextensivity beween sign and thing – while it works at the same time to generate and to sustain the permanent present established by epistemological finitude. The interplay between epistemology and representation generates its own history. It is this history that in allowing for its own distancing will occasion the introduction of judgement, a judgement displacing the Cartesian presentation thereof.

Returning to the text it is clear that the force of the 'aussitôt que' is to be located in its introducing a break where the before is marked by the absence of knowledge and the presence of either ignorance or prejudice. Any beliefs that existed before had to be either false or at least open to doubt. True belief rather than existing in itself is the necessary consequence of knowledge, i.e. of conceiving clearly of some truth. The central element is that truth is consequent upon an action that establishes it. This will relate as much to God (to the truth of his existence) as any other truth and therefore it will also be connected to beliefs concerning God in the same way as it would relate to beliefs about any other object about which it had become possible to have justified beliefs. These interconnected elements of Descartes' position will inform the response to Curley. In general they will form part of the inter-pretation of Descartes to come. Furthermore it will be suggested that the 'aussitôt que' can be understood as marking the moment that establishes the contemporary by defining a perpetual present occasioned by epistemological finitude, itself marked out by the limit established by the 'nothing more'. Establishing the con-temporary will therefore have the consequence of denying the continuity of history.

In relation to Curley's argument the immediate response is to suggest that despite its simplicity the Cartesian position is in fact far more radical. Using a formulation similar to the one used by Curley it is possible to argue that the basis of Descartes' position is that the truth of a given belief – its content – can no longer either be assumed or established within the terms that had hitherto existed for this practice. What are at stake therefore are two related projected movements. The first is formulating a new set of criteria in terms of which the truth content of a given belief can be either established or secured. The second is that this formulation must take place anew. (The interplay of the 'a new' and the 'anew' will provide a way towards an understanding of the 'not given'. In other words, if the 'not given' is that in terms of which truth is to be established, then these conditions have to be devised anew.) Consequently what is involved here is the problem of how, in the first place, a true proposition is to be identified and in the second how the truth of a given proposition is to be established. It therefore follows that it is not just that there is more at stake than a simple though rigorous review of past beliefs, there is also a profound questioning of how any 'review' would itself be possible. In any case, given doubt, and the basis of doubt, how would the conformity demanded by Curley's presentation be either noted or established? In responding to the actual formulation of Kenny's question, as taken up by Wilson, it has emerged that with God's existence what is central is not the existence as such but how that existence came to be proved. In the terms of the 'First Meditation' he was a 'thing' that could be doubted. He was therefore – *qua* object of knowledge – a thing like all other things (a position that is itself brought out by the French title of the 'First Meditation'; God is one of those 'things' (*choses*) that can be doubted). The doubt was initially epistemological in that it appeared as pertaining to no more than knowledge of the object. The radical force of Cartesian doubt – its intended destructive effect – means that it pertained to far more.

The possibility of overcoming the restriction of doubt to narrowly epistemological concerns can be further established by focusing on the implicit premise within questions concerning God's existence. The premise is that the conditions handed down for the acquisition and guarantee of such knowledge were no longer germane and that therefore the enjoined task was to establish anew new conditions. (The handed down is tradition operating in terms of a repetition articulated within the Same. Tradition is therefore the work of the already given. Destruction is the intended refusal of the gift.) That which is 'not given' but which comes to be given – a new present inaugurating the present, the contemporary – are the new conditions that emerge out of the posited centrality of a method articulated within the terms set by the certainty established by the methodological components at work in clear and distinct perception. (These components are those which lend themselves to universalisability as generating a method. The circularity here should be noted. It marks the new.)

Furthermore, to the extent that it is this method that establishes, within and for philosophy, the existence of God, then, as has been suggested, it must be method which has philosophical priority. (Even if God is reintroduced after the event as the ultimate, i.e. final, guarantor of method, it is still clear that this reintroduction is without real philosophical justification or result, thereby opening up the real problem of the atheist's actual and not simply potential access to truth – a conclusion noted by Gassendi.) It is therefore the method which is presented as having been established anew. The question that arises here is, how is the 'anew' to be understood? This question is central since the possibility of the 'anew' – here intended as devoid of any possible mediation – marks the Cartesian occurrence within philosophy. (It is an occurrence taking place in the opening marked by the interplay of *'erit'* and *'igitur'*.)

The problem that must be confronted at this stage concerns the possibility of resisting mediation. If mediation is inevitable, however, then, and of necessity, the 'anew' will confront – confront in its being proposed, in its being given – an 'again'. Once this confontation takes place then because of the necessity of mediation the confrontation will have to be approached from within the purview of repetition. This opens up a twofold division within repetition. In other words both the project, the philosophical inauguration, as well its impossible possibility and the ensuing results can be thought within repetition. It should be added that in both cases there is a fundamentally different conception of repetition involved. Difference points a way towards an understanding of naming as it indicates the difficulties involved in formulating any answer to the question 'what is named by repetition in the question, what is repetition?'

The first part of this divide within repetition relates to the consequences if the Cartesian project of beginning anew is shown to be impossible. What this state of affairs would entail is that the impossibility of constructing a new and original frame would itself be shown in the attempt to construct such a frame. It would come to be constructed, in part, from that which was intended to be excluded. The new frame would have become inextricably implicated in a reframing. The second form of repetition refers exclusively to Descartes' attempted inauguration. Here it is being presented as an attempt to end the repetition of tradition. Descartes can be read as working with the assumption that such an end is possible. Arising out of this assumption is the extent to which repetition will form part of the Cartesian philosophical strategy of destruction. It is this strategy which is announced in the texts.

Descartes argues in the 'First Meditation' for the need to 'destroy' all the old 'opinions' which he held. Doubt is from the beginning therefore inextricably linked to destruction. Cartesianism becomes a philosophy of destruction. The trap here would be to limit Descartes' argument to a claim being made by Descartes about himself. Clearly the claim is autobiographical but only to the extent that it pertains to all subjects and thus to all potential subject/object relations that are envisaged as establishing knowledge or certainty. Descartes' autobiography not only becomes the life, as written, of philosophy, it presupposes the intended universality of subjectivity (and with it of objectivity). Furthermore it is only when Descartes' writings incorporate autobiography that they are then not limited either by or to the biography of the particular self. Descartes intended to locate the power of a philosophical legislation – a legislation articulated in terms of imitation, i.e. by mimesis – within the confines of the singular in order that the philosophical power that the position then acquires is neither limited to the singular nor delimited by its singularity. The difficulty with this position arises because of the relation it envisages between the text and the reader and therefore with the reader's projected response.[28] While the position itself is of great significance the difficulty is not of immediate interest here since of more strategic importance is the internal time of tradition, itself the times of repetition.

Destruction is not in any straightforward sense part of a strategy of the withdrawal of a particular subject's judgement in order that things could then be judged again. If this were the case then not only would it personalise the argument, thereby obviating the inclusion of destruction in philosophy's biography, it would only be true if the 'again' – incorporated into the judgement taking place again – were understood as anew. Furthermore the newness in question would involve no more than that in terms of which judgement – Cartesian judgement – were to take place. For, as has already been suggested, what is of central importance is not the object of knowledge *qua* object but how it is known as itself and thus the conditions of possibility for knowledge itself. Developing this point will in the end necessitate that Descartes' conception of 'thing' (*chose*) or object of knowledge be taken into consideration. It will, in addition, be necessary to take up the subject/object relation conditioned by it. At this stage, however, it is essential to stay with destruction.

Destruction is far from simple. It demands a particular construal of that which is to be destroyed and therefore what has to be taken into consideration is the ontology of the object and temporality of movement. In broad terms destruction needs be understood in relation to repetition, in that the intended destruction is of the repetition of tradition, the handed down. Destruction is essential in order that tradition – the gift – not be, in fact, given, in other words that it be refused. The gift of tradition in being destroyed is thereby left to one side. It is only with the possibility of its repetition being over that the contemporary is then introduced. Destruction is therefore fundamental to establishing the contemporary as that which occurs with tradition's end. Destruction as the end of tradition entails that modernity arises in its wake. The relationship between the contemporary as that which is established by destruction and modernity is a difficult problem. The nature of modernity may involve a different discursive frame, especially as the contemporary established by Descartes will in the end necessitate those relations, the destruction of which was taken to found the contemporary.

Descartes' destructive argument is, in sum, that the repetitions of previously held philosophical beliefs and earlier philosophical arguments and positions are not to be repeated and that therefore the project that aims to 'begin anew from the foundations' undertakes this via doubt and the destruction of previously held opinions. In other words it intends to stem the work of tradition by ending its repetition; the refusal of the gift. It is this intention which, while not announced in the text as such, is one of the fundamental components of Descartes' overall strategy. Ending repetition is destruction. Moreover the centrality of repetition will also be seen to figure in the presentation of the body; its opening. It goes without saying that in broad outline the concept of repetition at work here is a repetition in and of the Same. The contemporary is taken to emerge at the point where the possibility of the same repetition – the repetition of the Same – has been destroyed. It is thus that Descartes is a philosopher for whom the contemporary yields the need for philosophy and philosophy in responding to that need is contemporary.

What exists at the moment of writing and thus that which dominates the present and which therefore must be destroyed is presented as *'préjugées'*. The destruction of 'prejudgement/ prejudice', in part enacted through doubt, involves two funda-mental moves. The first is ending the repetition of the criteria handed down as philosophy – its being handed down, the philosophical gift, is the work of tradition – and the second to deploy, or redeploy, the actual formation (and formulation) of repetition's end – e.g. doubt, destruction – as itself providing the basis for a new philosophical pro-jection. The processing of ending – of destroying and effacing – also concerns the body. Opening up the body will enable the development of a more sustained understanding of the conception of repetition proper to Cartesian philosophy. The proper here concerns that which is at work in, and thereby also sustaining, the Cartesian formulations that enact and depend upon a certain construal of repetition. (It should be noted that repetition can never be reduced to this construal.)

The formulation of Cartesian dualism not only demands a radical separation between mind and body, it is also the case that the centrality and supremacy of the mind and the subsequent reintroduction of the body are themselves premised upon this founding separation. The body is at first to be denied and then reintroduced afterwards. It is the advent of this 'after-the-event' which is of singular importance because it opens up the space of the problematic relationship between the body and memory. As will be noted Descartes signals the presence of this relation at the end of the 'Second Meditation'. The Cartesian point of departure which is of course a redeparture after the departure of doubt is clear: *'ego sum, ego existo'* (II, 184). If the 'I' (*ego*) were not a 'thinking thing' then, in Cartesian terms, it would be subject to the body; the body would have become subject. With the *'res cogitans'* as subject (as 'ego'), the body will have become an object of thought and thus is no longer strictly corporeal. The body is therefore twice removed.

The beginning of the 'Third Meditation' traces the gradual elimination of the body. It should be noted that it is a type of self-elimination. The body attempts to close itself off from itself. Its closure is bodily. The body is no longer at the service of the body. The body is only lost by becoming its own image.

Now I will close my eyes, I will shut my ears, I will turn away from all my senses (*omnes sensus*), I will even efface from my thought (*cogitatione*) all images of bodily things (*rerum corporalium omnes*).

(II, 191)

The last dramatic gesture of the endeavour to efface the presence of bodily images is modified within the same sentence in which it is announced. Descartes continues

or at least (*certe*) because of the difficulty of doing this I will deem them to be empty and false (*inanes & falsas*).

(II, 191)

While the need for the modification is marked by the '*certe*', what does the modification itself mark? From the start the modification involves a division introduced by the task. The division involves two related elements. In the first place there is the concession of difficulty, namely the problem of actually effacing all 'bodily things' (*rerum corporalium*). In the second place it is precisely because of this difficulty that such images must be considered 'empty and false'. This avowal which amounts to a type of disavowal arises because of the difficulty of a complete elimination of what could be called the work of the senses. Something remains – there is a residue. It is the remainder and its twofold necessity – to be present and to function – that is of interest. What remains after the event is rewritten, perhaps reinscribed, by and in the process that intended to write it off. It is the work of '*certe*' – at the very least – that must be pursued in greater detail. Again it is a question of the mark and the role it comes to play in relation to the work of intention.

The removal of the body is necessary in order that the primacy of the 'ego' as 'thinking thing' can emerge. It is thus that the body can come to be represented. Representation by the self to the self depends upon an initial separation that is overcome in the act of representation. The world, that which is outside of the self – self as '*res cogitans*' – is represented to the self in terms of ideas. In the *First Responses* Descartes argues that the 'idea of the sun' is the 'sun itself existing in the understanding' (II,520). Between the idea and that of which the idea is the idea there must be an intended radical and fundamental coextensivity. The coextensivity is the work of representation and the representation is maintained by its having been enacted in terms of this coextensivity. It is this strict relation – an identity marking the place of an identity sustaining reciprocity – that is captured in the definition of the sign advanced in *La Logique du Port Royal*:

> The sign encloses two ideas: one of the thing which represents; the other of the represented thing: and its nature consists of exciting the second by the first.[29]

It is the possibility that something could enter into the enclosure and cause the coextensivity to come undone that must be resisted. The threat of the arbitrary must be excluded, or at least reduced to the status of a secondary and 'confused' signification. The *'certe'* while attempting to preclude this possibility also opens it up. It should not be thought that with regard to its intention the Cartesian position allows for relation, let alone a mediating relation. When Descartes writes of 'closing', 'turning away', 'effacing', these are intended to mark an absolute closure. The necessity of the absolute must be insisted upon. The methodological correlate of this position occurs throughout his writings. An important example can be located in the first Article of the *Passions of the Soul*. In an opening in which the work of others is deemed *'défectueuses'*, he continues,

> I can only have any hope in arguing for the truth in distancing myself from the paths they have followed. This is why I will be obliged to write in the same way *as if* (*que si*) I dealt with material that no one had ever touched before.
>
> (III, 951–2, my emphasis)

What appears to be a concession in Descartes' formulation, the *'que si'*, is in fact the mark of an absolute non-concession that, in the end, concedes. (Despite the concession the intended necessity of the absolute should be paramount.) The distance announced and demanded in the first sentence quoted above is only possible by the adoption of a writing that is absolutely new. In other words, overcoming the defects of earlier work involves taking up the subject as though this were happening for the very first time. What cannot be present is the mark of an earlier touch. It is this untouched state that is demanded by the elimination of the body and bodily images as the source of error. Before returning to the *'certe'* a similiar formulation at the end of the 'Second Meditation' needs to be noted.

After having argued for the triumph of thought and the understanding over the imagination and the body, and thereby being able to conclude that 'there is nothing easier for me to know than my mind', Descartes still finds it necessary to add a concluding remark. The effect of the remark is to modify the preceding sentence by reworking it and thus, in part, undoing its own claim of having provided the conditions for certainty. There is an intermediary problem, however, that concerns the status of the text. The first line of the Latin text is

Sed qui tam cito deponi veteris opinionis consuetudo non potest. ...

(II, 190)

while the first line of de Luynes's contemporary French translation is

Mais parce qu'il est presque impossible de se defaire si promptement d'une ancienne opinion.

(II, 429)

Leaving aside any additional difficulties the obvious point of divergence is the addition in the French of the *'presque'*. *'Non potest'* has become *'presque impossible'*. Even though the 'not possible' has become the possible, even if that possibility is expressed in the extreme negative form of the 'almost impossible', it will be maintained that in spite of this the actual position being advanced remains unchanged. Both passages conclude with the expression of the necessity for a longer meditation in order that the newly arrived at knowledge (*'nova cognitio'*, *'nouvelle connaissance'*) be imprinted (*'infigatur'*, *'imprimé'*) more deeply into the memory. The need for further meditation resides in the difficulty of undoing the work of an 'old opinion', in other words of overcoming what amounts to the effective residues of 'prejudice/prejudgement'. Again the central issue is the possibility of ending repetition.

Both the Latin and the French texts attest to the problem of speed, and the subsequent length of the meditation. However, the question must still be asked of the effect of the shift in the French. Pursuing the French it is clear that the *'presque impossible'* marks the place of the *'certe'*. In so doing it opens up the question of whether it would ever be possible to undo the work of memory. In this particular instance what is at issue is the possibility of actually and finally effacing the trace of *'une ancienne opinion'* (an old opinion). In addition it must be asked if it is ever just as Descartes seems to suggest a matter of speed. Moreover there is the additional question of whether the imprint of the 'nouvelle connaissance' (a new knowledge) turns the memory into a palimpsest? (The coupling of 'old' and 'opinion' and 'new' and 'knowledge' should be noted in passing.)

Answering these questions necessitates taking up Descartes' own formulation of the memory. The reason for taking this tack is simply that the difficulty raised by the nature of memory is that if the 'ancienne opinion' (old opinion) has in fact been erased – and erasure here will stand for destruction and with it rehearse the determinations of a philosophy of destruction – then its presence within the memory of that erasure, the erasure as a memory that is always yet to be erased, means that the event of erasure will itself have to have been forgotten. There must in addition be a forgetting of that forgetting. The overlooked cannot continue to be looked over. If it were, then forgetting would become a form of re-membering, a memorial. As a consequence, therefore, the doubling of forgetting is essential. Forgetting denies the monument. The doubling of forgetting would seem to preclude even the event of its own monumentality.

In the *Passions of the Soul* Descartes develops his conception of memory in terms of human physiology, central to which is *'une petite glande dans le cerveau'* (a small gland in the brain):

> when the soul wants to remember something this will (*volonté*) makes the gland ... push the spirits (*les esprits*) towards different places in the brain until they encounter the one where the traces have been left by the objects that is wanted to be remembered: these traces are nothing other than the pores in the brain.
>
> (III, 985–6)

After which there is an explanation as to why 'the spirits' move to one place rather than another. Memory works by the gland causing the object that is wanted to be represented to the soul. There are two aspects of this description that are relevant for these present concerns. The first is the presence of memory traces and the second is the role of the will. The intriguing question that arises here is that, given the model, what would be involved in the overcoming of an *'ancienne opinion'* (old opinion)?

The first possibility is that the trace left by the opinion would no longer be willed and that therefore the object would not be represented to the soul. The difficulty with this answer is that the traces would remain and therefore there would always be the possibility of remembering – the possible unwilled presence of an inadvertent memory – or even the unintentional intrusion of one object into another. Destruction therefore would not have taken place. The gift and thus the continuity of its being given would endure. It is perhaps because of the presence of traces that Descartes suggests that time is needed in order that the 'new knowledge' leave its mark. The image of printing leaves open two important possibilities both of which are harboured by the residual possibility that the memory may have become a type of palimpsest.

The first is that the new printing eliminates any trace of the old. The second is that the new printing would do no more than substitute for the old. It need not eliminate it as such. In the case of the first this means that, while any trace of the original may be eliminated, what remains is the registration of the act of destruction. In order for this process to be effective there would have to be a related forgetting of destruction. Otherwise the effective presence of destruction would have to proliferate *ad infinitum*. In the case of the second it leaves open the possibility of the return, in whatever form, of that for which the substitution was originally made. The problem of memory endures. The mark of memory leaves its mark, a site that can only be countered by forgetting.

While the use of the *'presque impossible'* allows for a possibility that the Latin *'non potest'* does not, it is nonetheless still clear that what is registered here is no more than a gradation of difficulty. In the case of the French there is a concession to the inherent difficulty of supplanting one opinion by another, to the extent that it is possible that its happening will open up the necessity for forgetting. While the Latin is more straightforward, all that this means in this instance is that there is a necessity – a necessity not yet realised – to act in relation to what is deemed 'not possible'. The act does not take place even though it is thought, within the confines of the text, to have taken place in terms of the enacted consequences of the recognised need for a long meditation. Here, and without any doubt, the *'certe'* is rehearsed. Its rehearsal will come to be repeated in that the check it introduces figures elsewhere in Descartes' writings.

It should not be thought that Descartes was unaware of these problems. In the 'First Meditation', for example, it is because of the endurance of 'old opinions' that he has, in the end, to pretend that his thoughts – the totality of his thinking – are false and imaginary. The strategy of pretending (*'fingam/feignant'*) is itself problematic in that it always holds open the possibility of a slide to complete self-deception in which the deception vanishes due to its having become the norm. For Descartes this possibility was circumvented by the fact that he – the Cartesian self – is always aware of the pretence as pretence. The problem with pretence is that not only is it importantly dissimiliar to destruction it also cannot be forgotten. At all events therefore the *'certe'* marks the concession within destruction, a concession which in the end becomes the necessary impossibility of destruction, or rather that it is only possible to the extent that it is linked to the forgetting of an active forgetting contemporaneous with a holding back of forgetting from the work of pretence. The necessity of remembering pretence and thus the objects of pretence within the pretence will work to undo forgetting and thus destruction. Pretence is only effective if it is not forgotten that what is at stake is pretence; real pretence. Remembering must exclude forgetting. Here the reintrusion of the body cannot be overcome by a concession. If this failure is taken as symptomatic of that strategy that was articulated in terms of the absolutely new, then what emerges is that such a foundation marks the found(er)ing of Descartes' construal of a philosophical inauguration.

Finally, the attempt to end repetition and thus to preclude the possibility of any relation does in the end maintain relation. There are at least two reasons why this is the case. The first reason for the retention is the strategic concession marked by a generalised *'certe'*. The retention of pretence as pretence is the continuity of its own continual self-recognition. The problematic status of forgetting, its necessary presence and absence, means that its inherent instability – the impossibility of finally and absolutely ridding the memory of all traces – means that the strategy of forgetting marks the place of relation. The second reason stems from what could be described as another take on the strategy of pretence. Even if an earlier opinion is deemed false it may eventually be the case that the content of that opinion was shown to be true. Equally the content may be actually false and thus the pretence would have become real. (Its becoming real is the work of having established the transcendental conditions for the possibility of truth.) In both cases what can be said to have occurred is a reworking and thus a repetition of the content. In being reworked and repeated the relation to that content had to be presupposed. Not only, therefore, is there the presupposition of the retention of content, the move away from pretence – a move comprising the confirmation of either the truth or falsity of the specific content – positions the conditions of truth as secondary to that which occasions the repetition of the given. The repetition therefore reworks the relation that was already presupposed. Relation henceforth gives, gives the determination, in the move away from pretence, the status of an occurrence that involves repetition taking place for the first time. The full extent of this state of affairs will need to be traced in greater detail; nonetheless two inevitable conclusions can be drawn. The first is that inscribed within the show of pretence is the necessary presence of that conception of inter-pretation that affirms the centrality of relation while incorporating it within the temporality of reworking and repetition. The second is that it further attests to the impossibility of Cartesian inaugur-ation in that the latter depends upon the end of repetition and the necessary absence of relation.

In general terms it leaves open the space of inauguration and destruction – the names 'inauguration' and 'destruction' – and thus what is raised therefore is the question of their redemption. Since redemption will involve a specific construal of repetition and event – here again the event begins to mark out the stakes of naming, what is named and what intends to be named – it will be argued that pertinent to redemption will be the necessity of taking the existence of the event into consideration. What is involved is the mode of being proper to the event; hence the ontology of events.

Descartes' 'thing'

An important link between the overcoming of doubt and the conception of the object of knowledge has already been noted. In the *Second Responses* Descartes argues that once doubt is overcome and real belief is established then 'there is nothing more to look for ...'. The postulation of this closure, an epistemological finitude, has to raise the question of what is involved in the expression 'nothing more'. What is expressed? Any answer to this question must involve having to address the ontology of the object – the implicit ontology within Descartes' own formulation – because it is the implicit and structuring presence of this ontology that sustains the 'nothing more'. (Here object is used in a general sense in that it concerns the mode of being proper to the object of knowledge within epistemological finitude.)

In the *Discourse on Method* Descartes, in a description of the use he made of method, identifies the relationship between truth and the object in the following terms:

> there being only one truth of each thing (*de chaque chose*) whoever finds it knows as much about it as can be known about it (*on en peut savoir*).
>
> (I, 590)

The 'nothing more' of the *Second Responses* is given a far more precise articulation in this passage. It opens up further relations. Because truth always has to be represented as such – representation as coextensivity – it is vital to note the way that truth is articulated in terms of representation. The terms here mean that truth also occurs within representation, in addition to its presence as a representation. Effecting a radical separation between all the elements within representation – e.g. truth, idea, sign, thing – becomes therefore increasingly more difficult to establish. The centrality of representation is important because it delimits the domain in which the Cartesian system works. It is a domain where not only was there the intention to end repetition and relation, the refusal of the already given, there was in addition the necessity to reintroduce a form of repetition. The reintroduction occurs, and it must be added that nothing could have been done to obviate this occurrence, because of the specific construal of judgement. As will be indicated, if judgement is constrained to add nothing then it is obliged to repeat.

In a letter to Mersenne in which Descartes discusses *De Veritate* by Lord Herbert of Cherbury, he writes that the latter

> examined what truth is, for me I have never doubted what it is, seeming to me that it is a notion so transcendently clear that it is impossible to be unaware of it... it could be explained, *quid nomis*, to those who did not understand language (*la langue*), saying to them that this word truth, in its proper signification, denotes the conformity of thought (*la pensée*) with the object.
>
> (II, 144)

The conformity demanded here is already apparent in the theory of ideas. Furthermore in another letter – July 1641 – Descartes argues that the certainty of an expression (an enunciation) only occurs 'when we have in us the idea of the thing (*l'idée de la chose*) which is signified by our speech (*nos paroles*)'. The question that arises again is, 'what is this "thing"?'

Earlier in the first of the letters already cited Descartes provides a formulation of the idea as though it were a response to the question 'what is named by the name idea?' (As will be argued further on, the name itself will have become a site marked by transparency.)

> I call generally of the name idea all that is in our mind (*notre esprit*) what we conceive of a thing (*une chose*) in the manner that we conceive of it.
>
> (II, 345)

What is at stake in *'concevoir'* and thus also in the name idea is formulated by Arnauld and Nicole *La Logique ou L'art de penser* in the following terms.

> Concevoir is the simple/single view (*la simple vue*) we have of things (*des choses*) which present themselves to our mind; as when we represent to ourselves (*nous nous representons*) a sun, a tree, ... thought, being, without forming any judgement about them. And the form by which we represent these things (*ces choses*) to ourselves is called an idea.
>
> (59)

The representation of the thing, the idea of the thing and knowledge of things all involve either the same considerations or the same ontology of the object. This description also opens up the question of what would be added once a judgement has take place. Once again it is in the *Second Responses* that the interconnections between idea, representation, conception and thing are drawn more tightly together. It is as though one were defined in terms of the other.

> By the objective reality of an idea I understand the entity or the being of the thing (*la chose*) represented by the idea in that this entity is in the idea. ... all of which we can conceive is objectively, or by representation in the ideas themselves.
>
> (II, 587)

The 'thing' *qua* object must be – exist – such that it can be represented as itself and where the representation represents it in its entirety. Any interpretive or epistemological problems posed by a complex representation are overcome by reducing the complex to the simple. It should be added, of course, that the Cartesian complex is a collection or amalgam of simples. (This is a position that Descartes shares with a number of other seventeenth-century philosophers, most significantly Locke.[30])

Following the lead given by Arnauld and Nicole, a lead which comes from Descartes, it is essential to separate conceiving (*concevoir*) and thus representing from judgement. Judgement, in this exact content and thus in this precise sense, becomes a response to a representation; it is not, however, an integral component of the practice and process of representation. Judgement in responding to a representation constructs a relation to it. It has already been established that in Cartesian terms judgement is uncertain. In the *Principles of Philosophy*, for example, Descartes argues that judgements which take place without the proper use of reason can lead as equally to the good as to the bad; to the true as to the false. Indeed while this is a position that is more proper to children it is also the state of affairs which if repeated stands in the way of the knowledge of truth (cf. Principle 1). Again it is clear that what is at stake here is ending the repetition of this eventuality. If it is possible to hold representation and judgement apart then the question that must be answered is how their subsequent relation is to be understood. In answering this question it must be recognised that a false judgement is always able to occur. Epistemological finitude and the certainty attached to it is limited to the level of the representation and conception of the thing. A judgement bound by the truth – i.e. bound by the 'conformity' between 'thought' and the 'object' – must itself be in conformity with truth. Being in conformity with the consequences of epistemological finitude means that all that can take place is a re-presentation of that truth; its being given again, given without addition. The re-presentation would not just have a similiar status as a repetition within the Same; it would emphatically demand its absolute presence since here repetition would have to involve identity, not just sameness. In other words it would necessitate that nothing was added in the act of judgement. As such judgement, the process or act, becomes a repetition. Using the formulation of epistemological finitude provided by the *Discourse* it is clear that once the truth of the thing is known – a process indistinguishable from it being represented as such – and with it the recognition that that is all that can be known, then this brings with it an implicit, albeit productive, conception of what could be called the temporality of knowledge and judgement.

Epistemological finitude works to create a perpetual present. The ending of repetition while ending history by the cessation of the accepting of the already given also opens up a present which, if the relation between representation and judgement is taken as paradigmatic, works by becoming the site where nothing can be added. Judgement will involve no more than the repetition of ideas. Discovery will be possible but only because judgement will allow ideas, which had not been connected hitherto, to be joined or connected. Furthermore judgement will also be involved in the evaluation of the relation between ideas. It may identify attributes of ideas where this had not previously been done, however, no action may cause an addition of any form. If addition can be distinguished from the attribution of predicates then what this means is that what must be excluded is a reworking of the idea in the act of judgement. In other words if this were to occur – i.e. if a reworking took place – then it would be a repetition in which within the work of repetition the idea that came to be repeated would then have to take on an addition. (An addition which would not be a supplement. The logic of supplementarity is linked to the problematic of representation. Here addition gives rise to complexity.) What must be developed, therefore, is an under-standing of the stakes of this exclusion. The practice of judgement, working with the intention of not adding anything to the represen-tation, allows for the re-presentation of the coextensivity between idea and thing or the conformity between thought and object. Consequently within the confines of the question 'what is named by the name idea?', the answer must be the singular (and single) content of the idea which is the idea itself. The name names, since it is, this transparency. The repetition of the idea within judgement must be such that the idea as repeated must be identical with the idea prior to its being repeated. The relation is constrained to preclude the possibility of the introduction of any alterity. It is as though, here, representation, giving again, and repetition (a repetition in and of the Same) amount to precisely the same strategy. The idea could not be reworked. If it were it would mean that in the process the repetition, now a reworking, would no longer be commensurate with the act of representation.

Representation would have become an-other, a different, rep-etition. There are a number of elements at work in this presenta-tion of the Cartesian 'thing' which need to be brought out.

The first is that judgement as re-presentation, even if it is a re-presentation that intends to be evaluative, is itself only possible given two assumptions. The first is that the representation of the 'thing' must be such that it can be represented in its entirety, i.e. in its totality and thus as a representational absolute. The second is that the act or process of re-presentation ought not to introduce either an addition or an alteration. It has already been noted that the destruction that was necessary in order that the opinions which had been deemed 'empty and false' could be given, for the first time, a secure foundation involved a complex forgetting that worked against the finality of destruction. It should be added here that while it is always possible to show that the Cartesian attempted philosophical inauguration works by working against itself, it is far more significant to note that the inauguration and the destruction depend upon this forgetting. The significance lies in part in the fact that showing the latter allows for the redemption of the inherent potential of inauguration and destruction via their rearticulation or rethinking within repetition. An awareness of forgetting need not itself be forgetful. The problems posed by both the strategy and temporality of redemption will be approached in terms of the implicit, yet strategic, temporality of *Nachträglichkeit*. With it what is opened up is the time of interpretation. It will, of course, already have been opened. There is another aspect of these present concerns that needs to be noted. It figures, figures by founding, in the process of reworking.

This additional component pertains to the terms – here names – deployed by Descartes. In addition to the varying uses already noted it must remain the case that here 'destruction' and 'inaugur-ation' – the names destruction and inauguration – must exist such that they can be reworked and that therefore in being reworked they come to be repeated anew. (This is a claim that pertains to the ontology of names.) The 'anew' now is not the envisaged new resulting from Cartesian destruction. It involves a repetition in which the name in being repeated occurs again for the first time. (This is of course a potential already inherent, *pace* Descartes, in Descartes' own formulations.) The appearance of simplicity is belied by the fact that what is actually involved here is the relationship between ontology and naming, i.e. the mode of being proper to the name. It this ontology that allows for this particular form of repetition. (It will be suggested that it is in terms of ontology that the name becomes the event.) Again the complex element is the name as marking out, in terms of an internal spacing, the possibility of its own repetition; its being repeated in this way. It bears this possibility and in bearing it the possibility resides as potential within the name itself. What this entails is that the name, what it names and what it is – its mode of being – is originally complex. It is the site of what is called anoriginal heterogeneity. The consequence of this heterogeneous event is that it eschews its own presentation within representation because there is no explicit singularity to be represented. Using the language of Cartesianism it will emerge that the anoriginal does not lend itself to a 'simple/single view' because there is no such event that can viewed, in its totality, in this particular way. This does not mean that there cannot be a specific and actual designation; however, the stakes of this designation will themselves need to be reformulated. This cannot take place within representation and therefore what has to be thought is the possibility of a determination or presentation within repetition – and thus of being within a generalised becoming – that does not still the process of repetition. It is this possibility that is to be formulated in terms of the pragma.

Returning to the implicit assumptions identified above, the trap in which Cartesian judgement is placed is that its possibility works out to be its impossibility. If the event or 'thing' is such that it can be represented as it is, in its totality, and within the confines of epistemological finitude then there is quite simply nothing to add; indeed no-'thing' can be added; the 'thing' is complete in and of itself. It establishes the boundary containing its own ontological and semantic propriety. As with any boundary it cannot be breached without that which is harboured being altered. (Any boundary is always already pragmatic.) It is precisely this state of affairs that is named by the idea and it is this which the idea as name bears. Within the question 'what is named by the name philosophy within the more general question "what is philosophy?"', it now emerges that Descartes thought it was possible to give a radically new designation as the answer (a significant component of which was the intended complete absence of any relation). In other words what the name had named hitherto could be destroyed, the referent obliterated and thus its repetition ended. The consequence of this destruction is that not only could a new name be provided, the means by which the old was destroyed and the set up occurring in its place would provide it with its content. In sum it would be the name that was, in Cartesian terms at least, contemporaneous with science.

In discussing the Cartesian revolution Gueroult describes Descartes as wanting to condemn

> the history of philosophy in so far as it is just history. The spirit of history is, in effect for him, contrary to the spirit of science.[31]

While it may be objected on another interpretation that it is precisely the Cartesian conception of science that begins the modern in the wake of history (in the precise sense of the conception of modernity – though perhaps in this instance the contemporary – within Descartes' philosophical project) by its having broken the reign of a repetition within and of the Same, the split that Gueroult identifies is apposite. Science, in the Cartesian sense, creates a present in which nothing can be added and where judgement is constrained to repeat, a project that becomes impossible because of the eventual impossibility of sustaining forgetting within it. The consequences of the intermingling and consequent interdeterminations of time, judgement and repetition will continue to be taken up within specific works of Pascal, Leibniz, Hegel and Heidegger. In each instance what is essential is tracing that work, be it implicit or explicit, at work within or arising out of the work of the texts under consideration. Immediately it is there in naming, remembering, of course, that what is at stake in naming will be the event. With the event what will also emerge is the present in which the event can be said to occur. The occurrence is of necessity present. Its necessity is in part the event.

Intermezzo: conflict naming

Forgetting figures within the Cartesian strategy of destruction in clearly identifiable ways. There is another site, however, where consequences similar to those arising from forgetting are acted out. As a result, therefore, the effect of these consequences must be noted and their presence acknowledged. What is involved in this instance is the connection between forgetting and yet different forms of destruction. No longer is destruction simply to be linked to the presence and thus to the intended absence of tradition's continuity; destruction can in addition also take the form of an obliteration of the site of conflict obliteration as the effacing or denial of the name as event and thus with it either the obviating of complexity or the re-presentation of complexity as a construction of simples and therefore as no more than a specific totality of simples. It will be noted, at a different interval, that this reworking of the site such that its obliteration can be taken as being of significance arises out of the potential inherent in Leibniz's formulation of the monad. (It goes without saying that it is the consequences of this potential that suffer obliteration.) Its being *inherent* – an inherent potential – almost stakes out in advance the ontological state of affairs which it can be seen as addressing. Taking up the inherent, not necessarily in terms of the content that inheres but in regard to the ontology of inhering – understood initially as a type of presence – and the relation it enacts will form an integral part of any conception of complexity. Once again it is the complex beyond simple accumulation. With the monad the event is prefigured by the monads figuring, by allowing, the anoriginal presence of ontological irreducibility a site, i.e. locating the effective presence of a differential ontology, by being it.

Descartes' formulation of '*la chose*' is such that the intended ontology of 'the thing' is of an order that it – '*la chose*' – is always able to be represented as itself. The name therefore – the named 'thing', the 'thing' as named – demands a place within an intended coextensivity in so far as 'it' is itself intended to be coextensive with that which it names. The coextensivity does not preclude the arbitrary. However, the arbitrary involves a formal particularity;

in other words, any given signifier may be arbitrary in terms of its particular relation to a given signified. Arbitariness, however, does not describe the structural relation between signifier and signified. Staying within the Cartesian context it should be remembered that Arnauld and Nicole indicate in *La Logique* that, despite the absence of a natural connection within the sign, it nonetheless remains the case that the named (signified) still names (signifies) absolutely. Language and signification are constrained on the one hand to resist the Cratylian temptation of construing the name as in some sense arising out of the named while on the other to exclude the possibility that the name may be present as originally overdetermined and thus potentially polysemic. Both possibilities would demand both a radically different ontology of the name and temporality of signification. The differences involved are only explicable in ontological terms.[32]

The necessity at work here – a necessity marked in part by these two exclusions – is also found in the interplay between grammar and logic developed by Arnauld, Nicole, Lancelot, and colleagues at Port-Royal.[33] The interplay and the related levels of necessity within their differing though interrelated systems of logic and grammar have been formulated by Kristeva as including the following minimal determinations.

> Word and linguistic expressions dress ideas which refer to objects. The logical or natural relation, which reveals the truth of things is played out on the level of ideas; it is the logical level. Grammar treats objects, language (*la langue*) which is only the sign of this natural or logical dimension, thus it depends on the logical even while having its own autonomy.[34]

While there is an important difference between what is identified in *La Logique* as a '*definitio nominis*' and other names it remains the case that it is the linkage of both to ideas – and with it to the ontology proper to ideas – that unites them. It establishes a structural identity which unifies them within a more generalised structure of representation. However once both this conception of representation and the related and intended ontology of the represented are no longer dominant, then a different possibility within naming (as naming) can be allowed to develop. It is a possibility which, in distancing the interplay between representation and the classical conception of epistemology, reworks presentation within an ontology of becoming. It is this particular mode of being which when thought within repetition sanctions the presentation of the singular within plurality, a presentation which not only occasions but also will demand the response of judgement. Judgement rather than knowledge becomes the response enjoined by anoriginal difference. Again, this should not be understood as even suggesting that knowledge claims cannot be made; rather it is to be taken as marking the dis-placement of the aspirations of classical epistemology. They are reworked while the domination of epistemology and the structure of representation are held in abeyance. Displaced in the same movement therefore is the structure representation. What has to be thought through is how the hold of displacing and with it the presence of that which has been displaced is to be understood. Central to such a thinking will be time; time, that is, as being the site of its plurality.

The simultaneity of movement – of displacing – results from having to respond to the necessary interarticulation of knowledge (classically construed) and representation. One of the results of this is that knowledge becomes strategic by its always having to have been delimited. Foundations give way to the interplay of consequences and conditions of existence and thereby give rise to a politics of knowledge. The politics of epistemology – even a redeemed theory of knowledge – lies outside as well as within the theory's formal interiority. There is therefore a constitutive spacing that checks, again at the same time, any easily formulated distinction between inside and outside. More significantly, however, it causes the nature of the event to be reworked in order that its complexity is retained. Finally what is opened up – reopened as a question – is the way in which truth will or can play a role within such a reformulation. It may be that truth stands in the way of the actuality of the politics of epistemology in that truth, in being formal, can only pertain to the interiority and as a consequence would preclude attention being given to an exteriority of consequences and conditions of existence. What needs to be worked through, therefore, is the possible emergence of distance. Again, it should be noted that distance does not exist in itself. The presence of distance signals the necessity of relation.

Of the many sites in which it is possible to locate the occurrence of a distancing that can be taken as involving displacing rather than destruction in the Cartesian sense, one of the most productive is the work of another seventeenth-century philosopher, namely

Blaise Pascal.[35] It should not be thought, however, that Pascal was unaware of the contemporary construal of naming or that he eschewed any engagement with it. Pascal's own confrontation with the Cartesian heritage is far from straightforward. In the first section of *De l'esprit géometrique*, while not referring to the work of the Port-Royal logicians as such, Pascal nonetheless employs what could be described as the structure of the 'word' that is found in the *Logic* and which is also articulated within the structure of representation at work within Descartes' texts. Pascal argues that, in pursuit of research,

> one arrives necessarily at primitive words (*mots primitifs*) that can no longer be defined and of which the principles are so clear that there is little advantage in attempting to prove them.
>
> (182)

Despite the complexity of the text from which these lines are taken its importance is that it signals, as has been indicated, the retention of the same structure of simplicity and geometrical method that is found in both Descartes and *Logic*.

While there will be no attempt here to deny the importance of any undertaking that aims to trace the work of 'words' and 'names' throughout that text, or moreover of the effective presence of the theory of representation within the corpus of Pascal's writings, in this instance as an attempt to take up the relationship between naming and conflict, it will be essential to concentrate on that aspect of the *Penseés* which can be taken as checking the defined name and with it the actual possibility of a 'primitive word' and which therefore displaces the dominance of representation and its associated ontology.[36] It goes without saying that it is Pascal's recognition of 'definition' and its related conception of naming that makes the references to another possibility within (and for) naming all the more significant. The difficulty and thus the challenge resides in how this other possibility is to be understood. The presence of the problem of understanding as a question rather than as an already present conclusion – presented within Pascal's texts as an unequivocal conclusion – accounts in part for the contemporary force, perhaps the modernity, of the *Pensées*. Within the confines of Pascal's own writings this division is of considerable importance. It has both philosophical and theological consequences and as such would have to figure in any synoptic interpretation of the totality of his writings. Indeed it could be further argued that it is this very division – its ineliminable actual presence – that comprises the totality.[37]

Naming is other than straightforward; it is never simply present. As will be indicated naming names but always in addition. For example, it is as part of an attempt to take up the question of unity and with it the relationship between unity and diversity, in 65, that the 'name' comes to be reworked. It is the presence of the 'name' (in the end the name 'name', naming in addition the presence of naming) within this description of the process of naming that opens up the possibility of a different presentation of signification, one which in contradistinction to the Cartesian heritage will involve the necessary interarticulation of naming and conflict – hence conflict naming, the latter being a designation which will of itself demand a reconsideration of conflict. Here the reconsideration would stem from the recognition that conflict when taken as a name may be subject to – or at least mark out – the process that it names. As such conflict reintroduces the same set of concerns as 'repetition' when it is taken as a name.

Pascal's take on the name – the name that differentiates itself from the 'primitive word' – is presented in the following way:

> A town, a countryside, from afar it is a town, a countryside, but to the extent that it is approached there are houses, trees, tiles, leaves, grass, ant, ant's legs, *to infinity* (*à l'infini*). All of this enveloped under the *name* countryside.
>
> (65, my emphasis)

What is presented here is the complex interplay of three different elements. They can be provisionally identified as distance ('to the extent...'), time ('to infinity') and signification ('the name'). The complexity of these interdeterminations is yet to be clarified. Nonetheless what has already been presented is how, or in terms of what, those further determinations are going to be discovered. It is perhaps far from surprising that distance figures in other parts of the *Pensées*. As will be seen distance is linked to questions concerning signification and the responses to it.

At another point in the text (558), Pascal's overall concern is again with the possible conclusions that may be drawn from the inevitable presence of diversity. The important point in this instance, however, is that the concern is presented in such a way that it can be read as indicating that one result of the inevitability of diversity is an ensuing fundamental change in how objects are to be understood. While it is not argued for as such, the fragment can be read as suggesting that in their being reworked objects will come to have the same ontological status as the name.

> I have never judged of a thing exactly the same. I can never judge a work while making it. It is necessary that I do as the painters and that I distance myself, but not too far. How much therefore? Guess.
>
> (558)

What is significant in the above is that it is within a relation of distance that judgement (in this specific sense) becomes both possible and necessary. The co-presence of both needs to be emphasised. The nature of what presents itself is not such that it automatically presents itself as such, presenting itself in its totality at one and the same time. It is within this opening – the inscripted spacing – that time can be taken to figure. Part of this figuring is that its presence entails that the intended temporal simultaneity marking the coextensivity within the Classical conception of the sign, the Cartesian structure of idea, etc., no longer pertains. Coextensivity and simultaneity are sundered. In the separation the anoriginal presence of complexity is affirmed.

With judgement, again in the precise Pascalian sense, a necessary deferral has been introduced and as a consequence therefore a stand is necessary. But the stance, the posit-ion, is not given. It is neither posit-ed nor self-given; it does not come therefore within its law. The absence of the given – in both senses – also occurs in 41. Before returning to the individual 'pensées' cited above it is essential to note this further example.

> When one reads either too quickly or too slowly nothing is understood.
>
> (41)

With regard to this example, while there is an explicit reference to speed rather than to distance, what is being expressed is nonetheless still characterised, apart from the exclusion of a hermeneutical telos, by the absence within it of a given and thus already determined criterion of evaluation. It can be provisionally suggested, therefore, that part of what is absent is that which would give rise to the representation of any one given determination. The means of representation are no longer present and thus nor is what it is that would be represented – a singular content – were it able to be presented within the enclosure that defines the Classical conception of the sign. In other words, what seems to be absent is the actual structure of representation, i.e. that structure of onto-logical and temporal coextensivity between representation and represented demanded by representation and which it – represen-tation – intends to enact. What will have to be taken up is not just the possibility of this state of affairs but more importantly how that possible absence is to be understood. The inherent difficulty here is twofold.

In the first place it is thinking the advent of the different beyond the purview of destruction – in sum the obliteration of relation – while at the same time resisting the nihilism that enjoins the destruction of destruction. (As will be suggested at a later stage this doubling of destruction forms part of the dilemma arising from the logic of sacrifice, a dilemma exemplified by the acuity of the question 'How is sacrifice to be done without?') In the second place it entails disassociating absence from a more problematic loss. Absence need not stem from loss. It is precisely the latter possibility, namely a construal of absence that need not be situated within confines of melancholia or forgetting, that can be affirmed both by the identification of differing interpretive strategies and by structures of signification, a possibility of course which can only be accounted for by recourse to ontology. Affirmation would be linked to the distancing of dominance. Again the interpretive problem will be developing an understanding of this link. Again it must be assumed that the link is not just given. It will be essential to return to this point.

The content of 41 concerns an assertion that implicitly insists on the possibility of an appropriate speed. Understanding is possible; 41 will have been read. Speed itself pertains almost exclusively to comprehension. It is an assertion, however, that neither gives rise to relativism nor precludes the possibility of an adequate reading, i.e. a reading that is neither 'too quick' nor 'too slow'. (In the process, of course, the nature of adequacy is itself reworked away from the Classical conception of adequation – truth as *veritas est adequatio verbi et rei* – and towards its provisionality; a move which itself reworks the relationship between time and truth.) The absence of relativism is explained as due to the ineliminable link between relativism and the project of epistemology. Relativism is trapped by its having to imitate truth conditions without ever being able to enact them; a partial and to that extent negative mimesis. It mimics truth. Relativism is therefore no more than the possibility of the pathological within the Classical conception of adequation. Reworking adequacy will demand that it be distanced from its initial location with the reciprocity of 'words' (*verbi*) and 'things' (*rei*); again a relation which if it is not marked by coextensivity does at least necessitate a relation of what could be described as a one-to-one. The time of adequacy therefore – the temporality within this relation – is again simultaneity. Adequacy reworked, coming within the process of reworking to be linked to judgement becomes a response to that which presents the limits of *adequatio* while at the time actualising the potential already inherent in the name 'adequation'. Conversely the Scholastic conception of truth as adequation can therefore be interpreted as dependent upon the obliteration of that potential. It goes without saying that what sustains that potential – sustains by being it – is the ontology of the name.

What charactarises the implicit conception of signification in 65 is the interplay of time, distance and naming. The connections between them are such that no one element can be taken as standing on its own. Given the inescapability of these interrelations the question that must be answered concerns the presence of representation: how and to what extent can it be said to be present? Does the specific, though connected, presence of time, distance and naming allow for their own presentation within the structure of representation or are they already delimited by other concerns? In the case of the latter it would be concerns already occurring beyond that which is bounded, literally, by representation.

While describing the content of 65 in a slightly different way, Louis Marin in his *La Critique du discours*, and as part of a sustained interpretation of this fragment, writes that

> The undefinable character of distance discovers the infinity in the diversity of things which must be said and judged. The metaphor of distance, of point of view, constitute the elements of a model of representation in Pascal, but a model which functions negatively; this is the irony of metaphor.[38]

For Marin the structure of representation is maintained, even though its presence is given a negative function and thereby presented as ironic. He argues, for example, that 'Pascal utilises ... the model of representation in order to deconstruct (*déconstruire*) representation' – the intentional use of representation against itself. The claim of an already present deconstruction within the text must involve a more complex argument than that which amounts to the identification of the presence of irony. If the 'name' presented in 65 is taken as already explicitly involved in moving away from naming in the Cartesian sense, then the question that must be asked will concern the extent to which the name and the related conception of naming retain the structure of representation. This question is of fundamental importance, for what is at stake is whether or not Pascal can be read as advancing a theory of naming which, while alluding to Cartesianism, does in its being advanced take on a completely different orientation. In other words, is there a possible conflict between conceptions of naming where conflict, rather than working in terms of the mutually exclusive, marks the primordiality of relation. As such conflict is itself to be identified within the maintenance of relation. What will be argued here is that if the latter possibility holds then the structure of representation will have been dis-placed. It will have been neither destroyed nor 'deconstructed' (in Marin's sense).

According to Marin the introduction of 'pure differences' (introduced in part by *l'infini*) works against the structure of representation; a work that is only discovered once the question is asked of the status of that which is present – presented – to be represented. From any attempt to answer the question it will emerge that representation has set up, Marin argues, that which it cannot provide. The argument continues therefore that its possibility is its impossibility:

> in proposing a being which is only a differential play (*jeu différentiel*) and in obeying the demands of representation which aim to bring an evanescence in being by the means of signs, Pascal takes representation into the infinite play of difference. He puts it to one side. He destroys it as such since the differential element where it will be accomplished is an absurdity.

(121)

In this passage representation is presented by Marin as that which is used against itself. In trying to represent what cannot be represented the structure is 'destroyed as such'.

On one level there can be no dispute that within the frame of fragment 65, difference, perhaps even 'pure difference', can be said to figure. 'Diversity' can be read as another name for difference. Even conceding that 'putting to one side' is by no means the same as 'to destroy as such' the question that still must answered is whether what figures is a structure of representation that works against itself? With regard to the questions of how interpretation is to be understood and then how the object of interpretation is to be construed, the preliminary problem concerning how the presence of the structure of representation is to be taken is itself of considerable sigificance. Consequently prior to taking up the problem it is essential to try and state why its resolution is important.

A casual consequentalism would miss the point. In essence such a position would argue that, since it could always be maintained that if what is central is noting the demise of representation's dominance, then it must be asked why it is more significant that this demise occur one way rather than another. This type of response ignores the importance of what is involved. The issue here concerns the possibility of distancing the hold of representation, and with it of a distancing that resists the use of destruction. It is thus that the stakes are much larger. The interpretation developed by Marin entails that the actual structure of representation is used against itself and in being used in this way the basis of representation comes to be questioned; moreover it is the nature of this questioning that then opens up the possibility of a departure from the structure itself. (The latter movement is traced throughout Marin's *La Critique du discours*. Nonetheless what endures as an open question is the extent to which such a departure would necessitate the presence of forgetting.) What is at stake here is nothing less than the history of philosophy. For Marin the implicit conception of that history is of a totality working within itself for itself. It structures what is possible within it. This accounts for why the given, in always being given with the history of the Same, can only ever be deployed against itself.

While it is not precluded on any general or abstract level what is not considered in this formulation is the possibility that the fragment and its content were *ab initio* unthinkable within the structure of representation precisely because the conditions of existence proper to representation (i.e. the ontologico-temporal structure of 'thing', 'idea', 'sign', etc.) were themselves not present. Arguing that the conditions of possibility were absent would not be to argue that the terminology of representation's structure of signification – there with the word 'name' – was not present or that the possibility of time and place (the site of representation) was absent, but rather that their presence allowed itself to be interpreted in a different way (no longer absence as loss, or a present locked in a spiralling oscillation between irony and tragedy). The language of representation, while it announced the presence of the structure of representation thereby allowing it to be re-presented, the manner of its presence – its mode of being present – is such that it did not dominate the frame itself. The named presence of the structure of signification therefore need involve neither irony nor negativity but rather may be taken as signifying a different commitment within a range of differing strategies of naming. The way in which naming, citation and reference are present is as a reworked presentation incorporating the display of the dominance of representation but no longer being the display of that dominance. This is a move that is sanctioned by the inherent doubling there in display; there in the question of what the display displays and maintained throughout by ontology of the name sanctioning an inaugurating repetition and thus a re-presentation – presentation as pragma – of the name.

What is involved in the question concerning the importance of the presence of the preclusion of the structure of representation's dominance can be taken, not just as concerning naming, but as figuring within the plural possibilities of naming itself. More exactly it involves the relationship between naming and that which it presents, and therefore to the extent that this relationship is explored the simple opposition of presence and absence will be reworked. (The banality of simple antinomic thinking needs to recognised for what is.) In 65 the use of the word 'name' has been taken to name the presence of the structure of signification within representation in order that in naming – in naming it – it is present as such. It is not taken as simply re-presenting it. The relationship between 'name' and 'infinity' is assumed to 'destroy', to use Marin's term, representation since the structure of representation demanded by the 'name' cannot enact what is demanded of it by 'infinity', signifying the infinite till infinity. Representation therefore falls apart. It is clear that it is not simply negativity as irony that is at work in this construal. Perhaps more appropriately it could be described as the negativity of failure. The possibility of articulating this state of affairs in terms of failure is of great importance here for any assessment of Marin's argument.

However, its importance is even greater since negativity and impossibility will come to define, as will be suggested, the trajectory of a certain construal of the philosophical task (a construal which on the one hand presents philosophy's history in terms of the presence of a single monolithic dominant structure but which on the other precludes the possibility of an originating or inaugurating repetition distancing the dominant). Failure, the moment at which and thus the textual moment where the project runs up against its own impossibility, may become, within that trajectory, an end in itself. Indeed it is more than that since it becomes all that is possible. With negativity – with failure – a limit comes to be imposed and with it the range of the possible is delimited by the already existent border established by the then actualised impossibility of the projected possibility. On the other side of 'failure', marking its limit, is the redemptive move of affirmation. Affirmation in moving beyond the confines of an active forgetting is possible to the extent that the history of philosophy is understood as the site of conflict's continuity such that while the Same may be repeated – the repetition of dominance – with other differentiating repetitions, repeating in part the margins, what is held open is the continual possibility of originating repetitions. It is this particular opening that will be taken up. Again what is at stake here is whether the history of philosophy can be taken as sanctioning that which it had not sanctioned hitherto while at the same time the adventure is allowed to form part of that history. Both occurring at the same time will mean the necessary presence of relation and conflict. In other words the potential in the name is always being realised. These considerations must be taken as figuring in the *pensées* under discussion.

If it could be claimed that there was no suggestion of irony in 65, let alone the negativity of failure, and that on the contrary what was being proposed could be taken as a theory of naming, no matter how tentative and inexact its formulation, then the use of the word – the word 'name' – would be importantly different. On the one hand it would signal the presence of a theory of naming inextricably connected to time and distance, though no longer to what was taken as the *aphoria* of 'infinity' – loss of place/departure from path – while on the other hand because it was advanced within the vocabulary of the tradition it would, as a consequence, signal the ineliminable presence of relation (the mark of tradition within the pragma). The relation in question would be of course a relation eschewing homology and to that extent a relation of non-relation – a relation of distance, the mark of abeyance – to the dominance of the structure of representation. It is the latter possibility that still needs to be pursued. One way in which abeyance could be thought of and it is of course only one possible way – would be in terms of the theory of naming that allows it. Here it would be as though naming already contained the event's inscription at the same time as being an event. It would be as though it had become a *mise-en-abyme* for the event.

The specific question that has to be taken up concerns how representation is present. What is being argued is that even though Cartesianism is present it is the nature of that presence, which on the one hand signals the existence of a relation to it thereby maintaining relation over an intended destruction, while on the other hand allowing that relation not to impede the development of another conception of naming which is central. The structure of representation is named, its terminology is employed, and yet that terminology, the structure's names, are themselves never coextensive with that of which they can be taken to be the terminology etc. In referring though never absolutely the name is opened up. In the opening, with the recognition of an ineliminable constitutive spacing, the inscripted plurality is allowed to emerge. As will be argued this is an ontological claim and not just a semantic one. These preliminary points need to be taken a step further and therefore will be taken up again.

Within the context in which Pascal is writing the structure of representation is most straightforwardly present in the work of Descartes and the Port-Royal logicians. It is the dominant structure within that context. In part it is due to its dominance that it can itself be re-presented via the utilisation of a specific vocabulary. As has already been suggested Pascal's use of the word 'name' cannot help but raise the question of naming; raising it – allowing it to be given – within the context in which it is given. (The doubling of the given will be of considerable importance.) The question here is what is it that has been re-presented, given. It can be argued that the movement in which the word 'name' is given can be construed as a form of repetition; to re-present, to be given again is to repeat. The word has been repeated and as such what has to be determined is whether or not this is a repetition within the Same – a giving of the Same – or whether with this word, in its being repeated, can be said to occur again, now, for the first time. What emerges with this question – though it will, of course, already have emerged before – is that repetition lends itself and thus will already have lent itself to the incorporation and thus articulation of a plurality that checks the possibility of an essence and with it of essential thinking from the start.

What is repeated with Pascal's 'name', the 'name' presented and thus named in 65, is the structure of representation. It is named with it. Within that given context, the structure in some sense not being presented would be impossible. Accepting the abeyance of destruction means that here the structure's presence is ineliminable, thereby indicating that it – its presence – will figure as an aspect of the ontology of names. The structure of representation is presented with and in the name; the name 'name'. Again however the question arises of what does it mean to claim that this structure has been presented? Presentation need not be taken as either absolute (complete) or singular and therefore it needs to be recognised that the force of the question lies in the fact that it does not follow from its having been presented that it provides the fragment with the interpretive frame within which it, the fragment, is necessarily to be thought or understood. And yet this is to state too little. In the first place for the structure of representation to be more than maintained by the fragment, for it to be dominant and thus for the 'infinity' (l'infini) to offer a 'deconstruction' if not 'destruction' of representation (here only employing Marin's own terminology), certain additional elements would have to be present. They would moreover have to be more than simple additions.

As has already been indicated a fundamental component whose presence would be necessary if the structure of representation were to be dominant and therefore presented as implicated in its own 'destruction'/'deconstruction' would be the inscription and thus the effective presence of the temporality and the ontology and as such the ontologico-temporal concatenation proper to the structure of representation. It would have already been inscribed within a precarious dominance in order for it then to be destroyed. The time in question is the simulataneity marking both the coextensivity between sign and thing and the one-to-one of adequation. Ontology pertains to the ontology demanded in the formulation already noted in Descartes' conception of 'thing' (la chose). In each case what is of central concern is the nature of presence (remembering, again, that presence, the name 'presence', will itself have to eschew the possibility of an instilled essence and thus formally preclude the possibility of there being presence itself). Given this set up, what will have to be shown is the way in which the fragments enact a distancing of this structure maintained within its own abeyance.

In the case of 54 there is a complicating factor – that factor that marks the fragment's existence as a complex – which is the announced presence within it of distance. Indeed it will be suggested that what cannot be reconciled with (let alone within) the structure of representation is that which could be described as the mediating presence of distance; the effective presence of distance. Distance must be understood as more than the intrusion of narrowly geographical or cartological considerations. Distance marks the presence of an ineliminable opening. It is this presence – the presence moreover of this possibility – that is articulated in terms of the necessary impossibility of simplicity announced in 54.

> Inconstancy.
> Things (*les choses*) have diverse qualities and the soul divers inclinations, for nothing of that which is offered to the soul is simple and the soul never offers anything simple to any subject. This explains why (*de là vient*) we laugh and cry at the same thing (*chose*).

Here the twofold presence of distance presents difficulties bordering on the complex. First, 'things' having diverse qualities involve more than the claim that any one 'thing' may admit of a number of different predicates. Here diversity exists within – perhaps even as – the 'thing'. As such therefore 'things' are marked by an ineliminable and self-constituting spacing in so far as 'diversity' pertains initially to the absence of a unified essential quality that could be re-presented – repeated – as itself. The reason why what is involved here is not a simple semantic plurality is that to which diversity attests, and this will be equally true with the name, the impossibility of there ever being a coextensivity between that which is presented – what is deemed to have been presented and therefore taken over as such – and the totality that will also bear the name of the presentation. Spacing addresses the ontology of 'diversity', equally it will address the ontology of the name, Pascal's 'name'. Consequently spacing works to maintain the initial complexity – a complexity constitutive of the 'name' etc. and therefore anoriginally present – of that which is offered either by or to the soul. Things distance themselves from themselves in being themselves. In addition, therefore, diversity marks a distancing from the essential and thus the simplicity and unity of content, a distancing that no longer takes place within the determining ambit of the essential. The latter is the second form of distancing. In other words, also enacted within the fragment is a distancing of the Cartesian conception of the simple. (It is of fundamental importance to note that it is distanced only in being raised. Again it is this state of affairs that will work to inform naming, forming it as the event.)

The other term in this fragment that is of considerable significance is 'offer'. With it what is introduced is another description of presencing. What is presented to the soul and which the soul itself presents cannot be described as simple. What this means is that presentation is not such that the presented is a self-referring unity. The consequence is that 'offer' comes to mark out the possibility of a presencing and with it of a presentation in which the object – that which is given, presented – cannot be represented as such. The coextensivity demanded by the structure of representation, which has already been noted, for example, in Descartes' formulation of the 'idea' and even in the Cartesian construal of the work of memory, is no longer apposite because of the nature of what is offered. Offering becomes a tentative way of thinking presentation working within the distancing of the possibility of the simple. It is this point – the abeyance of the simple – that must be pursued. It should be added, again, that its abeyance is not its destruction. The simple will always be present though as secondary, perhaps as the pragma and therefore as never absolutely simple. The pragma will always be marked by its bearing the impossibility of absolute singularity. It shows, as well as showing in the ontology of the pragma itself. With this twofold showing the unity and simplicity of any 'itself' is itself distanced. Any presentation will always bring more than itself into play, thereby turning the 'itself' into the secondary while maintaining through its ineliminable presence in the presentation the insistence of an anoriginal plurality.

The simple is present throughout the Cartesian texts both methodologically and in the formulation of central terms, e.g. the 'idea'. The role of the simple is announced with striking force in *La Recherche de la vérité*. Within its presentation in this particular text the direct methodological consequences of simplicity are also brought out. The complex exists only because the complex is no more than the co-presence of things which are in themselves simple.

all the truths follow one another and are united between them by a common link. The entire secret consists in starting with the first and the most simple (*les plus simples*) and then lifting ... little by little and by degrees to distant and more complex truths.

(my emphasis)

The simple therefore is already articulated within and thus intends the articulation of the structure of representation; the site constructed out of the interplay of idea, sign and 'thing' – Descartes' 'thing' – and which therefore already contains that which will occasion its own deconstruction. The 'simple' moreover should be understood as being what is *seen* by 'clear and distinct perception'. Cartesian sight – in this precise sense of sight – both sees and sees that which is seen *in simpliciter* and consequently the simple is offered to sight as simple and its seeing, the seeing itself, is equally simple, equally singular. Again, the time of this singular seeing is temporal simultaneity. At the instant all that is to be seen is seen and the name will name – name by identifying – the singular all, totality as unity, given within simultaneity.

In specific terms what is suggested by this passage from Descartes – and it is of course one that could be supplemented with many others presenting the same formulation of the 'simple' – is an initially straightforward methodological movement involving the possibility of an unequivocal departure from the complex to simple and then back to the complex; a movement occasioning that understanding of the complex as the accumulation of simples where each simple is attributed the same ontological weight. The important aspect in this instance, however, is not the methodological. It is rather the implicit assumption pertaining to the ontology of 'thing', sign, idea, etc. that enables such movement to take place; the intention that it take place. As has already been noted the basis for any oscillation between complex and simple occurs due to a repetition of the same ontological preconditions that have already been assumed to figure within the more general conception of 'thing'. In other words the complex is a collection of simples. The simple exists in and of itself. As such it can be represented as it is. It is not as though the simple could itself ever form a complex by being complex in itself, or be the site of an already existent diversity and thus a plurality which was anoriginally present.

The project of simplicity is the pro-ject of that singularity – original singularity prior to complexity – that gives itself to consciousness to be received as such. This will, perhaps, become another description of clear and distinct perception. It is a giving that precludes judgement in the precise sense that what is given clearly and distinctly is true in virtue of its being thus given. Representation is a repetition that any additional judgement is constrained to repeat. Judgement in the case of the presentation of the simple and thus of a complex of simples can neither add nor introduce. Any additional move would introduce change – the change stemming from work – into the re-presentation and consequently it would undermine the continuity demanded by repetition within the Same. Pascal's offering brings with it the need for a constant evaluation and reckoning. When what is offered can never be coextensive with the thing itself – for there is no itself that is distinct from the totality of possiblities captured by the name 'name' or 'diversity' for example – then with the restriction of representation and the putative certainty it allows what arises is neither relativism nor scepticism but the responsibility of judgement. The preconditions for judgement, in this precise sense rather than the Cartesian sense, are provided by the ontology of the name once it is taken as naming beyond the confines of the Cartesian heritage.

The position advanced in 54, in part due as will be suggested to its retention of an elementary structure of subject/object relations, is not simply the negative possibility of representation, nor moreover is it implicated in a destruction of the structure of representation. It is rather that by the recognition of an initial complexity, one eschewing the possibility of a further reduction, while at the same time being linked to the obviation of that structure of reception demanded by clear and distinct perception – assuming that perception can be taken as a figure and thus as an exemplar for the reception of the gift of singularity – what is presented becomes what is unthinkable within the structure of representation. Here 'unthinkable' needs to be taken as that which cannot be thought because the conditions of existence pertaining to its being thought are not presented as dominant within and as part of the intended project.

Within 54 each component of the structure of representation

would be checked by the attempt to 'think' its presence within representational terms. However, and this is the point that in this instance needs to be emphasised, the attempt is not being made within the confines of 54. This is not to argue, however, that the structure does not figure within 54. It is there within the pro-ject and therefore relatedly there within the word 'simple'. Its presence, while on a formal level attesting to the anoriginal complexity of the word – of what the word names and thus with the word as name – does at the same time establish a relation of non-relation to the structure and therefore is what allows it to be present but only presented as distanced, present while held in abeyance. In Pascal's own terms it may be that its being presented but present as distanced accounts for why here 'we may laugh and cry at the same thing'. Furthermore the simple, though now perhaps more accurately the simple's complexity, a founding complexity foundering the positing of an original simplicity, opens up a way back to the name, Pascal's 'name', and thus with it a possible response to the question of how to interpret the presentation of naming within 65.

The point at issue is not therefore the simple question of the extent to which the presentation of naming in 65, taken in conjunction with the various other 'pensées' cited above, can be read as situated with the structure of representation such that what emerges as a consequence is their functionning as that which destroys the actual pro-ject demanded by the structure. The answer to that question is that there is another reading taking place as another philosophical possibility that in insisting upon an already existent complex – and thus already present complexity – precludes, by its work, this possibility. It should be added that a direct consequence of such an interpretation is the necessity to develop an understanding of the 'already existent'. However, the more general interpretive problem that has to be resolved is how to understand that the structure of representation is present but only present in being named. What will be argued is that it is precisely the theory of naming that emerges from 65 which when read in conjunction with other 'pensées' will allow for this possibility to be expressed.

Giving content to the formal treatment of complexity and simplicity can be begun by showing its present enactment. The simple, the simple presented in 54, is complex initially because it brings with it the Cartesian simple while at the same time introducing that which departs from such a conception of simplicity. The actual use of the word cannot but raise the possibility of the Cartesian adventure. It is to that extent present; named. Its presence, however, is neither 'destroyed' nor 'deconstructed' (maintaining Marin's terms) since its presence, understood as its present dominance, is not actualised as such. It is therefore not at work. Consequently the formal possibility that 54 allows is a way of thinking presentation that is neither situated within nor premised upon the destruction of representation. The suggestion of the impossibility of an initial simplicity which would have been either given, the positing of simplicity, or discovered, the repositioning of simplicity, is no longer the work of negativity (the latter being intention's impossibility shown in its coming apart). It is rather that the interplay of 'diversity', understood as descriptive of things, and 'offering', understood as a mode of presentation, provides the means within which to think presentation beyond the structure of representation. And yet it is a means which while alluding to the structure by its having been invoked via the use of the terminology pertaining to it does not at the same time sanction the dominance of that which the terminology invokes. Representation does not structure presentation. (Domination, however, need not involve its own success. Indeed Marin's reading of 65 turns around the possibility that the structure of representation dominates but that its attempt to realise that dominance undoes the project itself.)

The inherent theory of naming that is present within 65 and supported by formulations in other fragments, once either allowed to be generalised or assumed to provide a formal frame for semantics, will be, as was suggested, that which will allow for an account of its own distancing of Cartesianism to take place. Allowing for it to be named but at the same time not allowing for its dominance is a possibility that in marking the abeyance of the Cartesian conception of 'name', 'thing', 'idea', etc. will demand that a return be made not just to naming – i.e. shown semantic content – but more importantly to the ontology of the name. (It should be remembered that with the name it is the event that is coming to be named.) What has been designated *conflict naming* means that what 'infinity' names is an infinity. And yet of course this infinity is not to be taken literally. Infinity is not the other possibility, the op-posing counter to finitude. Here it is that which breaks the specular confines established by the interplay of reference and ambiguity. It is thus that it is not simply semantic. Infinity pertains to the ontology of the name, the showing of which is semantic; to which it should be added straight away that there is of course never the purely semantic. Developing this point involves returning to the fragment itself if only to take it beyond its immediate concerns.

As has already been noted what the fragment presents is the co-presence of time, distance and signification. There could, however, be a complicating factor for it could be argued that all that is involved in 65 is the relativity of collective nouns – i.e. what they stand for will depend upon the position from which the description is given – and is thus not applicable to naming in general. Arguing for this possibility would have to deny the force, now perhaps ironically, of the naming of Cartesianism within the fragment. Naming it allows for the essence, the 'idea', etc., to be brought up, raised almost as a possibility, only to be held to one side while naming opens itself up to a possibility occurring with the abeyance of representation, and therefore within the spacing opened by the re-fusing of the essence. What makes such a possibility real is that there is a fundamentally different ontology of the word (and with it therefore of the name) involved. In the absence of the Cartesian construal – the absence of its dominance – what is presented is radically different. The difference can be signalled by returning to the name; here this means – returning means – opening up the inherent plurality within time; within the name 'time'.

The temporal simultaneity of the construction of the sign in *La Logique* is no longer possible. Equally the judgement enjoined by representation – judgement as a repetition from which work is of necessity excluded – is in addition no longer apposite. The time of the presentation, and with it of another different judgement, has a given location and thus a given specificity. Any particular judgement pertaining to the name's content (its meaning) will involve a relativity only because the specific content can never be absolutely coextensive with the name itself; a relativity beyond relativism. Other judgements and thus other contents are possible, opening up thereby another space of conflict. Each, however, will demand another time and another site. The time of judgement and with it the ontology of what is judged will involve a different ontologico-temporal framework from the one found in 'infinity' and yet of course it will depend upon it. This dependence indicates why the pragma – and here even accepting the difficulties that must emerge for Pascal, the partiality of the formulation thus far, it remains the case that the regional, therefore the judged, is the pragma – will always be inscribed within that which will question the possibility of any attribution of any absolute singularity. Infinity, the 'infinity' within 65, should be understood as a generalised becoming in which presentations take place. And yet the provisionality of such an understanding will mean that the generality will need to be given a type of content and with it the formalism given a more precise range of application. It therefore follows that the recovery of plurality rather then simply enjoining a limit – again the spectre of negativity and loss – will open up philosophical work; it may become its work without ever being it.

What the name names therefore can never be an essence within any semantics, the singular essential meaning or referent, nor moreover does it identify the ontology proper to Cartesianism. None of these possibilities is applicable. This is equally the case for the adequation of Scholasticism – the self-enclosing universal in which adequation is always adequation to the same, presented within the Same – in being distanced allows for the adequation given by judgement. The source of this adequation is conflict since judgement becomes the response to conflict, responding to the inelimnable conflict arising out of the nature of the name; by extension out of the event since what the name names becomes the event, is it.

Hegel's 'need'

Here as a beginning two movements will be traced. Both occur in different Hegelian texts. The movement of the time devoted to writing marks out approximately thirty years. In this time Hegel's 'need' – 'need' as the given beginning – is formulated and reformulated. The theme introduced in the first movement is reworked throughout. What comes to be presented and re-presented is the continual re-enactment and thus repetition of *Bedürfnis*, the work of 'need'. Its presence, an effective presence, portraying and framing philosophy, is presented as given. 'The need is there.' ('There' is the contemporary, the actuality of the historical.) The preoccupation with the emergence of philosophy and of different philosophical systems occupies, by providing, Hegel's beginnings. What has already been identified as the process and manner of the 'attempt to formulate' not only patterns the very beginning, it provides the site of interpretation. This amounts to a provision whose work precludes the possibility of its being reduced to a simple addition. This initial obviation of the parasitism between complexity and addition works, again, to open up complexity.

By retaining the centrality of the name and thus that which its centrality names, and by working with the suggestion that has already been made, namely that Cartesian destruction was the attempt to provide the name with a new and original designation, one that intended to efface the presence of relation, what is thereby sanctioned is tracing the work of 'need' through naming. Naming provides therefore an opening within and thereby beyond itself. With such a provision another beginning is provided occurring as a beginning sanctioning re-citation. The Cartesian position is not itself unique. In general terms it amounts to the positing of an intended singularity, in the end existing without that singularity. Indeed it can be viewed, given a certain relativity, as exemplary. If Descartes had been successful, if, that is, it would have been possible to 'commence all anew from the foundations' and in so doing to have fractured, sundered, all possible relations, and furthermore if that position became one that could have been generalised – *pace* Descartes – such that it provided the means to account for other developments within philosophy's history, then the result would have been that history would have become no more than a series of disparate occurrences denying relation and resisting connection. The history of philosophy, in lacking any sense of continuity, would have become the history of the idiosyncratic and thereby of fundamentally different names/named relations. This generality can, of course, be given locality for in Hegelian terms the problem here is that of the *'eigentümlich'* (the singular, the idiosyncratic). Even though this is a problem that contains, while distancing itself from, its own internal yet unique sense of propriety, it still needs to be distinguished from that state of affairs identified by Hegel as *'Das wahre Eigentümliche'*; the 'true particularity' of philosophy (an identification taking place in the *Difference Essay* (88, 19) and whose consequences are repeated in the *Shorter Logic*). It is not just that the overcoming of particularity will still be constrained by having to retain it by holding to a version of singularity, it is also the case that particularity is itself constructed and conditioned by that which sanctions its appearance.

The particular is not given as such. Its presentation is a self-presentation within the Hegelian system. At stake here therefore is this construction. It is thus that the difficulty that arises in this specific instance concerns how the individual, the peculiar or the idiosyncratic – i.e. in more general terms the singular and as will be seen the expression or result of chance or the contingent (*zufällig*) – is to be thought. Is there, for example, a relation or a division that grounds the identity of the singular as the singular? If what characterises the intended claim of singularity is the absence of relation, then that absence automatically raises the question of how the singular could ever be identified as such. At this stage the recognition of the singular is not the central issue. What must be taken up first is that which is implicit in the question, namely the consequences for philosophy, not in itself but for the Hegelian take thereon, of the presence of singularity and therefore of the appearance of an already present division that is in some sense posited (or given) before either unity or universality.

In the *Difference Essay* it is the presence, the present appearance that is, of fragmentation and division that provides what Hegel describes as the 'need' for philosophy. Need and division are indissoluably related. The inability of one to function without the other must be noted from the start. This state of affairs is expressed by Hegel in the following famous passage from the *Difference Essay*;[39]

> Dichotomy/Diremption is the source of the need for philosophy (*Entzweiung ist der Quell des Bedürfnisses der Philosophie*) and as the culture of the age is the unfree given side of the whole frame (*Gestalt*). In culture the appearance of the absolute (*Erscheinung des Absoluten*) has been isolated (*isoliert*) from the absolute and fixed itself as the self-standing/as independent (*ein Selbständiges fixiert*). But at the same time (*zugleich*) the appearance cannot disown its origin (*die Erscheinung ihren Ursprung nicht verleugnen*) and must aim to constitute the manifold of its limitations as one whole (*als ein Ganzes*).
>
> (89/20)

This is neither a simple claim nor one made in passing. At work here is the possibility of the effectuation of system itself and thus its separation from the 'form' of philosophy. It is this strategic importance that has alerted commentators. Indeed in his apposite commentary on the passage Dennis Schmidt has observed that it announces what he identifies as

> the task of thinking as Hegel see it. More precisely, Hegel contends that thinking comes into its own once it sets itself truly to the task of overcoming the deep bifurcation (or diremption) that lies at the basis of positivity.[40]

The need enjoins a task. The conditions of possibility for this task are already inherent, announced, in the as yet to be announced construal of the relationship, and the identification of the relationship (the position of and for the identification) between the 'appearance of the absolute' and the Absolute. The difficulty within the actual detail of this relationship emerges for Hegel because the Absolute cannot be – in the strong sense of be present as itself – in the appearance as such; it is rather that the 'Absolute must posit itself in the appearance itself'. (The precise nature of this presence and its relation to that into which it is posited must be noted as it will help in accounting for why it is that relation is primordial.) Since these conditions need to be situated in relation to Hegel's articulation of the 'need', the above passage in which the 'need' receives its initial setting, warrants careful analysis.

What is *Entzweiung*? (provisionally 'dichotomy', 'diremption', 'bifurcation'). The immediate answer is that it is an emergence out of harmony. Its particularity is to be located in the specific individuality of that emergence. The context of this response to 'need', and moreover its identification, is the publication of the 'First Fascicule' of Reinhold's *Beyträge zur leichteren Übersicht des Zustandes der Philosophie beim Anfangs des 19. Jahrhunderts*. It is in order to counter Reinhold's construal, not just of contemporary philosophy but more exactly of the history of philosophy, that Hegel is writing. The 'need' also exists therefore within and for contemporary philosophy. It is Reinhold's understanding of the historical – an understanding that is, of course, contemporary – that, according to Hegel, fuels his conflation of the systems of Schelling and Fichte; a positing of identity engendering a failure to confront philosophically the implications of such an action. Identity and difference when taken as given indicate for Hegel that philosophy has lost its way, a loss that is itself the consequence, as will be suggested, of a particular formulation of the subject/object relation.

For Hegel, Reinhold is no more than a 'collector'. As such, philosophical systems become 'opinions' only existing – existing as 'opinions' – in relation to the collector. In themselves they signify nothing beyond their content and their content only has significance in itself. They resist the presence of the universal. They take place and have a place in so far as they are informative. They inform and thus are deemed to convey an opinion. The particularity and hence idiosyncrasy of this position means that all that can be seen in the work of others is the idiosyncratic. Hegel's own formulation expresses the twofold reciprocity of identity and with it charts the necessary interrelationship between subject and object. It is within that complex connection that each site is established. The reciprocity of sight demands that each position have the same quality.

> One who is caught up in his own idiosyncrasies can see in others only their idiosyncrasies. (*Wer von einer Eigentümlichkeit befangen ist, sieht in anderen nichts als Eigentümlichkeiten.*)
>
> (87/17)

The important element here is the nature of the internal relation between the subject and the object. It is only the 'personal view' that sees the history of philosophy and indeed the appearance of plurality in contemporary philosophy as a series of 'personal-views'. It is to this reciprocity, its sustaining of identities due to the interdependent subject/object relation, that Hegel's counter question – 'How could the rational be a personal idiosyncrasy? (*eigentümlich*)' – needs to be understood. As Hegel's question is one posed in response, what must be set out in greater detail are, first, what conditions Hegel's question such that it functions as a question, and thus second, what determines the position to which it is being addressed. In the latter case what is being sought is that which determines it as a position.

Working within Hegel's own formulation the first element that should be examined further is the subject/object relation. It is to begin with a relation of separateness and it is because of the nature of this relation that it is also possible to argue in addition that any given relation, any coming into relation, will be contingent. Any occurrence, the form of that occurrence, is the result of chance. There is however no pure chance. Chance does not happen by chance. There is a type of necessity at work here because of the nature of the subject/object relation. It is one in which, for Hegel, it is the attitude of the subject that determines the object. The 'collector' recognises philosophical positions only as separate elements of information. While Reinhold, according to Hegel, indicates that he will always allow for a certain philosophical perfectibility, in that he presents earlier philosophical positions as open to their own subsequent development, it remains the case that each particularity presents what would amount to its own world, its own self-presentation. As such it is, and can be, no more than an exemplification of itself. What for Hegel is a self-presentation without relation brings with it its own conditions of existence.

An implicit and sustaining element of this position – i.e. Reinhold's within Hegel's interpretation – is the conception of temporality in which it is articulated. From within the confines of the position itself, the history of philosophy not only allows for innovation and the advent of new 'opinions', which would amount to 'opinions' without heritage, it also sanctions the development of earlier 'opinions', a development that moves them closer to a desired truth. It is the latter movement that demands that their re-presentation take place in terms of a temporal frame in which any re-presentation would have to amount to an addition. The temporality in which addition takes place involves the continuity of sequence. It is the time in which something is added.

(The process of addition can be understood as marking out the exclusion of repetition in that time becomes a neutral place. It is as if time were an empty space for the representation and alteration of philosophical images; philosophical portraits that are adapted for different purposes. The centrality of the image works against any posited reworking.) The impossible combination let alone interarticulation of images and repetition will be of concern at a later stage. With the pragma the presentation will come to stand for itself – the complexity of any itself has already been noted – though always within the possibility of its own reworking.

With time one of the fundamental determining elements is introduced. It should not be thought, however, that temporal considerations are absent from Hegel's own formulation of the counter claim of Reason. There are three extremely important temporal markers that can be seen to figure in this formulation;

> if the Absolute, like Reason which is its appearance is *eternally one and the same* (*ewig ein und dasselbe ist*) – as indeed it is – then every Reason that is directed towards itself and comes to recognise itself, produces a true philosophy and solves for itself the problem which, like its solution is *at all times the same* (*zu allen Zeiten dieselbe ist*). In philosophy Reason comes to know itself and deals only with itself so that its whole work and activity are grounded in itself and with respect to the inner essence of philosophy there are neither *predecessors nor successors* (*und in Rükhsicht aufs innere Wesen der Philosophie gibt es weder Vorgänger noch Nachgänger*).
>
> (87/17; my emphasis)

The three temporal markers are first the description of the absolute as 'eternally one and the same'; here the temporal has a straightforward ontological component (an ontology already passed over). In the second place Reason recognising itself as Reason solves a problem while engendering a solution which are both 'at all times the same', again sameness will involve its own ontological guarantor, and third, taken essentially the work of Reason has neither a 'predecessor' nor a 'successor'. Its singularity is the philosophy of history. All that is able to figure as part of that history is to that extent already determined. The figure of time, its repetition, is self-evident. Nonetheless the question that must emerge is, what is being marked here? What figures?

The marks each articulate a temporality that involves continuity. (They are to that extent already articulated within such a temporality; the twofold of articulation.) It is not, however, the continuity linked to addition. Furthermore the possibility of a causative relation – i.e. a mediating relation – between philosophical positions, where each position is taken as an end in itself is also being ruled out. Once again such an eventuality would depend upon the possibility of creation: the advent of a new position that worked on a former one. It would also assume that the subject was only implicated in such an activity to the extent that the subject became the site of this innovative philosophical 'handicraft'. It is precisely the likelihood of such an occurrence that is checked by the claim that the Absolute is 'eternally one and the same'. It follows from this interplay of time and identity – an identity that will incorporate particularity – that any appearance, the form of Reason, is only ever able to enter into relation with another form because they are both forms of Reason and thus both forms of that which is 'eternally one and the same'. Relation between forms is conditioned by the Absolute. (The Absolute becomes the ontological *conditio sine qua non* for the possibility of relation.) The temporality in question therefore pertains to the already given. Any occurrence within the already given is both conditioned by the given and enacting, perhaps acting out, that which made its occurrence possible in the first place, i.e. the ontological precondition.

It has already been suggested that there can be no necessity in terms of the specificity of a particular occurrence. It is this eventuality that Hegel identifies in terms of 'contingency'. (Here therefore it will be 'contingency' as the translation of *zufällig*.)[41] Contingency will pertain to content. (The element of chance within contingency can never be precluded, let alone written out.)

> When and where and in what forms such self-reproductions of reason occur as philosophies is contingent (*ist zufällig*).
>
> (91/22)

This contingency, the occurrence of chance, cannot for Hegel, however, be allowed to stand on its own. There cannot be a pure occurrence since were that to happen it would serve to pose questions such that any attempt to provide answers would, in the *de facto* acceptance of them as questions, work to undermine the positioning of 'need'. There are at least two interrelated questions that arise here.

In the first place what type of identity bearing relation would such an occurrence have (again the implicit necessity of relation for identity). Given this question the next must be: with what could such a relation exist? It is the possibilities inherent in these questions, the demand that in being posed they would come to establish and in being established give rise to a different need (another need, not the 'need', and with it another difference) that Hegel seeks to counter by relocating the site of contingency.

> This contingency (*Diese Zufälligkeit*) must be comprehended on the basis of the Absolute positing itself (*sich setzt*) as an objective totality (*als eine objektive Totalität*).
>
> (91/22)

It is not simply that the advent of chance must be controlled or come under the control of Reason – the Absolute's self-given law – it is rather that its happening is, and of necessity, presented as the positing of the Absolute. Chance is thus never just chance.

A risk still exists, however. There may be an exception. It could be that chance allows for the possibility that what occurs by chance, the accidental contingency, may have become really 'isolated' from the Absolute. This isolation defines a present and is therefore historical or cultural in nature rather than purely onto-logical. (And yet ontology will be seen to intrude.) The question that will have to be addressed is the extent to which this isolation which is the occurrence of the contingent is itself the consequence of chance. Allowing this possibility would mean, therefore, that chance would be operating beyond its determination as chance; a determination that is given by the Absolute. If this were the case then another chance would have occurred within, though also as part of, the attempt to stem the productive presence of chance. The result could be that chance, by chance, comes to trip itself up. Chance being tripped up by chance will mean that what will have happened will be an occurrence without prediction. Here lies chance's chance.

At a later stage in this section of the *Difference Essay* Hegel argues that if the history of philosophy does not provide the history of the 'one eternal Reason (*ewigen und einen Vernunft*)' presenting itself in infinitely manifold 'forms' then

> instead it will give us nothing but a tale of the accidental occurrences of the human spirit (*eine Erzählung zufälliger Bege-*

benheiten des menschlichen Geistes) and of senseless opinions that
the teller imputes to Reason.

(114/47)

The risk identified in this passage comes from chance. It has
already been suggested that, because of the functional reciprocity
between subject and object, the position from which the history of
philosophy is viewed as the work of either contingency, chance
or the idiosyncratic is itself the consequence of a chance, contingent, accidental or idiosyncratic view, a state of a affairs
marked out here by the imputations of the 'tellers'. (The logical
necessity for a type of misrecognition is evident from this
formulation.) What still endures, however, is the already alluded
to possibility that chance may play a more significant role, in that
it may allow for an occurrence that cannot be precluded by the
tight reciprocity between Absolute and appearance. Again, its
occurring would be a role sanctioned by the doubling of chance;
part of the chance effect – a doubling releasing the already
present determinations of chance by repeating them. The conflict
between representation and repetition therefore will be seen to
figure within it. The conflict is, of course, not the site of an
antinomy. Antinomies do not happen as chance, let alone by
chance. The conflict here while not involving naming as such
indicates the presence of an ineliminable differential ontology.
Within it conflict is necessarily irresolvable – if only because of
the nature of the event – and in being thus will demand the
response of judgement. Having come this far it is possible to
return to Hegel's earlier formulation of 'need'. Of central
importance will be its implicit presentation of time and its
relation to the self-standing or independent.

The 'diremption'/'division' already noted is the result of an
isolation. (Even for Hegel diremption does not exist in itself.) The
formulation of what Hegel identifies as the 'self-standing' involves
a specific construal of appearance. Appearance has become self-
standing. Fixed it stands apart in its singularity. However, while
being singular, in standing apart, it is neither truly singular nor
truly apart. It contains, in addition, that which it cannot 'deny',
namely its origin. The apart, in spite of the work of intention,
becomes relational, it becomes therefore a part. Apart is now
inextricably linked to that of which it forms a part. What is
occurring here is that while Hegel wants to hold these two apart,

thereby rehearsing that construal of philosophy that denies rela-tion, what emerges in contradistinction to this intended result is the impossibility of holding them apart. The logic of diremption demands that they form a part of each other even though, as will be indicated, it also demands the opposite.

Appearance in appearing as itself is present in its singularity, as 'independent', and yet singularity, the presence of appearance, also appears 'at the same time' as an estranged delimitation containing, bearing, the marks of its own origin. The important point is that these marks are not contained as an appearance. They do not have the same mode of being as appearance. (Here is the possible location of a plurality – marked by a spacing that cannot be overcome – that reinforces the presence of relation.) Their presence outside of appearance thereby opens up the question of their relation to the Absolute and thus by extension the question of the mode of being proper to that appearance (again the possible inscription of anoriginal plurality). Is their appearance a chance occurrence?

There is, however, a necessity at work here for estrangement and the undeniable presence of the origin could not appear; were this to be possible, were it to have occurred, then the appearance would not be self-standing. Some other thing would have happened. It could not have fixed itself, established itself as independent, and thus be present, presenting itself, as the site of the singular. There would have been the addition of an acknowl-edged separation, if not loss; the melancholic sign neither of an absence nor of a lack but of isolation; a longing enjoining need, an isolation therefore to be overcome. The consequence of this is that if the singular or the appearance are themselves never, even in their own terms, the singular, the curious – all that which is marked out by the 'eigentümlich' – but are inevitably linked to something outside of themselves, where that outside is always marked inside, then this is going to question that formulation of the philosophical task that takes 'diremption/division' ('Entz-weiung') not only as central but as that which provides philosophy with a 'need'. (It should be noted of course that the 'diremption' is not given as such. It is rather that it is posited as providing a state of affairs that can and will be overcome. This is part of the logic of diremption. Diremption does not mark out the stakes of original difference but the inevitability of the overcoming and elimination of that difference. Its formulation – its inscripted presence – is as that which will be overcome. Isolation brings the possibility of its own overcoming with it.) Before taking up this questioning, the encounter of chance, a further consideration needs to be noted; with it time is reintroduced. Again its occurrence is not by chance, even though it figures chance.

The singular event, the appearance, involves in terms of its attempted formulation an addition, at the same time. It is worth repeating – as the repetition will announce something in addition – the line itself. Careful attention must be paid to the precision of Hegel's actual formulation.

> *Zugleich kann aber die Erscheinung ihren ürsprung nicht verleugnen* ... (But at the same time the appearance cannot deny its origin ...)
>
> (89/20)

The impossibility of disavowal takes place '*zugleich*', 'at the same time'. The equality here is temporal as well as spatial. The temporality and spatiality in question, however, do stand in need of greater clarification.

Time here involves space, a complex space present beyond the determinations of either the absolute or the point of relativity (the point in space). Here it involves spacing as the ineliminable relation and thus as a holding and relating incorporating distance. If it were not for spacing then the two events would not take place at the same time, they would be the same event. (This amounts to a variant of the law of the identity of indiscernibles.) The impossibility of the disavowal of the origin would be identical with the appearance. The fact that, as Hegel states, they take place 'at the same time' while also being held apart means not just the ineliminable presence of appearance's other within appearance but that the singular will only ever be singular if the singular is plural. Plurality, here present as spacing, is that which is marked by the '*zugleich*', marked, it must be added, at the same time. It is not simply that the problems that emerge here are complex; it is rather that they attest to the presence of a complexity that pertains to the nature of the event itself. It is the ontologico-temporal nature of what is named here, this event – the inherent plurality of the 'itself' – which gives rise to a specific task. The description of the event – perhaps the enactment of the task – will allow its implications to be traced. A connection can be drawn between the spacing – the ineliminable presence of spacing – marked and sustained by the '*zugleich*', and the isolation of the appearance, an isolation that designates or determines the being of the appearance in terms of its being 'self-standing' or 'independent'. Establishing the connection will draw on the already suggested doubling of chance. Again, it should be added that the time in question is not Hegel's, in other words it is not the time formulated in Sections 257–9 of *The Philosophy of Nature*.[42] It is the time inherent in the structuring of the position itself. It is, as it were, the time of transcendental constitution; the time that underwrites what comes to presence as that which is writtten out.

Hegel's formulation is multi-layered. The isolation that occurs is itself the sign of diremption. Diremption involves the appearance of the isolated as isolated. The logic of diremption works by presenting appearance only in order that its status as an appearance can be overcome. Indeed this is the function of the sentence beginning 'Zugleich ...'. The appearance of the isolated is represented as appearance. A relation is re-identified, a re-identification emerging out of an overcoming of the subject/object position of misidentification. The reason for insisting on the re-identification of relation as opposed either to simple identification or the establishing of a relation is that the relation must have been in a sense always already present. (A return will be made to the sense of this presence, for it is with it, with it as that which it is, that the effective presence of the anoriginal can be noted.)

It is the always already present nature of the relation that indicates why the appearance cannot 'deny its own origin'. Indeed it is possible to go further by arguing that the relation provides what has been identified as the 'impossibility of disavowal' with its conditions of existence. The object of impossible disavowal is the ontological construction of appearance; its mode of being. And yet it is the impossibility of disavowal that redefines this ontology. Returning to ontology will involve the reinscription of the event; the reinscription of the already inscripted. What is occurring at this stage, an occurrence gestured at by the 'zugleich', is the possible reidentification of the site of diremption. Rather than it merely delimiting the relationship between the universal and particular – appearance and Absolute – it will come to mark by marking out the event itself. The event as the site of diremption is here marked by the inevitability and hence effective presence of spacing. In this instance it is necessary, however, to continue tracing the movements taking place in relation to Hegel's positing of singularity and then with the overcoming of that singularity.

With it the relocation of diremption and thus the reworking of diremption in terms of differential ontology can be seen to take place.

If it is the case that the appearance in appearing as isolated is also marked by its origin, then it cannot be isolated but must bear its already existent relation. However, this, as has been suggested, undermines the ground of diremption and therefore of the 'need' of/for philosophy. There would not be as many problems here if Hegel were arguing that on one level of existence the appearance appears as isolated but on another, and viewed from a different subject position, that appearance only appears as isolated to the extent that the isolation is itself an appearance of the state of culture. Moreover it would need to be argued in addition that part of the recognition of appearance as appearance is the co-joint recognition of its containing the mark of its origin (a recognition based on the 'zugleich'; an occurrence at the same time). However, to accept this formulation would mean denying the force of diremption. It would be as though diremption could not exist in itself; diremption obviating the possibility of its own diremptive existence. In addition it would be a formulation that was inherently incompatible with the articulated mode of being of the appearance that has already been identified; namely an intended singularity, the project of being apart. The latter will be clarified by a return to the ineliminable and constituting presence of spacing. Prior to this it needs to be reiterated that if the various reworkings of Hegel's position were to be accepted this would cause the 'independent' nature of the projected singularity (the apart) to founder (to become a part). If 'independence', the sign of diremption, is necessary in order that 'need' give rise to the task of philosophy – Hegel's task – then that self-standing independence must be maintained. It cannot, at the same time, bear a mark that works against its being self-standing. Such a mark would once again betray diremption by showing its impossibility; in other words it would show that the absolute singularity demanded by diremption, and thus enjoining 'need', depends upon an independence that is denied by that which is marked out and is thus there 'at the same time' (zugleich). This denial is of an anoriginal complex. As such it attests the ontological nature of the event.

Reiterating a point that was sketched out above it is now clear that the force of the 'zugleich', its complexity, is that while it is essential that the presence of an occurrence, an event, that has to be isolated and singular be maintained in order that the logic of diremption work, it is also the case that in being singular it cannot be singular. Furthermore it is the latter impossible singularity that must also be at work – working within its own self-presentation – in order that the logic of diremption can be effective. The 'accidental occurrences' (*zufälliger Begebenheiten*) must be both accidental and non-accidental 'at the same time'. It is thus that they are never purely accidental and thus never purely isolated. There is a residue, a remainder, that marks the appearance, even if the appearance takes the form of radical contingency or even a foolish chance.[43] That which remains is what cannot be denied. The impossibility of disavowal cannot be an attitude, let alone a predicate of appearance. It must be a constitutive part of appearance itself. If it were not a constitutive part then the existential finality demanded by the logic of diremption – and inherent in the positing of that mode of isolation that contains a relation enabling its own subsequent overcoming – would itself be impossible.

Continuing this return to Hegel's attempt to take up the philosophical as occasioned by 'need', where the latter is itself parasitic upon the presence of what is identified as contemporary diremption, will take place within the terms set by the attempt made by Hegel in the *Shorter Logic* to deal with the presence of different philosophical positions. Once again what enables this task to be enacted is that the presentation of difference occurs in such a way that the 'difference' that is presented lends itself – perhaps more aptly gives itself – to its own overcoming. (Again what is at stake is the specificity of difference and thus its own self-presentation; a presentation inscribed within its own work.) The reciprocity marked out here is the logic of diremption; a positing that enjoins a need that brings with it the conditions of possibility for its own satisfaction and thus is always an intended absolute positing which is given within and thereby inevitably subject to its own law.

Once again it must be noted that Hegel's position, a position that will come to be advanced in terms of a metaphorics of fruit, is still constrained to posit chance as the threat to the work of Reason. The threat is tame, however, for its presentation occurs in order to displace any of its possible effects. The formulation is clear; chance will not have a chance. Chance therefore will be seen to play out a doubling that holds its relation to necessity. What remains to be seen is whether or not chance is reinscripted by chance and therefore as real chance; the reality being the actual presence of chance itself. The possible failure of the exclusion of real chance would be the consequence of the chance effect.

Hegel's fruit

In Sections 1–18 of the *Shorter Logic* Hegel has a number of different concerns. Apart from a general preoccupation with beginnings (*Anfang*) there is the attempt to articulate that concern within the more general strategy of differentiating philosophy from the 'contingent' (*das Zufällige*) while also trying to locate the necessity (*Notwendigkeit*) within the arbitrary. Again such moves locate 'need' (*Bedürfnis*), what Wallace in his translation dramatically and in the end misleadingly calls the the 'cravings of thought', as central. What is of interest here is how the attribution of necessity takes place; its positionality. The way it comes to be enacted will figure within Hegel's attempt to deal with the existence of different philosophical positions. The precise stakes of difference should not go unnoted. (There is no difference as such. Central to the procedure of this essay is the move away from the substantive and toward the actative which means here that what is of concern is the way difference figures and not the figure of difference. In other words the figuring of difference in continually displacing the figure lends itself to an active plurality, a variety of presence, which would be denied by the all too hasty import of the figure. What is thereby opened up is the possibility of a philosophy without either substance or essence.)

'Necessity' is posed in Section 1 of the *Logic* as part of the early strategy to differentiate the content of thought – the given content – from the necessity of that content. What this establishes is that necessity involves dealing with the content of thought as thought (hence the emergence of '*Nachdenken*'; the 'after thought of thought' on the way to reflection). This is a distinction that is mirrored in the capacity of 'experience' (*Erfahrung*) to differentiate between what is 'only appearance' (*nur Erscheinung*) and 'actuality' (*Wirklichkeit*). It is not surprising that it is in terms of this distinction that the contingent is introduced in order then to be distinguished from the actual. In Section 6 Hegel's argument is defined in relation to the contingent. The contingent is presented as an inadequacy to be overcome; the improper returning to, though significantly from within it *in potentia*, its own state of propriety.

> even our ordinary feelings are enough to forbid a causal/ contingent/chance existence (*eine zufällige Existenz*) getting the emphatic name (*den emphatischen Namen*) of an actual; the contingent is an existence (*das Zufällige ist eine Existenz*) which has no greater value than a possible existence (*eines Möglichen*) has, which might as well not be.
>
> (9/48)

Later in the same section the fortuitous (contingent) is again differentiated from the actual even though things which are fortuitous are nevertheless existent. The nature of the positing of chance is still such that it is chance that can never occur by chance. The contingent could never actually be contingent. Nonetheless these exclusions introduce a risk. They open up the possibility of a chance occurrence, the occurrence of real chance.

In Section 7 Hegel treats the emergence of *Nachdenken* – 'the after thought of thought' – in order to show that, while it is involved in what is there described as the 'Principle of Philosophy', it is nonetheless not adequate to the task of establishing necessity and thus of realising the principle. It is the precise nature of the failure, the defect, that for Hegel is of the greatest importance. The emergence of this mode of thinking, occurring as it does after the 'time of the Lutheran reformation', is concerned with what Hegel describes as the *'masslos scheinenden Stoff der Erscheinungswelt'*. A feigned world, perhaps even the feint of fiction (a literary appearance?), is captured by the play of *'scheinenden/Erscheinungswelt'* – hence the translation, the 'stuff of the world of appearance appears boundless'. Here philosophy, the form of philosophy, attempted to locate either law or necessity in

> *der scheinbaren Unordnung der unendlichen Menge des Zufälligen* (the apparent/feigned disorder of the boundless masses of the contingent).
>
> (10/49)

Again the image of the boundless, again the play of appearance. In both formulations the use of first *'scheinenden'* and second 'scheinbaren' work to introduce the feint, a situation in which what appears is not as it appears.

For Hegel what amounts to the defects within 'empirical knowledge' are chartered in Sections 8–9. Since they concern the relationship between the universal and the particular it is the ones identified in Section 9 that are of immediate relevance. Before taking them up it should be stated that Hegel's general procedure here has involved identifying the principle of philosophy and then showing how in a specific instance the principle comes to be thwarted by the way in which it is put to work, a work that works against the principle. The subject and the object within the specificity of the task set, a setting arising out of 'need', are both distanced and incorporated.

Sections 8 and 9 are similiarly concerned with the 'satisfaction' (*Befriedigung*) given by 'empirical knowledge'. It is shown to be inadequate. In other words it fails to answer the 'need'. In Section 9 this is described in the following way:

> in point of form the subjective reason desires a further satisfaction than empirical knowledge gives: and this form is, in the widest sense of the term, Necessity (*Notwendigkeit*).

(13/52)

In Section 39 Hegel identifies two elements within experience: one is the '*unendlich mannigfaltige Stoff*' (boundless diverse stuff) while the other is 'form', i.e. the determination of universality and necessity. What is at issue here is the distinction between diversity and unity. Empirical knowledge cannot move the former to the latter. The two defects within empirical knowledge are first that whatever sense of universal it may contain it is sufficiently 'indeterminate' (*unbestimmt*) that it fails to connect with particulars. Any relation would be 'external and accidental' (*äusserlich und zufällige*). They are outside of each other and relation comes about by chance. There is no necessary connection, on the level of empirical knowledge, between universal and particular; once again what is potentially at work is the chance effect. In the second place the conception of 'beginning' (*Anfange*) suggested by 'empirical knowledge' involves the simply given. What is given is the immediate and the found. It is in relation to both of these defects that 'the form of necessity fails to be satisfied' (*der Form der Notwendigkeit nicht Genüge*). It is this failure that opens up the possibility of satisfaction emerging from a different source.

When after-thought/reflection (*Das Nachdenken*) sets out to respond/satisfy this need (*diesem Bedürfnisse Genüge zu leisten*) it is proper (*eigentliche*) philosophy, speculative thinking.

(13/52)

The speculative therefore arises out of and within the propriety demanded by that emergence and it is therefore delimited by a response to a need which is itself a response to particularity, to the singular. (The *eigentümliche* has become *eigentliche*.) The speculative cannot be thought to exist in itself. It is conditioned by its ground of emergence; i.e. its specific conditions of existence. This condition is not 'need' as such. It is rather that 'need' – the play of *Bedürfnis* – is sustained by (and thus sustains) diremption. The speculative is to be thought, indeed within this presentation can only be thought, within these relations of an identity sustaining reciprocity. The positing of the speculative is, again, no more than a gesture.

The difficulties posed by the complex relationship between Philosophy as universal and the particularity of philosophy is, for Hegel, to be resolved by paying closer attention to the general relationship between universal and particular; a task undertaken in order to preclude finally the possibility that one might be set beside the other; an equality of site. It is to this end that Hegel employs a metaphorics of fruit:

> Would anyone who wished for fruit reject cherries, pears and grapes on the ground that they were cherries pears and grapes and not fruit? But when philosophy is in question, the excuse of the many is that philosophies are so different, and none is the philosophy – that each is only a philosophy. Such a plea is assumed to justify any amount of contempt for philosophy – as if cherries were not fruit.

(19/59)

The analogy that this passage is thought to have established is between cherry and fruit on the one hand and *a* philosophy and Philosophy (*the* Philosophy) on the other. Within the confines of the analogy a cherry is both itself and fruit. There is no apparent difficulty in moving from one to the other. The proliferation of kinds of fruit does not work against the use of the universal. A grape can be accepted both as grape and as fruit. In the case of philosophy Hegel suggests that there seems to be a difference. The presence of different philosophies (particulars) seems to under-mine the possibility of either Philosophy (the universal) being located within them or the particular being, in some sense of the term, an instantiation of Philosophy (the universal). Hegel's analogy is intended to show that its having broken down is due to and thus signals the limitations of such a conception of philosophy and more exactly of the construal of the relationship between universal and particular. Given the importance attributed to it, the internal force of the analogy – its viability – must be questioned, beginning, at this stage, by leaving the question of the analogy – its own internality as a way or method of argumental procedure – to one side.

A cherry when viewed on its own, as a singular occurrence, would be no more than a cherry. That the cherry is both itself – maintaining its particularity – and fruit indicates that it comprises, at the same time, a particular form taken by fruit. The pear is another form fruit takes; indeed as with the grape. The relation-ship between cherries, pears and grapes is based on the *fact* that they are different forms of fruit. It is at this precise point that the analogy should be evoked. In Section 14 Hegel argues that 'A philosophy without system' while merely giving rise to subjective expressions only 'has its content by chance' (*ist es seinem Inhalte nach zufällig*). The expression of contingency, existing as the contingent – as the philosophical 'one off' – is to be contrasted with that state of affairs in which the content becomes justified as philosophy. This occurs when they are taken 'as an element/a part of the whole' (*als Moment des Ganzen*). The important point is that, to the extent that this justification is not, in the language of the *Difference Essay*, 'a senseless opinion (*sinnloser Meinungen*) that the teller imputes to Reason', then the content given by chance – and as chance, the contingent – comes to be regulated and as such is shown to be part of the system.

The risk of chance would appear to have been undone. And yet the threat of chance endures to the extent that it may not always be possible to differentiate accurately between those moments har-bouring that which is without meaning, in its being attributed to Reason, and those in which meaning rather than being attained is identified. The site of such an identification would be the relationship between the particular and the Absolute. This distinc-tion is not the one prefiguring the movement in which the particular gives up its claim to particularity; it is rather the actual threat of chance, the realised chance effect. Now, however, it is no longer the chance that gives itself to its own overcoming; the latter being the positing of chance in terms of the necessary surrender, sacrifice, of chance. In other words the chance that does not have a chance. Here, on the contrary, chance has come to be given an-other chance – a different chance – and thus what arises is the threat of real chance, an outbreak. The latter would be a random occurrence and thereby a threat whose very realisation is no longer appearance, the contingent, but freedom itself. Freedom as madness. Not the madness that opposes Reason – a madness that is in the end just chance – but the event whose madness, and thus whose existence, falls beyond the purview of the opposition between Reason and its other. (It is, of course, at this precise point that freedom takes on the guise of experimentation and the advent of an occurrence beyond prediction and therefore happening beyond the restraint of the already existent relation.) In no longer being held by it the other chance is able to figure. In other words there is not just the threat of chance (*zufällig*) but there is another and now different threat. It is simply that chance may be the occurrence of chance, the break with necessity. It is to counter the force of the first of these threats that the analogy with fruit is presented. In tracing its viability what will emerge is its capacity, or rather incapacity, to deal with the secondary threat, namely the chance occurrence, real chance. The reality of this chance is its unpredictability.

The counter to the first of these two threats resides in the argument that while unsystematic philosophy may have content by chance, chance is not really chance. Chance is simply a designation that provides a way of dealing with what appears. The cherry appears as cherry but in appearing it is at the same time an instantiation of fruit, its appearance. The impossible occurrence would be the presentation of the cherry in its complete singularity as an isolated occurrence falling outside of any relation. While the strategic use of the analogy, its intended function, lies in its capacity to show that the proliferation of particulars does not work against the existence of the universal, and that furthermore the particular is a form of the universal, what still remains to be investigated in this instance is the status of this particular universal, i.e. fruit. What must always be remembered is the presence of fruit within and thus as constitutive of this analogy. Its own segments are in the end not of central importance.

Hegel's formulation of the analogy opens with a question. The force behind the question resides in the suggested implausibility if not impossibility that a response to the request for fruit would be deemed unsatisfactory, and thus not a response, because what had been supplied as fruit were in fact either cherries, pears or grapes. Within the realm of fruit there is no apparent problem moving from particular to universal or from universal to particular. Why Hegel asks is this not also the case with philosophy? Why is it that the plurality of philosophical positions are not recognised as particulars (as opposed to either singular occurrences, or universals in their own right and thus as the purely singular) all of which have a relationship to Philosophy (the universal) and are included in it as comprising its totality? Hegel's emphatic conclusion announced within a rhetoric of the self-evident – 'als ob nicht auch die Kirschen Obst wären' (as if cherries were not fruit) – captures the apparent force of the analogy. It is as though acceding to this assertion is in itself sufficient; a sufficiency that is on its own, however, far from being either self-limiting or self-sufficient because it only serves to raise the inescapable question of what would be involved in either denying or agreeing with the claim that 'cherries are fruit'. What is being apportioned by fruit?

The claim that a philosophy is the Philosophy necessitates a form of misidentification. It has already been noted that 'empirical knowledge' – taken as a philosophical position – is not adequate to the Principle of Philosophy. Moreover the relationship between them is defined by the lack of adequacy. In the case of the need to distinguish between 'contingent existence' and the 'actual', where taking the 'contingent' as providing the source of philosophy comprises a philosophical position, albeit an inadequate one, that which restricts the naming of the 'contingent' as 'actual' is what Hegel identifies as 'ordinary feelings' (gewöhnliche Gefühl). Feelings check the misuse or the misattribution of the name. While the distinction between the contingent and the actual is not identical to the one between particular and universal it is nonetheless the same since their difference is also qualitative. The consequence of conflating them would involve a similar type of misidentification as one that would occur when what was at stake involved differentiating between a philosophy and the Philosophy, or cherry and fruit. In spite of these similarities a significant difference between philosophy and fruit can still be located. It remains of course an open question as to the extent to which it is a difference whose presence could be either stilled or overcome by the response of 'ordinary feelings'.

The claim that 'cherries are fruit' does not involve time (time here in the minimal sense of the temporality of development – the problem of historical time does not as yet pertain). It is a claim that is made without any straightforward temporal dimension. Moreover the position from which it is made, fruit as system, is one that occupies the place of the ordinary. Systematic fruit does not involve the coming to fruition of a system that had hitherto been misidentified and thus misnamed. Two examples of such identifications (in fact misidentifications) would be first the failure to see any connection between cherries and grapes, i.e. failing to see that they are both fruit, and second giving the ontological status of fruit, namely universality, to either cherries or pears. Inadequate responses to the presence of cherries, grapes and pears, or indeed fruit, have not been made. It is not as though they were made but are no longer made and consequently the preclusion of a developmental time means that it is possible to argue that fruit (the universal) resists the movement of a progressive unfolding. The history of fruit is fundamentally different from the history of spirit. The former is always, perhaps always already, ripe.

That this is not the case in philosophy is also signalled by Hegel in this section. In an argument against that view of the history of philosophy in which it is seen as comprising 'principles' lacking connections (in sum the position already encountered in his presentation of Reinhold) his counter move necessitates the addition of development, i.e. the history of Spirit. More emphatically it is an argument that is dependent upon development and thus the overcoming of misidentifications, their having been sublated. They are interrelated to the extent that one does not appear without the other until that stage in which the totality appears as itself to itself.

> For thousands of years the same Architect has directed the work: and that Architect is the one living Mind whose nature is to think, to bring to self-consciousness what it is, and, with its being thus set as object before it, to be at the same time raised above it, and so to reach a higher stage (*eine höhere Stufe*) of its own being .... In philosophy the latest birth of time is the result of all the systems that have preceded it, and must include their principles; and so, if on other grounds, it deserves the title of

philosophy, will be the fullest, most comprehensive, and most adequate system of all.

(18–19/58)

The claim that a philosophy has been misidentified, such that either it is taken to be the Philosophy, where such moves can multiply without restriction, or the particular has been attributed the status of the Universal resulting in a plurality of philosophies, is a claim that can itself only be made from a position in which universality is self-present. Attaining this position, it having been attained, works as the sign of history. Once again recognising the Architect as the 'one living Mind' involves being in a position from where it is possible for the totality itself, in being a totality, to become an object for consciousness.

It is in relation to the recognition of the 'principle of philosophy' as the 'principle of philosophy' and the role of history, the movement through and sublation of earlier misrecognitions and misidentifications, that a point is established at which the analogy between philosophy and fruit collapses. Furthermore there is the additional point that the absence of a temporal or historical dimension in the relationship between cherry and fruit means that, rather than being a universal in Hegel's sense, fruit is perhaps more accurately a genre. Consequently agreeing with Hegel that 'cherries are fruit' does not impinge upon the more general question of the relationship between universal and particular within, and as, philosophy for the straightforward reason that different types of claims are being made in each case. Agreeing with one does not entail either agreeing or disagreeing with the other. What, however, of the opposite? What is at stake in the denial and thus in the claim that cherries are not fruit? This question will not only more aptly indicate why the analogy is pointless but it will serve to reintroduce the question of naming. With its reintroduction it will be possible to return to chance; the threat of actual chance.

Focusing on the denial, the analogy, the purported analogy, would mean that the claim cherries are not fruit is similiar to the claim that a philosophy does not form part of the philosophy. What, however, would be involved in the first part of the analogy? Initially it would seem that to assert that cherries are not fruit would provide the grounds for claiming that they did not fulfil the criteria that would allow them to be given in response to the demand for fruit, the 'desire for fruit' (*der Obst verlangte*). The same state of affairs would pertain for pears, grapes etc. and as such must raise the question of what would count as a response. With what would the demand, the 'desire for fruit', be satisfied? What satiates the need for fruit? There is no answer to this question and thus no satisfaction could ever be given. Fruit can never be presented. All that could ever be given in response are cherries, pears, grapes etc. Approaching the problem in this way means that while it is possible to respond both inadequately and then adequately to the 'need' of philosophy, there is no such response to the need either for, or of, fruit. A cherry while fruit is not fruit in the same, or even a similar way, as philosophy is philosophy when it takes itself as its own object. If there were to be an apposite analogy it would be that the relationship between cherry and fruit is similar to the relationship between 'empirical knowledge', as a form of philosophy, and the universal philosophy. In the case of the latter, however, it is the diremptive state that in being overcome moves towards that type of totality which philosophy, as universal, is.

Diremption is absent from fruit. It could never be argued that diremption gave rise to the need for fruit. Making this claim is not to deny the very real existence, at times, of the 'desire for fruit'; 'cravings' as hunger. Finally, that there is a necessity in regard to the relationship between cherry and fruit is not in question, that the analogy between fruit and Philosophy (the universal) establishes the presence of the same necessity between philosophies and Philosophy has not be shown and is thus simply an untenable conclusion either to have been reached or to have been inferred. The question that must be taken up prior to tracing the consequences of this breakdown is how the breakdown itself is to be understood.

After fruit

At an earlier stage in the Introduction – Section 6 – Hegel has identified 'ordinary feelings' as that which forbids the naming of the 'contingent' as the 'actual'. If this approach is taken a step further then the stakes of the metaphorics of fruit can be expressed in terms of the naming of the 'principle of philosophy'. While it is clear that 'empirical philosophy' can be named philosophy, it cannot bear the name if what is named is the universal, the 'principle of philosophy', philosophy having become its own object. The construal of the relationship between universal and particular in which the universal is the basis of the relationship between particulars is intended to guard against the misuse of the name. The relationship to the Absolute (universal) as already given entails in addition to the basis of the relation between particulars (appearances) the possibility of their inclusion in the universal (Absolute) and thus its inclusion in them and therefore their right to bear the name.

The intended viability of this presentation of naming is found first in the already present relation and second in the posited singularity or isolation of appearance, the self-standing. It depends upon the latter because the problem of naming arises out of – and as – a response to 'need'. The need is to show that what appears or the content of thought are not chance occurrences, unsystematic events or the purely contingent. They do, however, have to be taken as potentially, if not as really, singular in order that 'need' arise. Again, the initial difficulty of how the recognition of the singular as singular could ever overcome itself is dealt with by 'need' as the response to singularity. This formulation is still problematic because the recognition of the singular – here the self-standing – does not recognise them as singular because of a division or diremption. They are just recognised as singular and as it is singularity that entails diremption and thus need, that would of necessity have to involve a subsequent and therefore different recognition.

The existence of another problem, also arising out of Hegel's formulation, has already been noted. The presence of the word 'zugleich' marks that which is necessary for the logic of diremption. It is the presentation of the self-standing and that which while independent – and thereby marking diremption and giving rise to 'need' – also contains the mark of its origin; a residue, a remainder which is itself the mark of an impossible disavowal. It has been suggested at an earlier stage that these two elements have to exist at the same time (zugleich) and yet resist reduction, one into the other. The appearance, that which appears, must be other than the mark of the origin in that the latter cannot itself appear as such and thus it cannot have the same ontological status as an appearance.

It therefore follows that two distinct modes of being are in play and thus the difference in question is neither difference as variety nor even difference as diversity but difference as differential. What this involves is a singularity, an event, which is itself the site of two different and irreducible determinations; a present plurality. They are not aspects of appearance but are constitutive of the appearance itself. The anoriginally plural event, therefore, that which attests to the primordiality of relation, is present accounting for appearance. Identifying, contrary to the given intentional logic, the primordiality of relation will further the continual reworking of appearance in terms of presentation and thus of the pragma.

Moving on, it is not just that the singular is plural it is more significantly the case that the possibility of singularity is itself dependent upon plurality; a dependence that is maintained even if the plurality in question has to be denied by the assertion of the 'self-standing', an assertion that in being advanced is at the same time retracted by the spacing introduced by the 'zugleich'. Spacing repositions diremption; it is no longer descriptive of the relationship between either particular and universal or appearance and Absolute, it is rather that it pertains to the 'appearance' itself. It is the division within appearance, a primordially present division, that reworks the appearance in terms of an event. There is no longer the given relation between appearance and Absolute (particular and universal). Shifting the site of diremption is a possibility to which allusion has already been made when it was suggested that the presence of the impossible disavowal would work to redefine the intended ontology of the event – the mode of being of the appearance – though no longer as appearance in opposition to the absolute/universal.

If Hegel is constrained to deploy a plural event – the event as the site of anoriginal plurality – in order to secure the presentation of a singularity to be overcome, what amounts to the logic of diremption, then it is precisely that plurality that is effaced in the promulgation of singularity (and thus of diremption). Moreover even though the relation as always already present has to be assumed – despite this being an unstated assumption – in order that the logic of diremption be effective, it is also the case that there has to be, and at the same time, the assumption of the absence of all possible relations. The necessary presence of relation linked as it is to the plural event has already been marked out by spacing. However, with spacing relation comes, initially, to be located within the event itself. Plurality rather than designating certain qualities of the event is constitutive of it to the extent that constitution involves irreducible difference. Plurality is ir- reducible difference. As such therefore it is the expression of the ontology of the event. It comprises it.

The reworking of relation breaks the possibility of the already existent status between present, past and future occurrences. It is thus that time could have been said to have been reintroduced. (The temporality in question amounts to no more than the temporality of development – time as the interplay of sequence and subsequence.) The direct consequence is that Hegel's presen- tation of chance is no longer appropriate. The breakdown of the analogy between fruit and philosophy has opened up the chance effect. Chance has a chance in its positioning beyond the confines of contingency. Contingency in the Hegelian sense was contingent only because of the twofold presence of isolation and the always already existent relation. The result of this move away is not the introduction of pure contingency – that would be to confuse consequence with effect – but the break with the already existent relation. Stemming from this break is the possibility of an occur- rence – the subsequent occurrence – in a temporally progessive or regressive sense, that defies prediction. The question to which such a happening will demand a response will concern the nature of the relation to be established. The reconstituting of the given into an-other, another giving, the pragma – a movement the work of which is enabled by the ontology of the event – will demand that relation be the site of a continual negotiation and renego- tiation. Movements within this site are themselves possible because of the chance effect having been realised. It is with the advent of an occurrence without prediction happening therefore within the ambit of the event – the occurrence of chance and thus the chance occurrence – that the problem of the response and thus the conditions of possibility for the response to any occurrence is posed, conditions defining the ambit of response by inaugurating by establishing, either by a repetition within the Same or one taking place again for the first time, the instantiation of relation and thus, and with it, meaning and understanding.

It is at this precise point that tradition – the gift of the already given and thus the determination in advance – needs to be introduced. Tradition provides these conditions. (Their provision is the work of tradition, the presentation of the gift.) Their

pertinence, their capacity to incorporate the subsequent occurrence, opens up a distinction – a distinction that is itself the site of
evaluation – between relations, either potential or actual, within
tradition that involve either homology or dislocation. Again it
should be added that this either/or resists a ready incorporation
into the logic of the either/or. (With it the already alluded to
connection between philosophy and art is repeated.) It is this
problem that will have to be taken up in any subsequent attempt
to link temporality and judgement. Indeed it will be in terms of
this link that it will be possible to draw constitutive elements of the
projects of Descartes and Hegel together, elements that have
emerged with these interpretation and therefore which are involved in their constitution.

Both Descartes and Hegel worked to extrude time, extruded in
the end at the end by including it as a permanent presence;
occurring in the first place as Cartesian judgement and in the
second as the always already existent relation. At this stage it is
essential to stay with the event charting the consequence of the
emergence of plurality, an emergence not out of the singular but in
the re-positioning of the singular as that which is dependent upon
the plural and thereby taking place after it, as its effect; a reversal
overturning the predicted construal of singularity by recasting
singularity and complexity outside of the opposition of choice in
which they are invariably presented. Rather than either one or the
other their reworking will mean that they will be both one and the
other. Again, the primordiality of relation is central and again it
emerges as that which must be thought. Thinking here will involve
the complex relation to the dominant tradition in which relation is
always presented as secondary and thus as dependent on an
original self-referential unity.[44]

The recognition of anoriginal plurality and with it of a constituting spacing brings the question of naming to the fore. If the
event is plural how could it be named? How could one name name
a plurality? What would be named? Finally, what would be being
named entail in regard to both the event and the name? These
questions – questions evoking conflict naming, perhaps naming it
– must be seen here to arise in the context of Hegel's suggestion
that 'feelings' stop the misnaming of appearance. 'Feelings' restrict
the naming of the actual to the actual. Posing a limit to the range of
naming attempts to delimit and with it check the delimiting of the
named. (Attributing such a significant power to 'feelings' is not a

move that is unique to this text. It is also made in the treatment of national identity and nationalism in *The Philosophy of Right* and in the *Aesthetics*, where 'feelings' are presented as that which provides the possibility for overcoming the split, diremption, that is the mark of tragedy. In any return to 'feelings' what will have to be argued is that the threat of diremption will have become another name for tragedy. In general terms what this means is that what arises as a problem within the Hegelian scheme is the relationship between the history of Spirit and the historicity of 'feelings'. The place of 'feelings' may be that which preceeds and secures the role of logic. As such there would be echoes of Novalis's *Fichte-Studien*.)[45]

The initial response to these questions, in responding to them as being no more than questions as opposed to the mere presentation of symptoms, involves accepting a certain conception of naming and thereby of the name/named relation, one bounded by the strict and restricting unity of both name and named. In other words within these questions is harboured that relation between name and named which would amount to a variant of the conception of naming compatible with, if not engendered by, Descartes' 'thing'. There is a unity to be named and the name names that unity. As such the name represents the unity by re-presenting it by a name. At stake here is therefore the prob-lematic of representation; its presence effectively present, given the limits and constraints of intentional logic. The above questions are enacted within it. Spacing is itself the distancing of representa-tion and thus the repeating, the re-presenting, the presenting again, of presentation. If the event can never be reduced to a fundamental unity or singularity then there is no-one-thing to represent. Presentation takes place, but what it is that is taking place, the occurrence, demands an approach that works other-wise. Moving away from representation while retaining presenta-tion – the pragma – marks a shift in which repetition begins to mark the place of presentation by giving while maintaining as effective, rather than as excluding – the site of a mutual exclusion – the co-presence of being and becomimg. Plurality, the hetero-geneous event, eschews its own presentation within representa-tion because there is no explicit singularity to be represented. Presentation will therefore come to be rethought and with it to be repeated and thus in the end will be re-presented.

Intermezzo: necessary relations

Spacing and therefore relation are not to be taken as additions given after the event. It is rather that they play a particular role, one which can never be reduced to anything that could be described as taking place in addition and therefore only present as a supplement without necessity. Spacing – relation's mark, the presence of its constituting hold – may be taken as, in part, constitutive of identity (remembering the inherent complex, the complexity beyond the plurality simples, which is itself the construct of identity; identity's construction). The anoriginal is present as itself where that itself marks out an irreducible plurality. (Again the 'itself' marks the anoriginally complex; a set up repeating the open determination of the name within conflict naming.) The difficulty is thinking that construal of irreducibility which no longer figures within either diversity or variety. If irreducibility can be said to involve the undecidable or the indeterminate, then what is essential is that these qualities rather than being simply posited come to be described; where the description involves recourse to the transcendental act of constitution. Ontology has to figure – though more emphatically will always already be figuring – as part of this act. Ontology is not therefore a simple ground since its presence has consequences. It is effectively present.

If there is either undecidability or the absence of a fixed determination which are not taken as ends-in-themselves, then what is important is how the relationship between the elements comprising these states of affairs is to be understood. The reason for this importance is on one level quite straightforward, namely that even though there may not be an absolute determination or decision that is commensurate with the object and which therefore has to represent the object, it does not follow from this that no determination or decision can be given or could ever be given. There will always be one, despite the fact that one will never be the one. Indeed as has already been suggested the move away from the interplay of representation and epistemology and thereby towards the pragma and judgement mirrors this reworking of the 'one'. It is not that the one has become two, it is rather that the one can never be, and this for ontological reasons, just one. This 'one' becomes the locus of judgement. (The overall suggestion that will be made at this interval is that by reworking Leibniz's distinction between 'appetition' and 'perception' another formulation of the pragma will emerge. The mark that precludes absolute singularity and thus the ontology of the Cartesian idea will be perception's dependence on the impossibility of any coextensivity (either ontological or semantic) between perception and the monad.[46]

Retaining as a strategic device the term 'object' while nonetheless leaving open its possible determinations allows for the following formulation of what is involved in the opening of the 'one'; its being therefore in its being reworked.[47] What this opening will entail is that the existence of judgements which are themselves not intended to be coextensive with the 'object' will necessitate that a philosophical description of the object be given in order to account for how it – the object – can sustain different re-presentations (repetitions) and thus different and potentially conflictual judgements. Undertaking this task involves taking up the mode of being proper to the object since what is under consideration is the existence of the object as that which sustains different re-presentations and judgements. (The task therefore cannot but pertain to the ontological, where the ontological figures in part as a quasi-transcendental.)

As has been indicated the philosophical challenge is thinking this state of affairs, i.e. presenting the presence of necessary relations. A way towards taking up such a task is provided by the writings of Leibniz, a provision occurring – again perhaps *pace* Leibniz, i.e. despite intentional logic – first in the formulation of the monad as 'multiplicity in unity' and second in the nature of the difference between 'appetition' and 'perception'. What is at stake is on the one hand how this unity is to be understood and on the other how the difference is to be conceived. Given the difficulty of these questions what is essential is to trace – albeit schematically – Leibniz's own attempt to differentiate his formulations from the dominance of Newtonian and Cartesian formulations. Again a beginning occurring *in medias res*.

Leibniz's argument with Newton can be seen as having at least two fundamental premises. The first is that substances are not themselves spatial (space is not a predicate of substance). The second is that space involves 'an order of succession' and is therefore relational. The relativity in question is not to be counterposed to any absolute. Since space is the relation between monads any relativity could not pertain to substance in the singular but to substances in the plural. Monads themselves are not spatial. There is therefore no absolute space in which substances are located. Within an imaginary Leibnizian philosophical grammar a possible locative would always be determined by an 'in relation to. . .'. In other words the spatial location is established, positioned, because of a relation to another substance. Space does not exist as an end in itself, however. Despite the work of intention – the text's own intentional logic – which may be taken as demanding such an existence, space is neither self-referring nor does it admit of self-definition. Indeed Leibniz's presentation of space is defined in terms of time and thus depends upon the effective presence of a temporal base. The dependence on temporality – a dependence which means that space is articulated in terms of time – is clear from the 'Third Letter to Clarke':

> I hold space to be something merely relative, as time is; . . . I hold it to be an order of coexistences as time is an order of successions. For space denotes in terms of possibility, an order of things which exist at the same time (*en même temps*), considered as existing together (*elles existent ensemble*); without enquiring into the manner of existing. And when things are seen together, one perceives that order of things among themselves.
>
> (6, 363)

There are two aspects of the letter which should be noted in advance. The first is the distinction drawn by Leibniz between things 'existing together (*elles existent ensemble*)' and their 'manner of existing (*leurs manières d'exister*)'. It is essential to recognise that what is involved here is existence and with it the presence of that which exists. The second is his use of the term '*ensemble*' to describe a totality without parts and therefore without relations. While both of these aspects play a pivotal role in any understanding of Leibniz's position as it is developed in his response to Clark (and thus Newton) what is essential in each case is the particular construal that is given to 'existence'. What this means in this instance is the centrality of the modes of being proper to that which is presented as comprising spatial relations, a presentation articulated in temporal terms. What must endure at this stage as an open question is the possibility of maintaining precisely this absence of all possible relations.

The significant temporal element that arises from this presentation is the description of space as depending upon 'an order of things which exist at the same time' (*un ordre des choses qui existent en même temps*). This gives rise to two related questions. First, what is the time of this existence? And second, what of *its* existence? (time's existence). The force of this second question is its implicit recognition that time exists and that therefore it cannot be thought outside of its necessary interarticulation with existence. Working with the assumption of the necessary – and of necessity plural – interarticulation of being and time, what this second question seeks to elucidate therefore is the mode of being designated by this time, i.e. the specific ontologico-temporal concatenation. These questions, which emerge from Leibniz's own formulations, are of central importance as they gesture – though at this stage it is no more than a gesture – toward the unannounced, and of necessity unannounced, presence of a differential ontology. A significant split will emerge, a split characterised by relation and distance, in the differing ways in which plurality can be said to be present. The split hinges on the voicing and thus the presentation of this presence.

Given these strictures – the interarticulation of time and existence – there are two components of this passage that are of immediate interest. The first is the interrelated definitions of space and time. The second is the already mentioned projected twofold distinction within existence. The latter aspect comprises what, on the one hand, can be taken to be the assertion of the fact of existence, and on the other of identifying the 'manner' or mode of that existence. While this distinction can always be expressed in terms of the difference between quality and quantity advanced in Sections 7 and 8 of the *Monadology*, where Leibniz takes up an important distinction that can on one level at least be located in Aristotle and which comes to be redeployed by Hegel in the Doctrine of Being in the *Shorter Logic*, it will, nonetheless, be essential to find a way of formulating it with greater precision and thus with its having far greater extension. The interplay of formulation, precision and extension marks the site of an-other repetition; interpretation as an inaugurating repetition.

Space and time are both orders. In the case of space it is one of 'coexistence'. Again this repeats the exact formulation given by Leibniz in a letter to Des Bosses in 1712:

> Space is an order of coexisting phenomena (*spatium fit ordo coexistentium phaenomenorum*).

(2, 450)

This 'order' exists at 'the same time'. Time sustains space. Consequently it is once again clear that the possibility of space does not simply rely on the presence of monads, but that their existence is temporally defined in terms of a specific present. This establishes why division within the monad has to be precluded. Division, within monads, would mean that they not only were spatial but incorporated the temporal as well. It will be essential to note the extent to which, in the end, both these possibilities can be really excluded. The point of noting this is twofold. First it will indicate the point at which intentional logic can no longer sustain the project it has announecd as its own; the foundering therefore of the founding moment. And second it will show that relation is primordial, and thus that which demands a philosophical description is that in which this primordiality inheres. Complexity arises since 'it' inheres in it by constituting it. What this description will take up therefore is existence and with it a reworked question of being. Reworking here refers once again to the way in which ontology has effects due to its work.

The interrelated definition does not just work for space. Time is also defined as an order. Here it is not one that exists between monads at the present; the present time. But rather it involves a relation between monads that exist at different present times, i.e. different points in the 'order of succession'. Time therefore marks out the present as a continuous series of isolated points. As such the temporality involved thus far is time as the point(s) to which a date or various dates can be applied. It is at this stage that two related questions arise. Is this difference purely temporal? Is there not in the very formulation of the distinction between two different presents the involvement of an inherent and absolutely necessary spacing? In other words, even if the distinction is temporal the fact that they are held apart would seem not just to allow for spacing but, more significantly, would also necessitate the presence of spacing and thus of space. The presence in question would not take the form of an intrusion; on the contrary, it would figure as the *conditio sine qua non* for temporal succession itself. Spacing – involving the process that is always more than the attribution or identification of space – would be therefore constitutive of identity. It stops the points being the same. The challenge that emerges at this point stems from the recognition that if there is this additional spacing, and that if this spacing is necessary to sustain the identity as well as the formulation of time and space, then it is an addition that falls outside the ambit of the Leibnizian conceptions of both space and time. Pursuing this point will involve taking up the posited twofold nature of existence deployed in the description of space in the 'Third Letter to Clarke'.

The distinction drawn by Leibniz between things existing and the manner of existing is, on the surface at least, posed in terms of the difference between the form taken by that which exists and the fact of that existence. These relations will also determine possible existences; possible factual existence. In other words any future existence will not simply involve new spatial relations as though such relations were no more than a simple addition. The actual role played by these relations is far more significant than that which is suggested by the possibility that they were no more than a mere addition. (The temporality and reality of being an addition, in having to be rethought, opens up complexity.) Indeed it is the reality of these relations which, while being the articulation of subsequent existences (what Leibniz will have identified as '*les existants*'), will also provide future existences with their conditions of possibility; conditioning future. Leibniz makes this point in the *New Essays on Human Understanding* where he argues that space is

> a relation, an order not only between that which exists (*les existants*) but furthermore between possible existences *as if they existed* (*les possibles comme s'ils existent*).
>
> (5, 67; my emphasis)

Possible existence brings with it a specific problem. While it may seem that all that is at play here is the exemplification of the need to account, on the one hand, for the spatiality of possible future existences (the spatiality of relations to come), and, on the other, of the inclusion of time within space, there is considerably more at stake. Detailing this 'more' is complex. It involves that which is also formulated in the attempt to formulate.

The first element of this detail that must be noted is the use of the expression 'as if' (*comme si*). What this expression indicates is the necessity of relation and yet it is a necessity that exists as a potential. The 'as if' involves a twofold temporal division. In the first place there is a present necessity. In the second place, however, there is a potential that, even though it is unactualised, is nonetheless still present. This gives rise to the question of how the distinction between actual relations (which define space and the present) and futural possible relations (which open up Leibnizian time) is to be understood. Any answer must commence with the recognition that the distinction is not between the present, a specific present, and the future as such. If it were then the 'as if' would have been rendered otiose. The future is only present in terms of the necessary preconditions for the possibility of the future, namely relation and therefore space; the space of an inherent and implicit spacing. The temporality of the future will involve the 'order of succession' in which time figures as a series of distanced and hence spaced moments. In spite of this figuration, included within any present moment are precisely the preconditions for possible existences at future times. This means, therefore, that the present is always divided between 'that which exists' (*les existants*) at the present and possible existences whose presence at the present is, in this instance, always mediated by the 'as if'. What is emerging here is a diremptive present. (In emerging what is taken up, again, are the determinations within conflict naming.) The division is not sustained by the posited difference – a difference yielding eventual similarity – between universal and particular but pertains to the monad and thus to any of its present moments. The diremption, as with conflict, is not between appearance and universal, it is not present therefore within an alienated present marked by 'need'; it is rather that the object (name, monad and thus in the end the event) is the site of an already present division – the anoriginal – where the division in inextricably bound up with the ontological.

   The possibility of the diremptive present – a possibility building on what is presented by the 'as if' – receives further adumbration in Section 22 of the *Monadology*. Even though this example does not concern the 'as if', it still occasions the same result, namely that diremptive present in which the diremption though initially temporal is, because of the definitional interdependence between space and time, also spatial. Furthermore the co-presence of both space and time, coupled to the nature of that presence, will mean that the diremption is as much ontological as temporal. In other words spacing involves the presence of the ontologico-temporal. While this must be the case if time and being are always already interarticulated rather than simply delimiting each other, this on its own is not sufficient. The further point that must be made in addition is that spacing here is that which sustains the identity of space and time as well as being constitutive of the monad. It is this complex that is given in Section 22 with the presence of the already present future:

> so every present state of a simple substance is naturally a consequence of the preceding state, in such a way the present is big with the future (*le présent y est gros de l'avenir*).
>
> (6, 610)

While this may make the present plural, the nature of that plurality is yet to be specified, a problem compounded by what could be taken as the inscription of futurity in the present. While it will be essential to return to this description it should be noted that positing plurality in this sense raises the question of its relation to Leibniz's celebrated description of the monad as multiplicity in unity. The definition of the monad as multiplicity in unity needs to be understood in connection with elements of Leibniz's presentation of simple substance.

In the *Monadology* simple substance, in the attempt to present it beyond the confines of Cartesianism, is described as having neither 'extension' nor 'figure' nor 'divisibility'. The monad cannot be affected from outside; it is rather that its capacity for change comes from an 'internal principle'. As the monad changes there must be, Leibniz argues, elements that remain the same. This obviates the possibility of a radical transformation in which the monad would be recreated from within itself as the absolutely new. Change therefore takes place 'by degrees'. (The possibility of destruction and therefore of the new as that which arises from Cartesian destruction is, within this formulation, being displaced.) It is this description incorporating the co-presence of rest and change that generates one formulation of multiplicity in unity. Again what insists is how co-presence is to be understood. Again this is the question of relation. With its centrality – the centrality of already present relation – another task can be taken as having emerged.

At Section 13 of the *Monadology* this co-presence is expressed in the following way:

> it is necessary that in the simple substance there is a plurality of
> affections and relations (*de rapports*) although there are no parts
> (*il n'y en ait point de parties*).
>
> (6, 608)

Even though the consistency of Leibniz's argument in arriving at
this conclusion is not in question – since it stems from his
definition of a simple substance or monad – what does arise is the
problem of how to understand the presence of a relation in which
there are 'no parts'. The reason why there is a problem is obvious.
It looks as though the two claims are contradictory. How could
there be a relation when there are 'no parts'? Contradiction repeats
the structure of paradox in that both work within the logic of
identity. By showing that which is involved here falls beyond the
purview of the interplay contradiction and consistency, what is
displaced is the dominance of that logic.

While it will have to be approached via greater concentration on
the actual specificity of the 'parts' in question, the initial response
to the presence of this apparent contradiction must involve
indicating that it – the putative contradiction – is based on a
misconstrual of the ontological nature of the monad. The monad
while being a 'veritable atom' is not subordinated to an ontology
of stasis (even though such an ontology may appear to be included
as part of it). Moreover, taking it as being articulated within such
an ontology provides the basis of the imputed contradiction. (The
ontology of stasis and the logic of identity are themselves
implicated in an identity sustaining reciprocity.) The monad is not
a building block. Its mode of being is more complex and does in
fact form a complex. Leibniz can be taken as making his point in
his treatment of substance in a letter to De Volder, March 23/April
3, 1699. Within the letter, in arguing against Descartes and the
conception of substance as extension, Leibniz goes on to state that

> there should be no need to seek any other explanation for the
> conception of power or force that is the attribute from which
> change follows and *its subject is substance itself*.
>
> (2, 170; my emphasis)

The 'internal principle' that causes the monad to change is
therefore 'force' (in Latin *vis*). The initial difficulty here is description. Even though the monad is not static it would nonetheless
still be inappropriate to describe it as *in* a state of becoming. Such

a description would mean that there was something *in* that state and as such that 'something' would need its own preliminary ontological description. Force is neither a predicate of substance nor the monad's essence. Expressed accurately force is that which substance is. What this means is that the mode of being proper to substance is becoming. In other words substance *is* becoming itself. Here, however, becoming is not opposed to being. Restricting it to this opposition would mean maintaining as dominant the presentation of becoming within the Platonic tradition. (Trying to rework the opposition such that becoming is taken to be part of Being only reiterates the Platonic heritage.) Becoming takes place here beyond the logical exclusion informing Platonism and thus takes place with abeyance of that tradition.[48]

The way in which this logic unfolds and thus the Platonic heritage comes to be repeated – though repeated within reign of the Same – is that either one term excludes the other or that becoming is understood as a species of being and therefore subordinate to it. What is at stake is, on the contrary, the possibility of the co-presence of being and becoming. In other words one significant conclusion to be drawn from this redescription is that the assertion that a specific monad has a particular designation – its being a given X or in Leibniz's terms its having a given 'perception' X – does not occlude 'force' and therefore does not preclude its having an ontology of becoming. Force is present but not actualised within and as a particular. Rather than being actually present it is primordially present. It is thus that the monad comprises, in this instance, two forms of presence which are co-present in their difference. And therefore this is one way in which the monad becomes the site of anoriginal plurality. Here, again, the plurality is marked by the presence of an irreducibility that is ontological in nature.

Even though its being the site of anoriginal plurality may work against the text's intentional logic, it remains the case that the monad's presence as a site of irreducibility is nonetheless compatible with the way in which the monad's own logic constrains it to be formulated. It is this point that is of fundamental significance. It is the monad's own spacing – the nature of that spacing and thus the identity of the monad itself – which means that the monad has itself become the site of an ontological complex, a site in which complexity is anoriginal and as such involves ontological irreducibility; a belonging together that is unity, that is anoriginal difference. Identity, to the extent that identity is to be maintained, has become the plural event; the monad as plural event. It is of course a plurality always of admitting determinations, the pragma, 'perception'. It is thus there will always be two identities: the identity of the monad *qua* itself, the complex, and the specific identity or perception of the monad at a given point in time (time as the place of chronology). The elementary division between the two identities – two which here are one, the monad – is time. It is this complex that will be taken up.

Again, it is this description that is reinforced by Leibniz's construal of 'perception' and the nature of the difference between 'perception' and 'appetition'. As the difference is ontological and therefore differential rather than one where difference signals no more than the presence of mere diversity or descriptive variety, what is emerging is the need for a further elaboration of the monad as an anoriginally plural event. The presence of anoriginal ontological difference entails the primacy of difference (difference as differential) over the Same. The differential yields a conception of difference that comprises what can be provisionally described as incompatible values. (It may be that explicating the nature of this incompatibility will delimit a further philosophical task.) Despite this provisionality it is nonetheless still possible to argue that identity, in this instance, has become the belonging together of the ontologically different.

Perception, as is clear from *Monadology*, Section 14, is a representation.[49] In other words it is the state of the monad at a given point in chronological time. It is what it is and thus it is how it presents itself at a given present. However, what it is at the present, its self-presentation, is not and moreover can never be coextensive with the monad itself, because the 'itself' cannot be presented as such. In addition, though relatedly, this point can be argued for on the basis of the law of the identity of indiscernibles as well as in connection to the ontology proper to appetition. The monad is the co-presence of perception and appetition. It is the co-presence, therefore, of the ontology of stasis, its being what it is, its perception, and a potential which is present but which demands an explication in terms of the ontology of becoming. The result of this situation is that the monad contains, indeed is composed of, two different ontological realms. Their continual, though non-excluding, interaction is the work of the monad and to that extent the mode of being proper to the monad involves the continuity of becoming, evoking in its unfolding the ontology of the Heraclitean ῥέον ἀεί (always flowing).[50]

While this co-presence is not what Leibniz means by 'multiplicity in unity', it indicates that the unity is in fact composed of a plurality or multiplicity at a far more profound level than diversity. In Section 16 of the *Monadology* Leibniz formulates multiplicity in unity thus:

> We have in our selves experiences of a multiplicity in simple substances when we find that the least thought of which we are conscious involves variety in its object.

> (6, 609)

Multiplicity here is closer to the plurality to which he refers in the already cited letter to De Volder. It occurs only on the level of quality and enables one monad to be distinguished from another. What has been identified above as an ontological plurality is a state of affairs not recognised as such by Leibniz but to which his position is committed. Its primordiality as well as its effective presence is thereby affirmed (an affirmation taking place within interpretation and therefore in the text's repetition). The question that in the end must be answered is whether or not this plurality involves relations without parts; again a question whose very formulation opens up the possibility of the primordial presence of relation.

In a letter to Arnauld (30 April 1687), and as part of a larger argument that there cannot be a multitude 'without true unities' (*sans des véritable unités*) he goes on to argue that

> It has always been believed that one and being are reciprocal things. One thing is being, the other thing is beings; but the *plural supposes the singular* (*le pluriel suppose le singulier*) and where there is not one being there will not be several beings.

> (2, 97; my emphasis)

What is significant here is the description of multiplicity as involving singularity such that the multiple is a complex made up of particulars. While this is a position that, if only in part, is belied by his own description of multiplicity in unity as advanced in the *Monadology*, it characterises a general presentation of the multiple within a philosophical thinking that incorporates positions as apparently diverse as those of Descartes and Heidegger. In each case what is always excluded is a singular that is plural. Division or diremption will always demand external relations. The tradition, working with the assumption of an initial singularity, posits a movement into relation, e.g. the Cartesian simple becoming complex by the addition of further simples. The result is that diremption can only ever be envisaged as occurring between two given unities. It could never be taken as constitutive of identity. The division is also positioned as both ontologically and temporally consequent to that of the constitutive unities since they must, of necessity, be posited as already existing. The division, the plurality or the diremption can never be within either the unity or the singularity or the 'veritable atom'. It is of course precisely this state of affairs, i.e. a plural singular which is anoriginally present, that is at work, in different though foundational ways, in the work of both Leibniz and Pascal. It is in terms of this constitution that it becomes possible to argue that the anoriginal presence of a plural singular provides ways of rethinking elements of a transcendental idealism and thereby facilitating the incorporation of the transcendental – perhaps a repeated and thus redeemed transcendental – into ontological philosophy. The anoriginal provides that which has been provisionally identified as the transcendental act of constitution. It is in terms of the plural singular that it is possible to return to the question posed above as to whether ontological plurality involved relations without parts. It should be added that inherent in this question lies the problem of the possibility of thinking relation independently of spacing.

Ontological plurality cannot be straightforwardly identified with multiplicity in unity. And yet, however, there is a sense in which the possibility of such a multiplicity is dependent upon ontological plurality. This emerges with greatest clarity, as has already been suggested, in the distinction established by Leibniz in the *Monadology* between perception and appetition. What is important about this distinction is not the detail, in other words it is not there in the different ways in which the monad can present itself, but rather the nature of the co-presence of perception which presents itself as a representation and appetition. The nature of this co-presence is far from straightforward in so far as the possibility of a future perception – the monad presenting itself as a specific further X – is dependent itself upon 'appetition'. 'Appetition' is defined in the *Monadology*, Section 15, in the following way:

The activity of the internal principle which produces change or passage from one perception to another may be called appetition. It is true that the appetite (*l'appétit*) cannot always fully attain to the whole perception at which it aims, but it always obtains some of it and attains to new perceptions.

(6, 609)

The significant point is that this co-presence establishes what could quite appropriately be termed an ensemble. The ontologically plural event is a type of ensemble. It has 'parts' (*des parties*). However, the term '*ensemble*' already has currency. It should not be forgotten that Leibniz has previously used it (*ensemble*) in the 'Third Letter to Clarke' to describe the existence of an 'order of things which exist at the same time'. They exist together and as such establish relations that comprise space. Space can be said to exist in its being articulated in terms of a temporally defined simultaneity of presence. While '*ensemble*' – the original ensemble – is a term providing an apposite description of the presence of a relation between existent monads at a given and contemporaneous point in time, it is not, at this stage, descriptive of the monad itself. The ensemble thus far, and hence the plurality that can be thought at the present, is a collection of particulars, a plurality of constitutive parts, an ensemble.

The sense in which the monad is an ensemble is of course quite different. (As a methodological point it is worth noting that the term's repetition frees it from, while linking it to, its already existent uses.) Here the ensemble in question involves the belonging together of that which resists synthetic unity. The existence of the monad as an already existent ensemble means that the monad is an anoriginal ensemble, i.e. an ensemble in which differential plurality is not a consequence of the event, on the contrary it is constitutive of the event – the relational ensemble – itself. It follows from this that part of what would be involved in giving greater precision to the mode of being proper to the monad would be to explicate becoming in terms of anoriginal plurality. This is an explication sanctioned, if not demanded, by Leibniz's own formulations.

There are two reasons for maintaining the distinction between a perception and appetition and not allowing their difference to blur. The first is that in order for the monad to have a given perception X there must already have been a fundamental difference between perception and appetition. The identity of the perception is sustained by the presence of difference. It provides parts of the perception's conditions of possibility and therefore difference becomes a precondition for identity. The second reason is related to the first in that it underlines the monad's diremptive existence, remembering that the diremption is internal to the monad and not an external relation. Here the division refers to the possibility, already inscribed in the monad, of its having different perceptions. The consequence of this already present inscription is that it means that the perception *itself* can never be coextensive with the monad *itself*. (Even if in both cases the nature of the 'itself' is still to be clarified it should, nonetheless, be stated in advance that their difference – the difference of the 'itself' – involves both ontology and presence.) Describing this coextensivity necessitates, as has already been indicated, having recourse to ontological difference, difference marked by the co-presence of the different. The monad, as an ensemble, is ontologically plural. The possibility of thinking the monad, a possibility excluded by elements of Leibniz's own work and yet also demanded by them, is the possibility of thinking plurality at the present. What this envisages is a plural present, where the plural is no longer simple complexity, ornamentation or the multiplicity of particulars but is ontological and temporal in nature. It must be added that the plural is not an evaluative term. The plural is only to be opposed to the singular on the levels of intention and interpretation. Plurality must also be implicated in that which is intended to be monological.

The difference identified by plurality takes place within ontology (and is thereby definitionally interarticulated with temporality), and thus incorporated within the event – as the event – is a division, a spacing, that resists synthesis. (It is as part of this resistance that the anoriginal works, is at work, is effectively present and this despite the continual effacing or forgetting of either that which is at work or its effects.) The occurrence is therefore reworked and an initial diremption recovered. With it comes the recovery of the event, a recovery leading to the event's affirmation. Its affirmed presence – in this instance affirmed as a direct consequence of the act of interpretation – means that it has become the site of doubling or of repetition and as such will lend itself to those determinations proper to the event itself.

The problem that the resistance to synthesis poses arises with greatest force with the problem of representation – understood specifically as the attempt to instantiate, to present – when what has to be represented is a plural space. The acuity of the problem resides in the fact that it is exactly this state of affairs – anoriginal plurality – that cannot be thought within representation (now to be taken in its widest sense). This opens up the larger problem – a problem occurring as much in the visual arts as in philosophy – of the repetition and thus the re-presentation of complexity, plurality etc., while what is involved here relates to the impossibility of prediction once anoriginal plurality is affirmed and thus once the chance effect is sanctioned. Grasping the full force of this specific problem demands the recognition that the already present limits are historical in that they pertain to tradition, and with it to the repeated exclusion of anoriginal plurality.

Within philosophy and therefore relatedly within interpretation, history in being rethought as the continual interdetermination of repetition and tradition – the determination in advance whose determination need never be absolute because of the nature of repetition – allows for the possibility, and this despite the intentional logic working the dominant tradition, of an inaugurating repetition. What is present here, however, is more than just a redeemed hermeneutics. It should be clear that what is being staked out here is the interplay of freedom (the possibility of an inauguration beyond predication and thus as an occurrence within the abeyance of teleology) occurring within the recognition of the primordiality of relation. It is thus that abeyance becomes another form of relation; retaining of course the name relation. Again a similiar process is at work since relation's name is itself being subjected to the process that it names, the 'it' working through the presence of an ineliminable spacing, and thus the primordiality of relation admits its own plurality. The name relation therefore can itself (remembering the complexity of any 'itself') be taken as attesting to the primordiality of relation. Relation as with repetition and conflict will work once more as the *mise-en-abyme* for names and therefore for naming.

With Leibniz what has emerged is the insistent necessity of relation. Necessity here pertains to thinking and thus to philosophy. Its necessity entails a necessity. In other words what its presence means in this instance – its insistence – is the obligation to take up, and thus to think through, the presence of a relation. Again both the insistence and the necessity do not arise simply because the presence of relation cannot be denied, but rather and here more significantly it is because relation is that which works to constitute the monad itself and thus constitutes it in its multiplicity. While Leibniz has argued that relations are absent from the monad it is nonetheless still possible to argue that the irreducibility of 'presentation' to the monad demands that the relationship between the two be thought and thus the difference between them be given a real philosophical description rather than being simply noted. Again the importance resides in the fact that the difference is not just there as an addition. Citing addition, not presence, obviates work and thus precludes any recognition of the effective presence of relation. Necessary relations therefore are those which work to constitute while being primordial. The twofold nature of this necessity is the anoriginal.

Opening gifts

Again a beginning.[51] Here a return will be made to the question of the event. The return poses two initial sets of questions. The first concerns the nature of the return. What is it to return? Furthermore, what does the process mark and what is marked in the process? The second set, while involving the eventful project, would not be limited by the projection since it must also deal with the event as something to which a return can be made, emerging with a return, in part therefore imparting it. Working within these various moves means that a constituent part of the undertaking will be the way in which the event, its being and therefore the ontology of the event, figures in the process. Furthermore, implicated in a significant way in such an ontology will be the temporality of returning, the discontinuous continuity of the return, to be thought both within and as repetition. Occurring with the return, as one of its consequences, will be the concomitant bringing back into consideration of the interconnection between repetition and difference; an interplay that will in the end come to mark out the contours of the present. The situation is complex since not only is there a return to the event, its being given again such that the gift comes to be present as a form of repetition, there is also the occurrence of that repetition. What happens therefore is marked by the process of giving and giving again. How therefore is this move within giving to be understood?

The question of understanding hinges on an unannounced though nonetheless ineliminable doubling within giving (a doubling beyond simplicity and therefore other than a simple addition). The move away from simplicity means that the difficult element here – a difficulty based on complexity – is that part of this doubling has to be thought as work and thus as an original reworking; one in the end signalling the effective presence of the anoriginal. The work involved can be provisionally identified as that which is marked out by the name *Nachträglichkeit*. (The question of *Nachträglichkeit* must at this stage still remain a question. Its provisional designation of the interplay of repetition and identity articulated within the complex temporal relationship of the retroactive and the making present – presencing – will itself come to be opened up, an opening which – as with what is named within it – is only explicable in terms of work.) Moreover one of the inevitable consequences of the anoriginal will be the centrality of work.

In sum the specific problem that arises here concerns presenting repetition. The difficulty of the problem, however, is compounded once it is recognised that the process it names, names at the same time the impossibility of the essence and thus the impossibility of its own unique propriety. The singularity of the unique is effaced the moment it is announced. Repetition – once it is understood as always subjected to the process that it names – denies the very possibility of original singularity. What this opens up is complexity, the complex beyond addition and supplement. It is of course anoriginal complexity. Remembering that the presence of complexity is established neither by a further addition nor a secondary consideration will mean that what must also be undertaken is a reconsideration of the temporality of complexity. This is especially the case given that the temporality of addition and sequence are not appropriate. Complexity while not reducible to repetition is nonetheless bound up with it and thus takes its own time.

Even though the above has not presented it in either an unequivocal or a straightforward manner, and since it is that which will stand against complexity, what will need to be considered here is, once again, the possibility of the absolutely singular occurrence, i.e. an occurrence posited outside the hold of any relation (even the apparently paradoxical relation of non-relation). Only by recognising that singularity is constrained to occur *après coup* what is then opened up is the possibility of another presentation of anoriginal complexity. The counter to this suggested singular occurrence will involve an argument based on the recognition that even a putative giving gives, by repeating as an announcement the history that it gives to itself as what is not to be accepted. It is the effective presence of these relations – relations always mediating acceptance/non-acceptance – that would undo from the very start the possibility of a pure giving. Even in the limited case of a gift without destination, the gift will always be involved with that with which any involvement is most vigorously resisted. The relation will not be the resistance but its self-presentation as gift; a self-presentation that links identity and repetition. As it brings with it the question of the gift's own identity, it will be essential therefore to return to repetition. With this move, a return within repetition, the redemption of repetition figures; perhaps as a *mise-en-abyme*.

Despite the provisional nature of this opening – problems yet to be resolved, questions seeking answers – it has nonetheless two particular functions. It serves, in the first place, to rehearse some of the aspects inherent in any consideration of repetition, while in the second it introduces, in the wake of the impossibility of there being an original unified self-referential identity, the need to think the event as the site of ontological and temporal plurality; a plurality that will sustain the secondary singularity of the pragma. The gift is thus delimited by its having become part of a process of giving where both the process and that which is given within it take on the character of an event in so far as what is marked out is a necessary and ineliminable irreducibility. As such the problem of surplus is introduced; however, its presence is mediated by the reinscription of surplus – a reinscription to be presented in greater detail – within the interplay of ontology, tension and judgement.

The logic of the gift resists automatic summation.[52] The major reason is that even though the gift is given the nature of the gift, once the gift is understood as an occurrence – that which happens and which therefore rehearses the event even if that rehearsal and with it the rehearsed is not acknowledged as such – is *no longer* necessarily pre-given. Here the *no longer* marks the absence of a pregiven determination. However, regardless of this difficulty there would seem to be one overriding and necessary precondition that underpins the gift's existence as gift (a precondition that will emerge not as mere semblance, but as a paradox located at the borders of the logic of identity and with it formulated in terms of the intended obliteration of repetition). While it is a precondition that cannot be maintained and thus in its impossibility reinforces the primordiality of relation it is nonetheless worth presenting the argument whose viability would be necessary to establish it.

It is simply that if there is both a gift and hence a related logic of the gift it would then be argued that, in order that the gift be sustained as a gift, it is essential that both it and the accompanying logic be located prior to the emergence of an economy of exchange. The only way in which a gift can remain a gift, a pure giving, is if it is always being given. The gift 'is' therefore in its being given. If this were not the case, if that is, the gift reaches its destination and is given, then, it would be argued, it would enjoin the obligation that must inevitably result from its having been given. The gift could *no longer* be a gift. (It should be added that linked to emergence of such an economy is the separate question of the teleology of the gift. Its end as its telos.)

It will emerge that if there are problems associated with maintaining the very possibility of this particular construal of the logic of the gift, they will be discovered within the difficulties encountered in having to make more precise the nature of this *no longer*. The *no longer* must be taken – if indeed it is to be taken – as marking the point at which the status of being a gift is itself given up. Prior to the *no longer* the possibility of being a gift is held open. And therefore the only possibility of there being in fact a gift, in this sense of the term, is if its existence as a gift is delimited. Here this means that the gift 'is' – in the strong sense of its being as gift – in its always being prior to its being received. What follows from such a construal is that the *no longer* in marking a temporal division secures the priority of the gift. In other words, if after having been given the gift is *no longer* a gift, then this will allow for the gift to operate – to be – but only as that which is always prior to its reception.

There is, however, a complicating factor. A distinction needs to be drawn between the *no longer* at play here and the one already identified concerning the pre-given nature of the gift; a *no longer* emerging once the gift is presented as an event. In that case it was described as having a nature that was *no longer* pre-given. This additional *no longer* pertains to the interpretation of the gift – to that which is given – in so far as it relates to what is already given for its understanding, i.e. given in order that it be understood. The already given is, as has already been suggested, a way of understanding the work of tradition. The demand stemming from the already given – a demand rehearsing the work of tradition – is for a homological relation to be established between the already given itself and that which is given to it for interpretation. Here, in order that the question of the gift is reopened the interpretive already given is held in abeyance.

The *no longer* under consideration here refers to the gift's mode of being, its existence. (Here being and identity are intentionally posited as coextensive.) If there is to be a gift then it must exist prior to its actualisation as that which is given. What this particular *no longer* opens up as a field of investigation is the possibility of a pure giving located prior to an economy of exchange. Delimiting the field in this way draws a connection between the two uses of *no longer*. Holding the determining effect of the first, the interpretive *no longer*, in check, means that the question of the gift is yet to be determined. This serves to introduce a space where what is at stake is a reconsideration of the gift's existence; its mode of being. It is, of course, a reconsideration that may in the end only allow for the acceptance of the already given as a gift, if its acceptance will occasion different obligations and entailments than those which are given and therefore which comprise the varying intentions related to the gift and its reception. As such therefore not only will the gift of the already given have been reworked – reworking as repetition – but in addition the acceptance of it as a gift will have resulted in a fundamental change to the logic of the gift itself. This is the possibility of an acceptance, the gift reaching its destination, where its entry into a pre-given economy causes that economy to work in a different way. The specificity of this emergence of difference out of the already given defies prediction because it takes place in the withdrawal of the power of teleology; a withdrawal signalled by abeyance.

At this stage, however, what is important is the recognition that the *no longer* – the one pertaining to the existence of the gift as gift – means, as has been suggested, that the gift must in some sense be located prior to the operation of an economy of exchange. It is this location that provides a way of distinguishing, at least initially, the gift from a sacrifice. The only way in which it would be possible to maintain such conception of the gift would be if the divide marked by the *no longer* is also maintained. The *no longer* marks and sustains that point and thus the divide, both temporal and ontological, which were it to be crossed the gift would give up being a gift and in some sense become the sacrifice. It is essential therefore to stay with, while opening up, the *no longer*. The possibility of the pure gift – pure giving – is marked, as will be suggested, by the *no longer* and its correlates.

While what is central here is the gift, in more general terms what this signals is the possibility of absolute differentiation; in other words the possibility of a rupture in which a divide comes to be established, one where neither side of the divide could bear the mark of the other. The relation between them would involve the logical form of absolute alterity, perhaps what could also be described as the enacted presence of a completing indifference. (The function of indifference lies not in its actuality, and thus in its realised presence, but in its structuring presence within an intentional logic.) The mode of thinking proper to this, while complicated, can nonetheless be signalled, for example, by an expression of the form 'without regard to', a happening taking place 'without regard to' that which was thought to be implicated necessarily. This is, of course, a Heideggerian formulation that is found in *Time and Being*. With any formulation of this complexity the question will be of the gift of interpretation, from within whose gift will it be taken. Turning to Heidegger becomes a step with a general working though where what remains as central is the possibility of singularity arising with the abeyance of original singularity. Again the turn just cannot be to the plural event as though it were an eventuality that was itself simply given. There is an implicit temporal reversal that must be rehearsed in which singularity is an afterwards which has specific conditions of existence that always locate singularity within relation. As has been argued the nature of that relation needs to be thought beyond the Hegelian construal of the relationship between universal and appearance. As always there is more at stake.

In Heidegger's gift – sacrifice

And yet beginning is far from straightforward. The difficulty, again, is the Heidegger in question.[53] Here what is central is the attempt by Heidegger to formulate what he identifies as 'the thinking of Being'. While this may seem to limit, perhaps unduly, Heidegger's philosophical undertaking the project of such a thinking is central to his conception of the philosophical task and thus the attempt to formulate it as a pro-ject. Again this will demand emphasising the formulation within and as part of the struggle to formulate. Here what this will entail is the attempt to situate the presentation of the 'thinking of Being' within the frame of destruction. The latter is of course the attempt to establish singularity by the ending of relation and the obliterating of the event. Writing of destruction in relation to Heidegger is, however, already to run a risk. Heidegger writes of 'destruction'.

Heidegger's 'destruction' is presented in a number of places. The point of departure to which Heidegger returns is in *Being and Time* (1927), Section 6. His attempts to clarify the misconstrual of the passage in *Being and Time* are of great significance. In *The Question of Being* (1955) he argues that 'destruction' in that instance had

> no other desire than to win back the original experience of metaphysics as conceptions having become current and empty in the process of abandonment.
>
> (93)

Again in *What is Philosophy* (1955) he attempts to differentate his project from one which would involve a 'repudiation'(*Verleugnung*) of history in favour of an 'adoption and transformation of that which is handed down' (71). What is involved here is clarified in the same paragraph.

> Such an adoption is what is meant by the term destruction. The meaning of the word has been clearly described in *Being and Time* S6. Destruction does not mean destroying (*Zerstören*) but dismantling (*Abbauen*), liquidating, putting to one side the merely historical assertions about the history of philosophy.
>
> (71–3)

This gives rise to a specific philosophical project, though to be more precise it is rather that what is announced here is a reciprocity between this presentation of destruction and the project. One is inextricably implicated in the other. While it is tempting to try and determine in what way 'dismantling' and 'liquidating' form part of the same project and are thus synonyms in regard to both word and action, their disturbing synonymy will be left to one side. What is central for these present concerns is the task itself. (Any return to the synonymy will involve thinking its interarticulation within and as part of the task.)

The full force of the task is announced in the continuation of the paragraph under consideration.

> Destruction means – to open our ears to make ourselves free for what speaks to us in tradition as the being of Being. By listening to this interpellation we attain the correspondence.
>
> (73)

While this construal of destruction will in the end have to be investigated with greater precision it can nonetheless already be taken as implicated in another and of necessity unannounced work of destruction. The latter form will figure in a number of different ways. The presence of this other destruction will occur within, and thus in a sense also structure, the interplay of sacrifice, indifference, forgetting and blindness. It is this other form of destruction – unstated as such – that will allow for connections to be drawn between Descartes and Heidegger, connections that will have as a consequence the necessity to pose – though at this stage as no more than an open question – the possibility of the redemption of destruction.

The other destruction, its implicit though effective presence, will emerge from tracing the attempt to advance the thinking of Being as presented in *Time and Being* (1962). An opening for this presentation will, in this instance, be provided by an argument presented by Heidegger in *The Question of Being*. In taking up the question and with it the challenge stemming from Jünger's work, here identified by Heidegger as what is involved in thinking 'nihilism' and thus 'nothingness', Heidegger argues that the latter can only be approached, as in the case with Being, in terms of 'thinking its essence (*Wesen*)'. There is, however, an attendant risk, one which rather than having to be taken and therefore with its metaphysical consequences having to be endured, allows itself to be displaced and thus avoided by adopting the right way: *Weg*/ μέθοδος.

> Only this way can the question as to nothingness be discussed. However the question as to the essence of Being dies of (*stirbt ab*), if it is does not surrender (*aufgibt*) the language of meta-physics, because the metaphysical conception (*Vorstellen*) for-bids thinking the question as to the essence of Being (*es verwehrt, die Frage nach dem Wesen des Seins zu denken*).
>
> (72–3)

Thinking involves therefore the giving up, or surrendering, of metaphysics. This gift is the one that makes a thinking of the essence of Being possible. Here, if Heidegger's formulation is followed carefully, there is an intriguing reversal. In this instance thinking the essence of Being – even as a question – is only possible if metaphysics has already been given away. The divide in this instance necessitates that the giver – who is located within thinking and thus gives in order to be, and to have been, in the position of thinking – not retain any trace of the gift that was given. Therefore, rather than there just being a gift prior to an economy of exchange here, there must be both a giving and a gift with neither forming part of such an economy. Even though it is not argued for as such by Heidegger, thinking Being depends upon giving metaphysics away. There is, however, a price. In order that it be given away – metaphysics as gift – there can be no residue; nothing can remain. The price therefore is the presence of active forgetting and the absence of memory. Once again were this not the case then, by definition, there could *never* be a thinking of the question of the essence of Being. It would not be that such a thinking was difficult. It would be simply that such a thinking was always already forbidden, forbidden, it must be added, by and in the very structure that gestured towards its possibility. Interdiction is written into the actual structural formulation of the task's possibility. It is worth restating the actual line, the metaphysical 'forbids thinking the question as to the essence of Being'. The interdiction is inextricably present as part of the task.

Pursuing Heidegger's presentation will involve taking up the interconnection between 'surrender', 'overcoming' and the project of leaving metaphysics to itself. As will be suggested the dilemma that emerges here and which will concern the attempt to think the philosophical task that emerges out of this interconnection comes from memory; the work of memory. However, before turning to memory it is essential to reiterate the force of the denial of relation by locating it within its own economy, namely a logic of sacrifice.[54]

In developing such a logic the heritage of sacrificial thinking must be acknowledged, and yet rather than locate the following within it, here rather than attempting to rework sacrifice within the interplay of the literal and the figural – i.e. in terms of the question of whether its presence is to be taken literally or as mere figure (a figure which at the very moment of its inception will always be parasitic upon the possibility and thus the contours of literal presence) – it will be taken as already at work within the formulation of differing philosophies of destruction. In a provisional sense it can be suggested that to the extent that something is offered up in order that an end is achieved then that which has been offered is sacrificed. It is not just given away. Nor is it to be understood as forming the given. The gift while allowing for action and thus its own being imparted and received works, as far as the argument being advanced here is concerned, as marking out the space of an unavoidable reception; even a refusal is a type of fusing (re-fusing) or taking over. This accounts for why tradition has been presented as the already given. Sacrifice – in terms of this logic of sacrifice – as it figures in both Descartes and Heidegger is the sacrifice of this gift; a present differentiation of the present from itself that in denying the possibility of relation and in eschewing any eventuality of working within abeyance must, as a consequence, sacrifice the present for the future. Moreover the present is construed as a site given to be sacrificed; it is the locus of error, the site of irreconciliation etc. The interplay of the present as calling for its own sacrifice and the necessity of that sacrifice in order that a particular task be either enacted or achieved gives rise to what can be called the politics of sacrifice. There is an additional point that needs to be made here concerning the relationship between sacrifice and ritual and thus their differing enactments. It is a point that will be developed further on. Ritual involves a cyclical repetition in which the same is repeated; a repetition within the Same. Within it the consequence of sacrifice is assured by the continuity of its repetition. Within ritual that which is sacrificed can stand for the whole. Substitution and hence mimesis are fundamental. With Descartes and Heidegger because sacrifice can only take place once it occurs outside of ritual and is posed therefore beyond ritual's time. It is thus that the whole must be offered. The totality is given away. Finally it is the necessity of the totality's destruction that gives the question of memory its acuity.

In the passage cited above from *The Question of Being* what is essential is that 'the question of the essence of Being' is saved. Its death needs to be prevented. Its being allowed to die off only repeats the current determinations of the present as the site of metaphysics. Saving the question demands action. Were it not for action, the right action, then what would be 'forbidden' would be the demanded task, namely 'thinking the question as to the essence of Being'. While on one level it is clear that what still needs to be stated is that which is precluded by the necessity of sacrifice, in having 'to surrender' – give up – the 'language of metaphysics', its removal means that any possible redemption or reworking of that language is also precluded. What this demands is the subsequent attempt to rid the enacted task of the effective presence of repetition. In other words in having been surrendered 'the language of metaphysics' cannot simply be brought back, repeated; this is the necessary and unavoidable constraint of sacrifice. The reason is that bringing it back would involve the process of having either to maintain a critical relation to the metaphysical determinations of that language, or at the very least to maintain those determinations in abeyance while allowing their reworking to be dominant. Relation and abeyance have themselves been surrended in and as the realisation of sacrifice. This is in part what is necessitated in order to realise – perhaps to ground – the singularity of the thinking of Being.

It goes without saying that these tentative conclusions concerning sacrifice appear to be directly countered by Heidegger's claim, already cited, that he is not concerned with 'repudiation' but with the 'adoption and transformation of that which is handed down'. There is an extent to which part of Heidegger's project can be explicated in precisely these terms, e.g. his radical reworking of the language of theology and ethics beyond their proper concerns in *Being and Time*, Section 38. (It remains of course an open question how these actual moves are themselves to be interpreted once the domination of intentional logic no longer holds sway.) And yet the contention that will be developed here is that the overall task of 'thinking Being' – thinking it in its radical singularity, that which will be explicated further on as thinking 'without' – demands a fundamentally different approach.[55] No matter what type of transformation or adaptation could possibly take place the demand to think Being 'without' relation to either 'beings' (*Seiende*) or the 'language of metaphysics' nor indeed the cited need to 'surrender the language of metaphysics' thereby leaving 'metaphysics' to itself, none of these essays can be construed as employing either modes of adoption of means of transformation. Indeed the force of 'surrender' (*aufgibt*) lies in the inescapable necessity of the logic of sacrifice. And yet it is a process that remains unstated in Heidegger's presentation of the task of thinking Being. Sacrifice is only present in that it provides such a thinking with its conditions of existence and as such is enacted within it.

In sum therefore sacrifice figures in the philosophy of destruction to the extent that destruction resists repetition and thereby fails to think the possibility of renewal as a form of repetition. Sacrifice is thus the stand against the ineliminable presence of plurality that is essential if what is to be maintained is singularity; the occurrence outside of all relation. If sacrifice is not possible – in this instance if the 'language of metaphysics' cannot be 'surrendered', given way as such – what then follows is the necessity to rethink the present, no longer as a site of potential self-reconciliation and unity but as marked by the inevitability of tension and plurality and therefore as demanding the continuity – the retroactive continuity – of the process of judgement.

Giving again

Writing on *Time and Being* is already a challenging task. Tracing the unfolding of sacrifice, the logic's work, within it only compounds the already existent problems. The daunting difficulty of the text works to check any hasty evaluative move. The text's opening as well as its final moment states then reiterates the difficulty. Consequently rather than just positing difficulty as though it existed in itself what is essential in this instance is Heidegger's own formulation of difficulty. The passages in question need to be noted in order to identify the precision of the formulation.

The first occurs as part of the lecture's opening. Again, in part constitutive of the passage's force is what is opened thereby.

> Let me give a little hint on how to listen (*das Hören*). The point is not to listen to a series of propositions (*Aussagesätzen*) but rather follow the movement of showing (*dem Gang des Zeigens*).
>
> (2/2)

The second passage – which ends the lecture – concerns the stating, saying, of *Ereignis* in which the possibility of its being said as itself is held open.[56] Here this is linked to the 'overcoming of Metaphysics' as forming part of what is involved in the thinking of Being. Heidegger goes on:

> If overcoming remains necessary it concerns that thinking that explicitly enters Appropriation (*Ereignis*) in order to say It in terms of It about It.
>
> What is necessary is unceasingly to overcome the obstacles that tend to render such saying (*Sagen*) inadequate (*unzureichend*).
>
> The saying of Appropriation (*das Sagen vom Ereignis*) in the form of a lecture remains itself an obstacle of this kind. The lecture has spoken merely in propositional statements (*Aussagensätzen*).
>
> (24/25)

Without entering here into all the detail of what is presented in these passages it is nonetheless still essential to note the constitutive contrasts (if not opposition) between 'propositions' (*Aussagensätzen*) on the one hand, and 'the movement of showing' or another and different 'saying' (*Sagen*) on the other. In the first of these formulations Heidegger is providing a method for responding; responding to what is said in the propositions. Propositions are inadequate in relation to the 'movement of showing'; the latter must show itself as itself, i.e. show its own unique propriety. What is being said in such a movement cannot be said in propositions. Propositions only deny by betraying 'the moment of showing'. (What remains an open question – though in the end inevitably *pace* Heidegger – is the extent to which the twofold within betraying – the co-presence of showing and denying – could ever be overcome.)

The difficulty of a 'saying' that is appropriate to *Ereignis* is presented in terms of 'obstacles' (*die Hindernisse*) that need to be 'overcome'. The need is part of what determines the nature of the philosophical task; presented as the task of thinking. The effect of such 'obstacles' is that they render the 'saying' of *Ereignis* 'inadequate' or 'insufficient' (*unzureichend*) and moreover they turn the present into a site that is not reconciled with the propriety within it, i.e. the present is estranged from Being even though the present is the 'release of Being'. Specifically in regard to the lecture there is the further point that the lecture itself in its being spoken in 'propositions' is also inadequate. The lecture cannot complete – either by finishing or enacting – the task that it sets for itself. Again, however, it is only inadequate within the terms that are established by it. As such it can only betray; but only betray its own self-given propriety. Consequently it follows that the task set within the frame of these contrasts is best explicated, if only as a beginning, in terms of adequacy or sufficiency. In other words the actual force of 'overcoming obstacles' and the 'saying' of '*Ereignis*' should be provisionally formulated in terms of adequation; a self-adequation that is continually being betrayed, the demise of its self-sufficiency, a reiteration of estrangement. (Here, clearly, there is no simple re-enactment of the structure of '*adequatio*'; the adequation of the scholastic conception of truth, that would be too easy and besides Heidegger has already examined that particular formulation in considerable detail in *On the Essence of Truth*.)

Adequation, in this specific instance, involves two components.

The first is an implicit – and of necessity implicit – conception of signification. The second pertains to the nature, incorporating in the end the ontology, of that which is said. What is the 'it' that is said either adequately or inadequately? Answering this question, which cannot be done at this stage, will involve recourse to the ontology of the 'it' – to that which gives itself to be thought – and in so doing the ontological will have to be posed beyond its structured presence within Heidegger's own construal of onto-logical difference. (A difference, in his case uniquely posed within the attempt to realise singularity, to effect it. The problem will always be thinking a singularity that is no longer incorporated within a logic of sacrifice.) Adequation sets the scene for sacrifice. The way through the scene – here *Time and Being* – will consist of choosing markers which need not have already been given as chosen; in other words the continual encountering and distancing of the given way.

One of the most succinct early formulations of the project contains within in it the presentation of an economy that will determine, route, the project itself.

> We want to say something about the attempt (*Versuch*) to think Being without regard (*ohne die Rücksicht*) to its being grounded in terms of beings. The attempt to think being without beings (*ohne das Seiende*) becomes necessary because otherwise, it seems to me, there is no longer any possibility of explicitly bringing into view (*eigens in den Blick zu bringen*) the being of what is today all over the earth, let alone of adequately (*hinreichen*) determining the relation of man to what has been called Being up to now.
>
> (2/2)

The relation to 'Being' – the putative 'Being' of the 'up to now', this latter being the epochal present – is the mis-stating of Being.[57] A mis-stating that still states Being. Not only is the Heideggerian problematic of revealing and concealing shown thereby, the way into the present, and thus his present analysis, is based on the non-coextensivity of these statements. Determining what is at play in this mis-statement, as well as the present epoch of Being, being brought to sight – brought with its own implicit sense of unity and propriety (*Eigens*) – turns around a 'necessity' (*Notwendigkeit*), one stated as such.

The necessity is that the two stated tasks must be undertaken.

Achieving such an end will necessitate the denial of relation; a denial enacted as thinking, taking place within thinking and thereby marking an ineliminable doubling of 'necessity'. The 'attempt' demands the 'without'. The 'without' attempted is a necessity which is to be attempted of necessity. It is enjoined. An attempt therefore though while essayed in *Time and Being* yields more general conclusions that will demand to be followed since they are found as presenting the mis-stating that is the lecture, the presentation of 'propositional statements' that is *Time and Being*. There is therefore a complex obligation, evinced by 'necessity', named by it, that structures and enacts the text's intentional logic. The failure to follow would mean having overlooked or resisted the force of necessity and thus equally of having resisted the force of its lead.

From this passage there emerge two components of considerable importance. The first is the 'without' and the second is the incorporation of the effective presence of 'necessity'. The formulation of the second within its relation to the first re-enacts the logic of sacrifice. For an end to be achieved, to be an end, something must be offered – given away/given up – the achievement of the end, as an end, depends upon the offering; furthermore the end is marked by necessity. (The incorporation of surplus will be signalled in this instance by the necessity, here, of either blinding or forgetting; forms of oblivion that bring with them different consequences.) Finally the end must enjoin itself upon others with an equal necessity; the latter element generates what has been called the politics of sacrifice. The 'without' identifies the offering; the problem that confronts Heidegger in the formulation of the attempt is how to think 'without', the thinking of having done away with beings; *ohne das Seiende*. How are beings maintained as sacrificed? A question which, as shall be argued, highlights the already present question of the differing possible ways of construing the relationship between memory, forgetting and destruction. Part of the reason for their existence as open questions relates to sacrifice. And yet sacrifice, the logic it enacts, is itself far from simple.

Were sacrifice to be present within and as ritual then repetition would be essential to its practice. While this claim is accurate greater precision is necessary here. Ritual does not involve repetition *tout court*. It is rather that it would be repetition as rehearsed continuity; the intended reiterative simultaneity thought within identity. It is this construal that holds the above formulation of the problem of memory and forgetting in check. In other words sacrifice, in this instance, is repeated and thus its continuity means that its effect is continually renewed. The difficulty that emerges here is that for Heidegger, as for Descartes, destruction, and here sacrifice, are not thought as ritual and are therefore not continuous and hence are placed outside of any articulation within the specific repetition that forms the temporality of ritual. In both there is a sense of completion that in the case of Descartes is presented as the actualisation of the project of rebuilding, and for Heidegger of being in a position in which Being is able to be 'heard' – the there of hearing (exploiting thereby Heidegger's own play with *gehören*) – and more emphatically 'heard' in its singularity. Again it is the temporal singularity of sacrifice that will demand either blindness or forgetting in order that its effects be maintained. In other words the important point here is that blindness and forgetting are essential if the construal of the contemporary established by Cartesian destruction is to be maintained and that the continual openness to the future – its realisation as future – enjoined by Heidegger be held open with(in) reconciliation.[58]

Both of these moves, moves which are themselves necessary, necessitate a reciprocal denigration of the present. In the case of Descartes this involves, at its most minimal, a critique of the scholastic heritage coupled to its institutionalisation in both school and the university.[59] The present provides nothing else than the conditions for the repetition of error. For Heidegger the present is the locus in which the question of Being is misposed and mis-answered; as such the question is given within the epochality of Being, but only in order to be done without. (Its being given but then effaced means that the present is that site which at the present is necessarily not reconciled with that propriety announced within it and thus which is proper to it.) In a sense this will provide an important component of the strategy of *Time and Being*. Thinking 'without' will open up the possibility of the future in part because 'Metaphysics' understood here as a concern with Being and the continual mis-stating of Being defines and delimits the present. Thinking 'without' will be thinking without the current determinations of the present. It will be, of course, a move that is made possible by the present in the sense that the present is given by Being; Being's release. The reworking of the 'without' in terms of 'leaving metaphysics to itself', because it entails leaving the 'age' to itself, is an inherently futural gesture in the precise sense that it means abandoning the present to itself. What must be investigated of course are the conditions of possibility sanctioning such a move.

The lecture begins and thus the 'attempt' is presented with the offering of 'a hint' on how to listen to Being. And yet this curious evocation of the ear must face the eye's own textual presence. Already within the presentation of the task sight becomes the predominant guiding figure. Moreover sight is linked to the necessity within sacrifice. Enacting the 'without' is in part undertaken in order to bring into view the propriety – and with it the singularity – pertaining to the epochality of Being, pertaining, that is, to its own giving from out of concealment. The strange combination means that what is brought 'into view' (*in den Blick*) is to be heard. Despite this initial awkwardness of expression – an apparent confusion of image and function – that which is given within any privileging of sight will itself be given within *this* use of sight. An important point to note is not just the centrality of sight in both Descartes' and Heidegger's formulation as presented thus far, but the possible similarity of the construal of the object to be viewed. The particular presence of sight will always demand its seen.

The body of the text opens pivoting around 'naming' and 'giving'; specifically the provision of an occasion to name Being and time. Moreover determining what the 'titles' 'Being and time' and 'time and Being' name will mean 'cautiously thinking of the matters (*Sachen*) named here' (4/4). With naming there is the move from the simple advocacy, almost a positing, of Being and time to the more difficult 'there is Being' and 'there is time'. The reason for this movement is that once thinking concerns itself with the 'matter' of Being and time, rather than with their simple existence (which would almost amount to their existence as beings, *Seiende*) the project will need to be reformulated such that the formulation already marks the move away from a simple posited existence. In a sense this is the stylistic correlate to the strategy of thinking the 'without'. However, there must always be more than style; what matters can never be reduced to the idiom within which the adoption of a different expression is enacted. More will always have been said, will always be being said. Heidegger identifies precisely the potential for this problem with his own reformulation. The important point, however, is that the nature of the identification indicates in addition the way in which it can be resolved.

> For the moment we have only changed the idiom with this expression. Instead of saying 'it is' we say 'there is', 'it gives'. In order to get beyond this idiom and back to the matter, we must show how this 'there is' can be experienced (*erfahren*) and seen (*erblicken*).
>
> (5/5)

Independently of any evaluative consideration of the move from 'it is' to 'there is', what is significant here – here within a series of 'propositional statements' – is the stated recognition of the need to 'show' (*erweisen*) what is involved both in the experience of the 'there is' and in its being seen. There is no distinction being drawn here between, on the one hand, the 'there is . . .' being either seen or experienced simply in itself, and, on the other, seen and experienced in its differentiation from its more metaphysical entrapments. In the first case it is singular while in the second it emerges *in medias res*. The gift to sight and experience while important is doubly thus once the nature of what it is that is 'brought into view' is itself put forward. The 'thinking of Being' (*nach Sein . . . denken*), perhaps more literally the 'thinking towards Being', or 'on Being' and even 'of/on Being in its withdrawal', takes place

> in order to think its unique propriety (*um es selbst in sein Eigenes zu denken*).
>
> (5/5)

The thinking of the 'unique propriety of Being' marks every presentation of the task of thinking Being and time. In addition it is almost invariably presented within the logic of sacrifice and along with the figure of sight.

The effect of co-presence of sacrifice and sight emerges with great force in the following passage. Again it is a passage situated not far from the beginning of the text and can therefore be taken as a further presentation of the task of 'thinking Being'; not of course its representational enactment. Its strategic interest lies in its presentation of two different formulations of the thinking of Being and thus it allows for a greater understanding of a task that while the same will always allow for different presentations. It should be noted, however, that it is a task whose actual sameness is none-

theless inscribed within and thus shored up by the proper.
'Unique propriety' in this case is that which sanctions difference.

To think the unique propriety of Being requires disregarding
(*abzusehen*) Being to the extent that it is only grounded and
interpreted in terms of beings and for beings as their ground, as
in all metaphysics. To think the unique propriety of Being
requires us to relinquish Being as the ground of beings in favour
of (*zugunsten*) the giving which prevails concealed in unconceal-
ment. That is, in favour of the It gives (*das Es gibt*).

A question that can be asked here is: What is it to 'disregard'?
However, there is a more complex question (in this instance
complex means the incorporation of time is).The question is
simply: How is 'disregarding' to be maintained? These questions
are demanded by the incorporation of the logic of sacrifice. In no
longer utilising the temporality of ritual – repetition as continuity
within identity – the question of how the sacrificial effect is to be
maintained is constrained to emerge. In this specific instance the
question pertains to how it is possible to extrude definitively
Being as ground? 'Disregarding' and 'relinquishing' are presented
as synonyms for the same function in so far as they mark out and
in marking it out hold open the same possibility. At this stage
'disregarding' holds the key to 'relinquishing' for it brings with it
the figure of sight and thus re-enacts the dominant motifs of action
and perception within the text (*Blick, Rücksicht, Hinblick, Einblick,
Vorsicht* etc.). It should be added that while the possibility of the
denial of sight, its blinded overcoming, is eventually questioned,
the dominance of the visual at this point works through and thus
works the actual attempt to formulate the specificity of the
thinking of Being. It is unthinkable without sight.

'Disregarding' is that which is necessitated therefore by the task
of 'thinking the unique propriety of Being'. At a slightly later stage
the metaphysical or grounding relationship between Being and
beings is formulated 'as Being with regard to (*im Hinblick*)
beings' (8/8). In addition the obscuring of the 'original sending of
Being' demands their 'removal' (*Abbau*) in order for thinking to
have 'a preliminary insight' (*einen vorläufig Einblick*) into that
which shows itself as 'the destiny of Being'. Again, it is not the
presence of mere images of vision that is important but rather their
presence as part of a logic of sacrifice. Metaphysics is offered up
but how is its return to be precluded? The reason why such a

question is not simply sophistic is that what must be precluded absolutely is the possibility of either an enduring relation or a recurrent relation. What cannot be maintained is a relation to metaphysics, to Beings as the ground of beings, etc. What cannot be thought, what cannot exist as a subject for thinking, is relation. This is the dramatic effect of the logic of sacrifice. Relation has to be sundered once sacrifice is no longer articulated within ritual. Thinking in having a singular task must take it on in its singularity.

The complete denial of all relation and the subsequent presentation of singularity as its result are the *sine qua non* for the formulation of destruction that is found in Descartes and, as is being indicated, in Heidegger. In both cases relation cannot emerge as a subject for thinking. Metaphysics for Heidegger is the province of philosophy and thus descriptive of an 'age' that re-enacts the continual irreconciliation with that which is demanded by the propriety of Being, once its call were to have been heeded. Compounding the presence of singularity means that the question of its being maintained returns with greater acuity. In sum, therefore, how is the 'without' (*ohne*) continually done without? The actual formulation of the question indicates why the problem is inherently difficult. Within the question what is brought into question is the possibility of it, the question itself, providing the means of its own solution. Within the negative realisation of that possibility what is announced thereby is the necessity to take up relation. Once the 'without' cannot be done without then what is opened up – opened by it – is the possibility of a different mode of thinking. And perhaps a thinking that will occasion as part of the reinscription of relation – a reinscription affirming its primordiality – the possibility of a reworking and thus the repeating anew of destruction.

Even though it involves a passage that occurs at a later stage in the text, at the point where the reformulation of Being in terms of presence (*Anwesen*) has already taken place, its importance at this stage is that it reinforces the general claim that what is essential to the thinking of Being is singularity. Having recognised that one of the difficulties of speaking of the 'It' (*Es*) of the 'it gives/there is' (*es gibt*) is of providing what appears to be no more than an 'arbitrary positing' of an indeterminant quality within every 'giving of Being and of time', Heidegger having stated the problem then offers what can be taken as an attempted resolution.

It is of course a resolution that is structured by the problem's formulation.

> we shall escape indeterminacy and avoid arbitrariness as long as we hold fast to the determinations of giving which we attempted to show, if only we look ahead toward Being as presence and toward time as the realm where, by virtue of offering, a manifold presencing takes place and opens up.

Again it is the strategy that is essential. The differentiation or disengagement is signalled by the terms 'escaped' (*entgehen*) and 'avoided' (*vermeiden*). As possibilities both can be realised but only to the extent that what is maintained is a looking ahead towards Being (*der Vorsicht auf das Sein*), as presence etc. The 'looking ahead' is a singular view. Simplicity here is not the pragma, i.e. the assertion of the singular within a general becoming. In the case of the pragma the specificity of its designation involves maintaining the inscription of the primordial relation in which it is sustained. This being the case thinking the pragma involves thinking the presence of that relation and thus thinking its presence, its being present, and thus the manner – perhaps the nature – of its presence. Presence cannot be taken as essential; it will always depend upon that which is presented.

Returning to 'disregarding' – the turning away of sight – it now has been linked to a sightful redirection. An insight leading to the point of a 'looking towards (*Vorsicht*) Being'. Looking away takes place in terms of a looking elsewhere. Again the problem of what holds the 'eye' must return (accepting the eye as a figure within the more general con-figuration of sight). It is a problem whose acuity becomes clear when Heidegger is trying to formulate the unique propriety of Being and time 'in their belonging together'. This site is called '*Ereignis*'. The apparent complexity of the site demands that it be approached with caution, one retaining what has been gleaned thus far about the place of sight; its site.

The question whose perdurance marks the text is how is the 'It' (*Es*) – of the 'it gives' (*es gibt*) – to be thought? (remembering that with this question comes the problem of how that thinking is to be presented). The trap posed by the 'It' stems from the temptation to think it within the confines of traditional grammar and therefore as part of the subject/predicate structure of a sentence. The way around this trap is to think Being not in terms of its instantiation but there as the continuity of its giving; the continual giving of being. This 'gift' there within the German 'Es gibt' as the 'it gives' as much as 'there is', allows for a thinking of Being as the interplay of presencing and giving, presented/given in terms of a continuity that stakes out the place of its own self-encounter, becomes it, is it. As this situation pertains to Being so it will pertain to time. Being becomes a giving forth or 'sending' (Schick) and with it comprising that which is proper to Being it becomes its destiny (Geschick). The interplay of sending and destiny accounts for why it is that the initial formulation leading to the above mentioned introduction of the Ereignis takes the following form.

> In the sending of the destiny of Being, in the extending of time, there becomes manifest a dedication, a delivering power into what is their own, namely of Being as presence and of time as the realm of the open. What determines both, time and Being, in their unique propriety (in ihr Eigens) that is, in their belonging together, we shall name (nennen) Ereignis.

(19/20)

The importance of this passage is considerable. Despite its obvious difficulty what occurs is a presenting, perhaps even a presencing of Being in which there is the attempt to avoid the snare of the proposition on the one hand (a snare whose hold becomes obvious, as Heidegger concedes, when a few lines later there is the attempt to move out and state Ereignis), while on the other resisting the charge of having offered a formulation of Being and time that provides no more than an indeterminate presentation. Being becomes its own self-presenting, its own self-giving, given and thus seen through time while belonging together with time. (In passing it should be noted that this 'belonging together' is not a primordial relation because maintained within it is the Same. The latter works within ontological similitude and therefore without needing to take relation as constitutive of identity.)

Continuing this investigation of Heidegger means returning to one of the earlier passages where the attempt to think Being and time did not involve taking Being as a being, but rather both as 'a matter' (eine Sache). The same is said of time. After posing the question of their relation Heidegger continues:

> What lets these two matters belong together, what brings the two into their own (in ihr Eigens) and, even more, maintains and holds them in their belonging together – the way the two

matters stand, the matter at stake is – *Ereignis*. The matter at stake in not a relation retroactively (*nachträglich*) superimposed on Being and time.

In contrast to the retroactive imposition there is a presencing in which the 'there is' is there and where its self-giving presenting gives itself. Despite its problematic status what this summation brings to the fore is the presence of an opposition between that which is proper to Being and time, themselves, on their own and with it their relation, and a relation that either the work of history of even interpretation has come to impose, after the event, on that relation. Indeed the elimination of an occurrence working after the event serves to bring out the original given propriety of *Ereignis* itself. With the intended elimination of the retroactive what is refused is the interrelation of time and work, the latter term marking the presence of a certain economy and with it the place of an effective presence, both already in place and thus placed within philosophical thinking. The retroactive is not simply that which checks the origin, it is more emphatically the site of the origin's reworking because it entails that the giving again incorporates work such that what comes to be given (re-given and hence repeated) always incorporates within it the result of the work of repetition.

However, with the addition of the term '*nachträglich*' an additional time has been introduced. Moreover with its introduction a more significant, albeit implicit, contrast to the 'without', and thus to the necessity to think the 'without', comes into play. Marked out by the presence of the term '*nachträglich*' is that which will figure – figure in finally being overcome – in the move that occurs in the closing section of *Time and Being* where the sacrificial logic can be taken to concede the problem of memory and repetition and opts, an option enjoined here of necessity even though with equal necessity unannounced as such, for the effective presence of forgetting. It is, of course, a forgetting imposed on the task of thinking Being, demanded by it, and is thus present as a necessary even though implicit element of the task, itself occurring within the actual attempt which is the task's realisation. Its presence generates what could only be described as the oblivion of relation; an oblivion realised by forgetting, to which it should be added that the term '*nachträglich*' can be taken as naming the primordiality of relation as well as the temporality of repetition in/as interpretation. These moves must be shown at work in the text's final stages.

The two sequential paragraphs in which this occurs are the following. In the first instance there is a reiteration of the strategy of thinking 'without'.

> The task of our thinking has been to trace Being to its own form of Appropriation (*Ereignis*) by way of looking through (*Durchblick*) proper time without regard to the relation of Being to beings (*ohne Rücksicht auf die Beziehung des Seins zum Seienden*).
>
> (24/25)

In the second the overall viability of that initial strategy is put into question and this despite it predominating throughout *Time and Being* and another move – a move more emphatically sacrificial – comes to be presented.

> To think Being without (*ohne*) beings means; thinking Being without regard to metaphysics (*ohne auf Rücksicht auf die Metaphysik denken*). Yet a regard (*eine Rücksicht*) for metaphysics still prevails even in the intention to overcome metaphysics. Therefore our task is to cease (*abzulassen*) all overcoming and leave metaphysics to itself (*die Metaphysik sich selbst zu überlassen*).
>
> (24/25)

As a point of departure what must be noted is the interplay in Heidegger's first formulation of 'sight' and the thinking that takes place 'without'. The vision through 'proper time' (remembering the interplay of propriety and unity – ownness – signalled within the formulation 'proper time' (*die eigentliche Zeit*) even if the actual specificity of this propriety, i.e. proper time itself, is here not taken into consideration) occurs without sight falling onto the relation of Being and beings. What is outside of this site/sight is the relation. In a straightforward way the turning away from relation grounds singularity. It is not seen and is not to be seen. The latter withholding of sight introduces a philosophical directive, perhaps even a philosophical or interpretive imperative. The doubling of seeing in this passage is therefore of fundamental importance for it serves to open up the potential risk that inheres in trying to hold the original apart from the effect of the 'retroactive'. What must be maintained is a holding apart that can never become the holding of a part. The former is the enacted 'without', while the second is the consequence of having to remain with without. The actual consequences of this remaining cannot, once again, be simply posited. The matter in question will demand explication.

The doubling involves a dependency. The first seeing is the 'looking through' time taking place while not looking at the relation of Being and beings. The second is the sight that views the relation; the 'regard' itself. In regard to both it goes without saying that sight is present as a figure. Actual seeing – the physiological process of vision – is not being suggested.[60] How then is this figure of sight to be understood? Perhaps, and here it is essential to remain with the figure – remaining by remembering that it is a figure – it is in the first place to be understood as the singularity of vision which, of necessity, envisions the singularity of its object, while secondly understood as the figurative occlusion of an object of sight. The second must be maintained in order that the first take place. However, with the first, the singular seeing, what is of interest is the relationship between seeing and the seen, an interest that endures despite the impossibility of 'stating' the seen; the limit Heidegger has identified in 'propositional statements'.

At its most elementary there is a homological reciprocity beween subject and object. And yet once this relation is recognised for what it is, then what will have to emerge as central and thus as inescapably given for consideration is precisely the ineliminable presence of that relation. It is a presence – an effective presence – that, in resisting obviation because of its having the force of a quasi-transcendental, demands recognition. It follows from this that singularity can only be upheld by the 'unique propriety' of the object of vision. The singular therefore is maintained within a relation, and thus as part of it. There is no point trying to give any specificity to that which is seen, if by that what is intended is to provide a description of content. On the contrary emphasis should be given to the specific determinations demanded for it by the nature of the seeing (still remembering that what is involved here is the unfolding of a figure; an intended figure). Such a task means taking up a problem that while posed is still to be addressed. At an earlier stage what was highlighted was the task of delimiting a construal of *Ereignis* which in its being presented allowed for a presentation adequate to *Ereignis* itself. Standing in the way of this possibility were 'obstacles' that had to be overcome. In being overcome what would then be sanctioned would be the possibility of a presentation, perhaps more accurately a presencing of it as it, in other words a presencing of 'unique propriety'; what could be described as *Ereignis*'s ownness. Again 'this' – recognising the problem of this 'this' – does not exist in itself but as the object of figurative sight. What remains is the question of what is it that is seen.

The answer to the question of the nature of what is seen is provided by recognising the interconnection within the doubling of seeing. Looking in this instance depends on the effective presence of another necessarily ineliminable 'not looking'. It is this twofold movement that is essential for the overcoming of what Heidegger identifies as 'metaphysics'. The singularity of the seen is given but only to the extent that the relation of Being to beings is not seen. Even accepting the presence of figures the question that endures is how the interrelationship is maintained in its effectivity. Heidegger does not ask this question but, as will be noted, in the end concedes the impossibility of overcoming the regard of 'metaphysics'. However were it to endure then, given the problem that arises because of the singularity of sacrifice and preclusion of ritual and thus the re-enactment of the sacrificial logic, each component of the doubling would need securing.

The singularity of sight would be maintained by the 'without'. And yet the without cannot be maintained by singularity since singularity depends upon the 'without'. Precluding sight – still the figure – drifting towards the relation between 'Being and beings' will necessitate that sight will either have to be blind – figure – to such a possibility, or sight, though more precisely the source of the 'regard', would need to have forgotten that what was being maintained was the 'without'. Forgetting thinking 'without' means forgetting that which needs to be done without. Forgetting and blinding are not options; they help constitute the task as such. Consequently to the extent that blinding or forgetting fail then what returns is not simply the sacrificial object, 'metaphysics', but rather the necessity to take relation as an object of thought; that relation whose presence it was essential to overcome if the 'destruction' (*Abbau*) of 'metaphysics' were in fact to be possible. Despite their obvious differences it is once again at this point that the projects of Heidegger and Descartes interconnect. For both, the importance of destruction lies in the impossibility of maintaining and thus thinking relation.

Heidegger does however recognise the impossibility of maintaining the lack of 'regard'. The suggestion that 'a regard for metaphysics' endures in those aspirations to 'overcome' allows itself to be read as acknowledging the difficulty of overcoming relation and differentiating the present from itself; the present being the relation of the 'age' to itself appearing as 'metaphysics'. Indeed it is possible to go further and argue that what is identified by expressions such as 'the end of philosophy' or the 'overcoming of metaphysics', expressions which dominate his writings, need to be interpreted in terms of relation. As such they mark out the project of thinking the singular where the singular is that which exists without relation. Being is, of course, the singular itself. The difficulty is that it cannot be thought or expressed as itself without first dealing with the tradition that has always mis-stated it in stating it and yet which has continually presented the unique propriety of Being, though always as lacking reconciliation with itself.

The recognition of the growing difficulty, perhaps impossibility, of sustaining the 'without' in regard to 'metaphysics' gives rise to a different formulation of what needs to be done in order to think Being 'without regard'. There are two moves that are involved. The first is to cease the project of 'overcoming', in other words to end a certain type of philosophical undertaking. The second is 'to leave metaphysics to itself', opening up thereby the possibility of a reconciliation denied in the present, to the present, by the present. Estranged and distanced from itself the present – the epochal present – and Dasein with it construct, by taking over the propriety within the present, as a futural act which in its being acted out brings futurity and reconcilability together. What they mark out is neither an identity nor a oneness but a definition of the future as the site of relation arising out of the present.

Metaphysics left to its own devices becomes a way of doing without it; doing without its present determining effects. As is clear from the text there is no intention to indicate let alone to say what this entails; showing has taken the place of stating. *Time and Being* is to that extent opening up a path and with it a way from philosophy and thus a way for thinking. As a text it can be taken as a foreword. However, there is no explicit goal or telos given as such; the future is given as an opening in which the propriety of the present, improperly presented at the present, becomes reconciled with itself.

The lecture both in content as well as in form presents obstacles. Nonetheless the way is indicated. What emerges is the need to put 'metaphysics' to one side; its concern with itself is not the concern of thinking, it is a present concern and not the future's. Both metaphysics and the present, one relating to and in part defining the other, are to be given up by being left alone. Again, and despite certain protestations to the contrary, 'metaphysics' as the present is the price that is paid for thinking. Leaving 'metaphysics' to itself is a reiteration of its being 'given away' and thus sacrificed. Again what is important is not the sacrifice in itself nor the project of thinking Being in its singularity but rather that both involve the obliteration of relation and with it the denial and effacing of the present, the sight of indifference. Its being obliterated means that not only will this obliteration itself have to be maintained, a strategy that will, once again, involve the infinite regress of forgetting. More emphatically, the very impossibility of destruction and thus of a philosophy of destruction (in the implicit sense of destruction outlined above) entails that its being maintained will only be possible with the retention of the effective interplay of sacrifice and forgetting. Outside of ritual and and therefore beyond the hold and effect of the continual repetition of the sacrificial act, the one-off nature of sacrifice will demand that the offering be forgotten. It must be, therefore, that which is and which will always have been offered up in its entirety. Maintaining such an offering as having been offered absolutely, i.e. in one entire self-completing act, will, once again, turn on forgetting working to preclude a return even in the form of either legend or irony. In the final analysis what must cause the pro-ject, this thinking – thinking 'without' – to founder is precisely the impossibility of overcoming this instability. The sacrifice beyond ritual will in the end have to become a legend and in so doing it will necessitate the reintroduction of relation, remembering that what is central here is relation and metaphysics as such. In this instance the foundering of pro-ject is of direct philosophical significance.

There still remains, however, an element of the text that has to be taken up. It will necessitate reworking the distinction advanced by Heidegger in his treatment of the *Sache* of Being and time between what is there as such ('the matter at stake') and that which would be there and thus would be, were it to be possible, a 'matter at stake' because of the retroactive process. The implicit distinction that is being drawn here is between taking up the relation of Being and time in terms of the unique propriety of that relation – a move that will be thought in terms of *Ereignis* – and what he terms 'a relation retroactively imposed on them'. Central to understanding this distinction is time; indeed what is at stake here is what could be described as the constitution of the event itself. As part of the interplay of event and time what will also have to be taken up is memory. The trap would be to think that what was involved in this instance amounted to no more than a simple choice, one given within the structure of an elementary opposition and thereby giving rise to the demand for a decision between one or the other. Here it would be between that which on the one hand was given originally – recognising the complexity of this origin – and came to be taken over as such, and what on the other, in denying the force of the original's propriety, attributed to 'it' an identity – i.e. a specific determinate identity – by a retrospective imposition.

From here to eternity

Even though the distinction between the proper and the retro-active may be the one that Heidegger might well be taken as wanting to draw, and moreover, while it could be the distinction that the text is suggesting, to think that such a distinction estab-lished a difference, a difference between two actual positions, rather than the presence of simple diversity, the difference of approach, is to misconstrue the actual force of difference. The choice, if that is what is in fact involved, would be between the origin (to which it must be added that it would be an origin thought beyond the confines of *arché* and *telos* and thus has to be construed in terms of ownness) and the after-event. However, this is no simple choice for what matters, once again, is how the difference between the possibilities is to be established, let alone understood. Choice seems to suggest an equality of opportunity. Opposition seems to suggest choice. In both cases it is as though the status of that from which the choice were to be made did not differ in any fundamental sense. Here while Heidegger's implicit suggestion is that the retroactive is a denial of original propriety, and that opting for it therefore fails both to take over, as well as on, the unique nature of what is for Heidegger almost literally on offer, the choice is presented within an intentional structure. It is as though it is possible to hold the movement that is retroactive in place and thereby not just to restrict it but to rid the present of the possible actualisation of its potential and in so doing to open up a future in which the possibility of the retroactive would have been eliminated precisely because what was allowed to emerge with its dismissal is that which would render singularly absent the retroactive effect as a structural possibility. As an intentional act it would no longer be possible as part of the task's practice.

Pursuing this point the question that must be asked is how the retroactive is either avoided or stilled. What is being asked for therefore is that which makes such an avoidance or silencing possible; again a question that turns in part around the presence of the transcendental since any answer must pertain to particular conditions of existence. Here the reason why the 'matter at stake' – the belonging together of Being and time – does not involve a 'retroactive superimposition' is formulated within a series of reciprocal if not symbiotic possibilities where a beginning is effaced by the continual turning out from within of that which was always an eventuality. Such a formulation will run, for Heidegger, the risk of all 'propositional statements' in that it will attempt to represent what is more appropriately experiential.

> The matter at stake first appropriates (*ereignet*) Being and time into their own/unique propriety (*in ihr Eigens*) in virtue of their relation and does so by the appropriating that is concealed in destiny and in the gift of opening out.
>
> (19/20)

In this instance the actual specificity of this claim is not central. Here it yields its place to what could be provisionally described as the ontologico-temporal concatenation of 'ownness', the 'unique propriety' of Being. What this description means is that they come into their own in virtue of a relation – their relation – by a giving, an establishing, in which their unique propriety is 'their' being established there, and that where they are is in their own process of coming to be, 'their' coming to be there. Being is no longer, Being 'as' (*als*) . . . where the identification takes it outside of its own propriety, its ownness, but rather is – is itself – in the process of becoming itself. A site, one intended to be self-effectuating, is thereby established and it is 'this' which stands opposed to the retroactive.

The context of the distinction is not in question. The difficulty of that which stands in opposition to the retroactive is not to be doubted. Indeed its difficulty can be taken as essential given that what it posits is the actual possibility of the giving of the singular, where its being given and its being are the same. What must be questioned is far simpler than 'this'. It pertains first to the restriction of the retroactive and therefore second – though this consequence even here is far from straightforward – to the ontologico-temporal nature of that from which it is held back. (For Heidegger this 'holding back' is not to be thought, it is not and nor could it ever be implicated in the task of thinking. For these present concerns, however, it can be taken as attesting, once again, to the ineliminable primordiality of relation. 'Holding back' is relation at the brink. In attesting to relation's primordiality the brink is central. It is important to note the reoccurrence of relation emerging at that precise moment at which its exclusion is demanded by the nature of the task. Its exclusion resists chance. Its necessary reinclusion is the chance effect.) In addition it should be remembered that rather than taking the contrast as either a simple choice or working within the variety of options it will be assumed to mark out the presence of difference and thus is to be thought as involving the ineliminable presence of both ontology and time. As such the interplay of time and being (though now the potential complex of ontology) will be allowed to figure; figure again, thereby figuring the again.

What has been designated thus far by the term 'ownness' is of singular importance. Its singularity inheres in a complex set of determinations all of which inhere at the present, structuring it as a site, as the present – the epochal present – and this even though ownness itself is precluded from coming into its own by that present. What this means is that the present is marked by an inevitable though more importantly constitutive divide. It occurs between the form taken by the epochality of Being – what is meant by form is a particularity that would enable one presentation to be distinguished from another – and the present as the 'release of Being', in other words the present as the site of Being's presence, its being present despite both its continual mis-stating and the repeated identification of itself (ownness) outside of itself. Resisting the task of thinking Being, when it is a task posed by the present at the present, would be to succumb, within the task's terms, to a complacency that demands to be understood as the presence of an unannounced resistance to propriety (a demand which also works to determine the task at hand). The force of the distinction between that which would be uncovered retroactively – were such a move even to be thought as possible – and the given 'matter at stake' resides at the point of division. In other words it occurs at the point at which the task of thinking Being emerges. It arises out of the tension of a relation that is necessarily irresolvable; irresolvable as formulated. And yet what occurs, again, is the refusal to allow this tension, the irresolvability and thus the relation, to be thought as that which is itself implicated in the task to which it gives rise. Formally it would have to be thought since it accounts for the task itself; the task arises out of and is sustained by a relation. However, overcoming it, leaving it to one side, in either case the present – metaphysics – is differentiated from itself such that what is intended is the absence of all possible relations. The questions that emerge therefore must concern how the task arises and how it is to be taken over. The importance of such questions is that they are linked to the distinction between ownness and the retroactive. What they indicate is that the task must arise such that the restriction of the retroactive is itself thought to be possible. Perhaps the difficulties encountered at precisely this point can be presented with greater acuity by switching emphasis and thus by turning to the other part of the divide to ownness.

While it may take the formulation beyond the construal given by Heidegger, one of the most important elements in the distinction concerns the presupposition that whatever it is that comes into its own, such that the force of the retroactive is not necessary, must in some sense therefore predate the intrusion of any retroactive addition. And yet to argue this position looks like doing no more than attributing an *arché*-ological quality to the original and ignoring thereby the force of Heidegger's utilisation of 'destiny' – 'destiny's gift of presence' – as that which counters, or at least can be taken as countering, the *arché*. A way around this problem would be to try and give a further explication of *Ereignis* since this is what is being opposed to a 'retroactive superimposition'. However, while this would be important it is not of immediate significance for the present undertaking. It is rather that what must be taken up is the force of the distinction. What is it that is held apart from the retroactive? Answering this question need not mean detailing the content of that which is held apart since the significant element is that whatever quality it has is there, or will be allowed to be there, or will come to be there, outside of any attribution taking place *après coup*. As such, therefore, what must be taken up is that ontologico-temporal dimension at work within the distinction.

What this will mean here is trying to give a description of that which is held apart from the retroactive. It may seem that a lot is being made of the presence of what could in fact be simply an opposition formulated to be no more than that which is noted in passing. However, this would be to miss what, it could be suggested, Heidegger has noted, namely that the importance of the distinction is that it allows first for the possibility of an inherent propriety that gives the present but is unavailable to the present, and second that this state of affairs does not demand a pre-given origin such that the enjoined task becomes its uncovering. It is as though that which is original in some sense comes from the future, a futurity it must be added that is structured by the interplay of 'sending' and 'destiny'. However, it is precisely this construal of the future that generates the problem, since while it involves a necessary differentiation of the present from itself, it does at the same open up that possibility which, while not being an origin to be uncovered, is precisely that which was there in terms of the possibility of its actualisation, its being present(ed) was there. If this is the case then it is the future that reworks the present in order to allow 'the matter at stake' to come to presence as itself. In addition it is a conception of the retroactive that does involve work in so far as while 'that matter at stake' may come into own in virtue of itself this does not occur of itself, it occurs in their opening presencing; its coming to itself. The question of the 'it' that comes to itself cannot be answered as such. There is no answer other than itself. Again this is the problem already identified by Heidegger of 'representation' and 'propositional statements'. And yet 'it' can be questioned; even though it is a questioning that has to take place outside of its own proper domain.

'It', in being uncovered by a giving of itself in which it comes into its own, is formulated as that which prefigures any representation of it. What is prefigured belongs uniquely to it. Even though its completion – a state of affairs in which it comes into its own – will always differentiate itself from the present and thus involve the future, its completion is of that which was already there. This is why Heidegger writes, to return to the passage under discussion,

The matter at stake first appropriates (*ereignet erst*) Being and time into their own (*in ihr Eigens*) in virtue of their relation (*ihrem Verhältnis*)

(19/20)

The difficulty here is no more than the inevitable consequence of Heidegger's attempt to provide a formulation of original presence that denies the convention of the origin and links presence to the action of the future. To this extent the language of metaphysics may be found wanting. And yet there is an element – not an addition but a constitutive part of the project – that reintroduces the mark of a certain metaphysics. Again, however, the difficulty must be recognised. The metaphysical mark occurs with the word '*Eigens*' translated thus far as 'unique propriety' or 'ownness'.

Of this word the first thing that must be noted is that its contents eschew the possibility of representation, it is to be experienced rather that re-presented (to what extent this signals the presence of a residual Platonism within Heidegger's attempt to formulate remains an open question). It is this 'ownness' that the *Ereignis* will 'name'. The name when used with propriety, that is, in differentiating itself from the hold of representation, will, in addition, have to resist any conception of naming that would allow for overdetermination, polysemy or even an inherent and residual ambiguity. The temptation here is to argue that what cannot be avoided is this possibility. And even if such an argument were advanced successfully the problem with it is that its force is simply semantic rather than ontological. What will always be argued to counter any posited semantic priority is that the reason why overdetermination, polysemy etc. are possible is because of the effective presence of the ontological. Making this point allows it to be turned around such that it will then become possible to suggest – at this stage no more than suggest – that 'ownness' and the naming of *Ereignis* as the naming of the unique beyond representation are only possible for ontological reasons, i.e. the assumed ontology proper to 'ownness' and that which is inherent in the conception of naming underpinning *Ereignis* as name. Moreover it is precisely ontology which sustains such projects by providing them with their conditions of existence. Making the latter point will allow for the possibility that it is those conditions which will at the same time indicate the project's impossibility.

The assumed mode of being proper to 'ownness' is of a singular existence whose determinations are such that any possible relation is precluded as a matter of definition. 'Ownness' therefore marks out the possibility of the absolutely singular occurrence that stands apart from any act of constitution or reconstitution which would demand that it was the site of a reworking that could be repeated such that it could come to be given again. What is excluded therefore is that possible ontology in which the occurrence is never absolutely commensurate with its presentation despite the presence of a presentation. It is the preclusion of a possible after-life in which the event is re-presented (though beyond the purview of representation where as a consequence the re-presentation would need to be understood as the pragma) that serves to introduce the temporality of 'ownness'. Again it goes without saying that what is involved here is an implicit temporal dimension. The time of 'ownness' is not going to be just the time of singularity but that time in which 'ownness' is neither dissipated nor reworked within the passage of time. The latter time, the time that passes, is chronology, the simple passage from one moment to the next. The time of 'ownness' differentiates itself in a radical way from this passage. It is not only that it cannot be reduced to it, it must not be marked within it. 'Ownness' gives rise to its own eternity in the strict sense that its singular unique self-identity must be maintained as itself through time. Indeed while it involves a slight shift in register it can be suggested that it is precisely this move that is at play in the structure of thinking 'without'.

If metaphysics is taken to be descriptive of an 'age' as well as a mode of philosophy, and if the preoccupation with Beings in which Being is only ever defined within that preoccupation as providing its ground could be taken as descriptive of a particular present, then in both instances while the 'age' in question, the given 'present', cannot be reduced to that which bears a date, both allow themselves to be given a location, at times a precise location, in chronological time. Heidegger's own conception of technology, his references to the political systems of 'Russia' and 'America', coupled to his own political engagement serve to underlie this possibility. It follows from this that if the task of thinking 'without' entails thinking 'without' the intrusion of the 'age' and thus the present's intrusion, the time of the 'without' becomes an eternity. Neither the eternity of theology nor the atemporality of the Platonic forms could be involved, for both are concerned with the possibility of presence – of a presenting – within the passage of time. It is rather that what is at work in this set up is the obliteration of the hold of chronology and the complete, and thereby completing, overcoming of its presence; in other words the removal of chronology, of the chronological possibility and that which is continually done 'without' or left behind in its entirety. The time in question is not explicable in either transcendental or universal terms. Both maintain relation; here, in contradistinction to this state of affairs, relation is once again precluded by the 'without'. (There are therefore important links between this construal of eternity, the denial of relation – especially the denial of its primordiality – and the pro-jected future.)

Furthermore, there is going to be an important parallel between eternity, as presented here, and the impossibility of 'propositional statements' and the language of 'representation'. The results of thinking 'without' cannot be represented, cannot be said. They are to be experienced, shown, heard but not taken over by an interpretive act that could then be re-enacted in writing, i.e. in their presentation and thus inevitable re-presentation in language, presented as such within it. If writing, in this instance understood as the presentation or instantiation of representational language, is taken to be acted out within narrative time, namely the time of sequence and progression, then the consequences of the thinking of Being, the thinking itself, the thinking taking place 'without', must itself resist its incorporation into that time, in the strict sense that it must completely overcome the possibility of narrative presence. Again this is the eternity in question, the removal, its removal of and from the possibility of any present and therefore of any datable presentation.

The time of 'ownness' is this eternity. It is not an eternity thought within repetition but on the contrary is that eternity which is given by the intended radical differentiation of itself from any 'age' and thus any re-presentation (the opening marking the giving presenting within repetition, the pragma) or representation. Eternity, this eternity, brings with it the eternal. Here the eternal – itself marking the presence of an ontology, the mode of being proper to the intended 'object' – the continually differentiated must be maintained as differentiated. In the same way the eternity must be maintained as itself – in its self-sustaining being – outside of any possible relation. Relation in both senses would undermine the intended ontology and temporality of eternity. Again what it is that will maintain this state of affairs is forgetting, the forgetting of relation, blinding, being blind to the possibility of any other possible seeing, and the elimination of the effective presence of repetition sited/sighted within work and thus allowing for the possibility of a continual reworking. And yet that which is other – other than these possibilities – is neither remembering, nor sight, nor moreover is it the simple recognition of relation. The given must itself give way to work and thus to that whose existence is denied by ownness, namely work, reworking and thereby the effective presence of repetition.

Approaching events again

Within the impossibility of a founding singularity – within, to be more precise, the grounding and thus the placing of its putative possibility in the twofold movement of sacrifice and forgetting (allowing here, as an opening, destruction and sacrifice a similiar logic) – the question of the abeyance of sacrifice and forgetting inevitably comes to the fore. Its coming to the fore, its possible presentation, should not be taken as in any way attempting to restrict its difficulty as a question and thus as a mode of philosophical thinking. (The opening here will have to involve in addition therefore the consideration of a series of topics – sites within the complexity of movement – and with them their combination as well as their interarticulation; a twofold comprising a form of translation.) Sacrifice as has been indicated becomes part of a strategy of establishing singularity and with it of the necessary denial of the primordiality of relation and this despite, as will have already been shown, the implicit maintaining of that primordiality, precisely maintained it should be added in being repressed – precisely – because of the effective nature of its presence.

The task given to sacrifice was specific and yet with that task and consequently with its possible abeyance there still endures the complex possibility of thinking abeyance, a thinking all the more difficult because of the pervasive presence of sacrifice and destruction. Abeyance, however, will have already been involved in an opening out that is never a pure giving since thinking abeyance will already be to think relation. In other words the very nature of abeyance will involve it in a relation, an always already existent relation. Abeyance in order to avoid forgetting will be constrained to have already acknowledged – acknowledged by its being enacted – the active presence of vigilance. Again this will not be to eliminate sacrifice since such a mode of approach only repeats and thus mimics sacrifice's logic. The repetition would be of course a repetition within the Same. Here what will have to be under consideration – a consideration enjoining its own continuity – is the possibility that abeyance will reopen repetition by inscribing an-other repetition, one which will in turn involve an-other remembering and thus a different differentiation; a differentiating bringing with it the twofold distancing both of the violence and the complacency of destructive forgetting, as well as the displacing of the false finality of sacrifice. Central to this other will be work, work taking the place of sacrifice, and thus holding itself in its place by working through it. Part of the logic of sacrifice in Heidegger took the specific form of the sacrifice of metaphysics, offered up for the thinking of Being and thereby reinforcing the point that sacrifice and destruction, as presented in the texts just considered, are not reducible, despite their on occasion being named, to their named presence, a presence reductively taken to be there only in the name sacrifice as though the name were all that was necessary for the evoking and with it the presenting and enacting of a sacrificial or destructive logic. (What is opened up here is the relationship between naming and being. A relation to which a return will be made.)

Within the context and thus the specific formulations of Heidegger's *Time and Being* and *The Question of Being* it was not just that the 'thinking of Being' was only possible to the extent that the sacrifice is achieved and thus thinking 'without' was itself thought to have been possible, it is also that the specific form taken by its achievement involves, as a consequence of its being achieved, the necessary singularity of the end. Maintaining that singularity demands forgetting. And if not forgetting then a silence that obviates the possibility of any 'propositional statement' (*Aussagesätze*) enacting, instantiating or presenting that end. One possible result of this silence would be the counter-instantiation of the poetic, the replacing of poetry; the replacing of the propositional by poetry. It goes without saying that what is involved here is a specific construal of the poetic, one in which the poetic revealed a quality whose unfolding took the form of a type of mysticism; mystical precisely because poeticising arises out of and is thus conditioned by the 'failure' of the propositional and therefore the poetic – poetry as mystery – occurs with the abandoning of the propositional. Poetry only arises when its counter – the propositional – is left moribund in its failure. In other words poetry/poeticising in this construal comprises a state of affairs that derives its identity – an identity thus determining its content, a content determined as the poetic – by its being the other side of the propositional; an other to which a turn was made because of the failure of the propositional. (The possibility of poetry should of course not be thought to have been delimited thereby.) The failure of the 'propositional – the necessity of its inadequacy (recalling the analysis of 'unzureichend') – should be understood as involving, and involving of necessity, an acceptance of the opposition between the propositional and its other; an acceptance normalising the 'propositional', and which therefore is that which allows it to fail, and the mystical, as its other to emerge in, and thus out of, that failure. The poetic is – poetry exists – but only in its difference from the propositional. As has been suggested what determines and legitimises, in this instance, the propriety of poetry's content is that which sanctions the identity of the poetic as the poetic. The problem lies in this symbiotic reciprocity maintained with what is in the end the impossible fragility of the distinction between the figural and the literal.[61]

Noting the difficulty of maintaining its result – a difficulty incorporating fragility – will mean that sacrifice cannot escape being questioned. And therefore it must be asked, to what end is this sacrifice – the sacrifice of a language, of metaphysics – with its all attendant risks being undertaken? (A question that despite its introduction of the language of ends, a teleological language thought to be inappropriate in the case of Heidegger, is sanctioned nonetheless by the necessary presence of the logic of sacrifice within the formulation of thinking 'without'. Its presence conditions its formulation as thinking. The logic of sacrifice involves ends.) Here the answer to the questioning of sacrifice is that sacrifice projects an end that cannot be, an end whose projected singularity came undone (and comes undone) the moment it is thought, and which therefore in its thinking only reintroduces the very primordiality that it hopes to avoid, to sacrifice. 'Ownness', its propriety and thus the attendant logic of sacrifice sanction their being checked at the same time as they are announced. Despite this check there is a necessity to go on. To go on by not going on with either sacrifice or a repetition of the self-same. To go on therefore by not going on, to go on, that is, by recognising the impossibility of just going on (a going on which may forget that it was just going on). The choice therefore is not between going on and not going on, but rather of having to work with the inelimin-able necessity of going on while not just going on. What is distanced therefore is the hold of the either/or. Within the appearance of paradox – appearing only for its posited centrality to be displaced – there emerges the terms that enable going on to go on; a movement which, as shall be indicated, in no longer unfolding the repetition of the self-same, no longer takes it to unfold within it.

In the place of progress, with both its denial and exhaustion, there lies repetition and work. In not being limited by the effusive though at times melancholic display of positing and counter-positing offered by the logic of identity as the only alternative, there is the possibility of working and repeating. Repeating is now, however, a repetition that in not being bordered by the Same and thus by its mimicry – the mimesis of the self-same – will have become a conception that needs to be thought within its own frame; a frame which while maintaining propriety and specificity also maintains relation and thus gives rise to the necessary absence of a founding and originating occurrence. (A set up not constructed by loss and thus not to be taken as the place of mourning and as a consequence one in which this pair of 'nots' has to be thought beyond the negativity of absence and therefore as a countering move in terms of affirmation. The 'nots' need not turn around a loss to be remembered but rather can take place in relation to an overcoming demanding vigilance.) It is thus that what is at work in this process of maintaining and distancing – abeyance – will involve what has already been identified in terms of the logic of again and the anew and the constructive interplay of 'a part/apart'. Both of these modes of thinking and interpretation – their work, their being their work – will need to be taken up (if only to be restated). With this general taking up what will be maintained, as it has been maintained throughout, is an approach approaching events again.

Working through

Again, what is on offer is neither paradoxical nor contradictory but, more emphatically, is the possibility of thinking within repetition without the dominance of the Same; in other words an already present thinking within and thereby also of abeyance; a thinking which in its own enactment differentiates itself from destruction. The immediate problem is how to formulate such an ad-venture. How does it come to be stated? As has been suggested Freud's concept of 'working through' (*Durcharbeiten*) provides a beginning, an opening. Here that opening will be traced initially within the confines of his technical paper of 1914, 'Remembering, Repeating and Working-Through'.[62] It will be in terms of this paper that the presence – perhaps even the named presence – of the process marked out by the term *Nachträglichkeit* will come to be reintroduced.

Within the context of this 'Paper on Technique' Freud's ostensible and stated concern is to provide a reminder to students of pyschoanalysis of the varying changes that have taken place within the development of psychoanalytic techniques, a reminder that in some way works through the history of that technique. The earliest form of the process involved enforced remembering via hypnosis. While Freud does not formulate it as such what this involved was the attempted recovery and thus identification of a one-to-one correspondence between the symptom and its forgotten cause. Giving primacy to what was taken as the structuring presence of causality meant – as was thought by Breuer and Freud in their earliest writings – that the patient's having remembered the cause would give rise to and thus secure the cure. (The internal difficulty lay in the patient remembering it *as* the cause.) In the wake of hypnosis and causality, and thus in the wake of this one-to-one relationship, what emerged was the importance of the activity of remembering and thus of working with the resistances to that memory. Limits were discovered with hypnosis, however, and while Freud does not detail them in this paper – indeed they are not taken up by him in a systematic way in any of his writings – the departure from hypnosis is plotted nonetheless:

When hypnosis had been given up, the task became discovering from the patient what he failed to remember. The resistance was to be circumvented by the work of interpretation and by making its results known to the patient.

(147/207)

For Freud the giving up of hypnosis led to what he takes to be the current prevailing psychoanalytic technique. It involved leaving to one side the centrality of the process of bringing a 'moment or problem into focus' and concentrating on the resistances, and then on the consequences encountered within the analytic secession of that concentration. It is of course this procedure that introduces transference. In the earlier model based on hypnosis the analyst could not have formed part of what was going on. Analysts were only ever apart. Transference can only be thought and thus its presence acknowledged by recognising that the analyst is both a part and apart. The site is no longer explicable in terms of a subject/object opposition. From which it follows that the constitutive presence of the analyst means that any quick formulation of the relation in terms of an intersubjectivity privileging consciousness must be questioned from the start.

Within the actual structure of the text and after adverting once again to the importance of hypnosis for its having highlighted the significance of memory, Freud then decides to 'interpolate a few remarks'. (With such a decision what must be remembered is the importance attached to the attempt to formulate.) Initially what is odd about this interpolation is that its content is thought by Freud to have been dropped from the rest of the paper. This is not to deny, however, as is made clear by Strachey's footnotes, that they are taken up by him again in the case of the 'Wolf Man'. However, far from being dropped and thus left to one side they play a pivotal role in the formulation of 'working through' and thus in the way it comes to be linked to the interplay of acting out and repeating. The straightforward subject matter of the interpolation is made up of the differing forms of forgetting and their related conceptions of memory. The important point however for this present undertaking is that as part of his enterprise Freud uncovers two formulations of 'remembering' in which what is remembered can be said to be consciously present for the first time, in its being remembered. What makes this problematic is that what has to be understood is the time of this first time; the temporality of an occurrence which takes place again for the first time. (The effective presence of temporality will mean that ontology will also figure – effectively – within what must be understood and thus in its understanding.)

The first formulation concerns the 'psychical process' of 'phantasies, process of references, emotional impulses, thought connections'. While the internality of the content is obviously significant the real importance at this stage lies in the temporal considerations they engender, or perhaps the need for the temporal reconsiderations they demand. Here Freud argues that they must be treated as special cases because, in

> these processes it particularly often happens that something is remembered which could not have been forgotten because it was never at any time noticed – was never conscious.
>
> (149/208–9)

The immediate act of forgetting falls beyond the range of conscious intention. It is thus not an act of consciousness as such. The result of which is that recovery comes to occupy the present, moreover what occupies the present was never past. (In fact outside of the interpolation though still within the same text Freud will make use of precisely this formulation of the temporality of psychic presence in the more general argument that the patient's illness should be treated, 'not as an event of the past, but a present-day force (*eine aktuelle Macht*)' (151/211).) The distinction between present and past has thus been reopened. Freud then goes on to suggest that in most cases the occasion of forgetting is based on what is described as

> dissolving thought connections, failing to draw the right conclusions and isolating memories.
>
> (149/209)

With such a formulation the question of how to interpret this break-up and division is immediately posed. As a beginning it can be understood in terms of an original narrative that has come apart and with it that the constitutive elements have become separated and in so doing have become forgotten. Despite its problematic nature – its harbouring certain truths in spite of itself – this particular formulation is not of immediate interest. What is far more significant is the move away from the fragmentation of an original narrative and towards a state of affairs where the 'understanding and interpretation' and thus the construction can be said to occur afterwards and which therefore are occurring subsequently. Again, it is the ontology and the temporality of being subsequent that is central, a centrality that will continually be at work in any attempt to answer the question, subsequent to what? How is this prior site to be stated? These questions are sustained by the complex of temporality.

The existence of 'understanding and interpretation' also needs to be understood and thus interpreted in terms of the presence or creation of narrative (narrative being defined by its temporal form). What this means is that the inclusion of the remembered into a narrative forms an integral part of the attribution to it of meaning; a necessity that is later identified by Freud in 'Constructions in Analysis' (1937) in terms of an analytic 'construction' (even though in the latter text Freud distinguishes between 'construction' and what is there identified as 'interpretation'). Freud describes what is to be distinguished from narrative breakup in the following way.

> There is one special class of experiences of the utmost importance of which no memory rule can be recovered. These are experiences which occurred in very early childhood and were not understood at the time but which were subsequently (*nachträglich*) understood and interpreted.
>
> (149/209)

After having made this claim Freud then sets out to leave both it and its consequences to one side on the basis that their 'novelty' amongst other things is such that the whole 'matter' demands 'separate discussion'. And yet it must be asked whether even here in the context of the structure of this 'technical paper' there is anything that has really been left to one side. It is almost as though such a possibility is precluded by the implicit temporal and ontological considerations comprising the interpolation's content. Returning to them means continuing with them.

There are many difficulties that emerge with the above formulation. Perhaps one of the most obvious pertains to what are identified in the passage as 'experiences' (*Erlebnisses*). With this word what is raised is the entire problem of the founding and originating occurrence; the question of the reality of what occurred. The problem is first raised in the *Project for a Scientific Psychology* in regard to the case of Emma (the case in which

Nachträglichkeit first appears), it figures in the letters to Fleiss, most notably in the famous letter of 21 September 1897 in which the theoretical basis of the project begun with Breuer is finally questioned (letters it must be added which contain important evocations of *Nachträglichkeit*), and then it comes to occupy and preoccupy his writings even in the final revisions signalled for example by 'Constructions in Analysis'.

Given the phrasing of the passage the immediate question that must arise concerns what it would mean for there to be an 'experience' that was 'not understood'. The question is both more difficult and yet more elementary than it seems. What is being asked for is how could it be said that the 'experience' occurred if there was no contemporary understanding of it as an experience. A similiar question must be asked of the slightly earlier passage taken from Freud's interpolation. Here what must be questioned is the status of that which 'was never conscious'. What was the 'it' that was never conscious? Any clinical answer to these questions will have to involve recourse to the process of repression. And yet even with repression the complexity endures since repression is not to be understood let alone equated with what is repressed; with what 'it' is. Consequently with repression what will be essential is not simply the disguised return of the repressed but the acting out of its consequences; in other words the continual presenting of its presence. It is the continuity of this presenting – a continuity necessarily unknown in the beginning to the analysand – that will come to be taken up in terms of what is identified a few pages later in the paper as 'the compulsion to repeat'.

It is precisely this point that Freud develops, even though it is a development situated outside of the interpolation, in differentiating between types of remembering. In distinguishing cases that 'behave like those under hypnotic technique' from some others, he writes of the latter group that,

> in order to bring out the difference, we may say that the patient does not *remember* anything of what he has forgotten and repressed (*verdrängen*) but *acts* it out. He reproduces it not as memory but as an action: he *repeats* it, without of course knowing that he is repeating it.
>
> (150/209–10; Freud's emphasis)

Acting out is a form of repetition and is approached by Freud in terms of the compulsion to repeat. Within this formulation and with the subsequent addition of 'working through' as being the response, albeit the clinical response, in the first instance, to the compulsion, what is provided is the key to repetition's redemption, and thus an opening in which repetition can be seen as subjected to the process that it names. As a beginning it is this threefold division – between remembering, repeating, acting out – that must be taken up.

The first element that must be considered is the repetition given within the passage. What does repetition mean here? At its most preliminary repetition accounts for the presentation of the 'forgotten and repressed'. What is repeated is a continuity that is itself the consequence, in part, of acts of repression. The relationship between repression and that which would disrupt continuity is another and perhaps more difficult problem. Here recourse would need to be made to pleasure and unpleasure and the way in which repression operates in order to secure a continuity that is then acted out; acted out, that is, even if it is a continuity in which the 'repressed' and the 'forgotten' return and intervene. The importance of the distinction between repeating and remembering is that it allows for the presentation of a continuity in which neither the nature of the continuity nor the continuity's content are opened up as a question since such an opening would demand remembering. The analysand views what is repeated and thus what is acted out 'as his destiny (*als ein Schicksal*)' (150/210). The compulsion to repeat is the enacting and therefore the acting out of this 'destiny'. A form of remembering, however, is not foreign to this repetition even though it is inherently paradoxical. For as Freud adds,

> As long as the patient is in the treatment he cannot escape from this compulsion to repeat: and in the end we must understand that this is his way of remembering (*seine Art zu erinnern*).
>
> (159/210)

It is of course a remembering in which nothing is remembered. (The question of whether anything can be remembered will at this stage be left open.) In the place of remembering there is the adoption of a seamless continuity that is always fraying and tearing and which can only be maintained by the successful continuity of repression, a success that is impossible because of the presence of the repressed's return and the interrelated formation of symptoms. The unending repetition of the self-same – its continuity as norm – is inherently pathological, hence both the pathos of repression and the pathology of 'destiny'; the pathological as tradition.

The repeating and thus the acting out take place under what Freud describes as 'conditions of resistance'. The resistance will be to remembering. And yet remembering is not the remembering of occurrences as such. Nor is remembering the recovery of a founding and originating moment. Remembering pertains to the present. The desired result of remembering, not the remembering of the compulsion to repeat but another and more complex remembering which, as will be suggested, draws on the temporality of the 'subsequent' in that it will be a remembering occurring for the first time, is described by Freud in the following way.

> The way is thus paved from the beginning for a reconciliation (*Versöhnung*) with the repressed material which is coming to expression in his symptoms, while at the same time place is found for a certain tolerance for the state of being ill.
>
> (152/212)

The key term here is 'reconciliation'. It can be taken as marking the intrinsic eschewing of destruction since it also involves the implicit recognition that destruction – and with it the logic of sacrifice – could only ever be other forms of repression; forms which, as has already been indicated, will demand another forgetting. What must be taken up is this 'reconciliation'; itself, of course, a form of abeyance.

'Reconciliation' does not occur by chance, even though its occurrence may involve the chance beyond predication inherent in the process of 'free association'. 'Reconciliation' is inextricably linked to work and thus to 'working through'. Even though it occurs in a lengthy passage it is essential to trace the actual emergence of 'working through'. In Freud's presentation what can be seen as taking place is the formulation of a complex semantics which is itself dependent upon the temporality of the subsequent and the related displacing of destruction. Freud begins the passage in question as though he were recounting an anecdote;

> I have often been asked to advise upon cases in which the doctor complained that he had pointed out his resistances to the patient and that nevertheless no change had set in .... The treatment seemed to make no headway. This gloomy foreboding was always proved mistaken. The treatment was as a rule progressing most satisfactorily. The analyst had merely forgotten that giving the resistance a name could not result in its

immediate cessation/coming to an end (*das Benennen des Wider-standes nicht das unmittelbare Aufhören*). One must allow the patient time to become more conversant with this resistance with which he has now become acquainted, to *work through* it, to overcome it, by continuing, in defiance of it, the analytic work according to the fundamental rule of analysis. Only when the resistance is at its height can the analyst working (*Arbeit*) in common with his patient discover the repressed instinctual impulses which are feeding the resistance; and it is this kind of experience which convinces the patient of the existence and power of such impulses.

(155/215)

Leaving to one side the fact as opposed to content of the analyst's forgetting the obvious point of departure is the implicit presentation of the interplay of naming and destruction announced in the passage. The figure of naming is never distant.

What had been forgotten was that the identification of the resistance and its naming, where naming is assumed to be identical with what is named, is not sufficient to give rise to the resistance's 'cessation', its having ended and thus effectively to what would amount to its having been destroyed. The implicit assumption behind the move whose inadequacy is being indicated by Freud is that naming and being are the same. In other words the assumption would entail that once the resistance is named, given the premise that in its being named the resistance is identified as itself – as what it is – then the naming understood as comprising the giving of the resistance to the analysand, its being given as itself, will mean that it will be able to be overcome, i.e. to be a resistance no longer and therefore *qua* resistance to have been destroyed. It will be destroyed precisely by having been identified as itself. Each of these moves is premised upon a mistaken assumption. Freud can be read as suggesting that, contrary to what is assumed, if naming and being are to be assigned a single and unified quality, then naming and being are not the same. One does not denote the other. As its presentation indicates there will always be more to naming than just naming. (It will be essential to keep returning to the consequences of this addition for if there is an excess it is always one in which specificity – the pragma – is possible.)

Rather than identification, naming and thus knowledge providing a way of dealing with resistances, in neither being able to be ignored nor destroyed what is demanded is an approach that works with them – they have to be 'worked through'- by working with the site of the self-same's repetition. A way of understanding what this means is given by the equation, within the passage, of 'working through' and 'overcoming': 'to work through it, overcome it' (*ihn zu überwinden*) (155/215). 'Overcoming' here involves neither destruction nor the Heideggerian 'without' (*ohne*), the latter marking the site and with it the necessity of sacrifice. What accounts for the absent dominance of sacrifice within the thinking of 'overcoming' is the juxtaposing of 'overcoming' and 'continuing' (*fortsetzt*). One works with the other, working within the logic of a part/apart. What is overcome is a part of while at the same time being apart from the resistance's effect and the related working through. It is precisely this juxtaposition therefore that marks out abeyance and shows the movement of its presence at work. The analysis continues in 'defiance' (*Trotz*) of the resistance. Working through that which is repeated does not allow for either the destruction of the resistance and with it the repetition of acting out, or the denial of its content, but rather occasions an interruption of the repetition of the self-same by an interruption within it. It is this twofold interruption that will involve the 'subsequent' in the precise sense that what will be given will be formed within that which occurs for the first time.

'Working through' provides an understanding of what was not understood and thus which only acquired meaning by its iteration, and yet of course it was an iteration, a repetition, in which what was given was given to be understood for the first time. Its being given for the first time means that in the giving – that 'first' giving taking place again – there is the effective presence of the temporality of the 'subsequent'. 'Working through' allows for the forgotten and the repressed to be presented, to be worked through – figured resistances – such that they are understood subsequently for the first time. Taking these considerations a step further necessitates a type of translation. A move in which what is carried over from the straightforwardly psychological – if such a designation has any viability – is a structure of thinking. It is of course a complex structure since the translation has already started with the presence in Freud's description of 'destiny' and the link between its fateful presence and the compulsion to repeat. With this repetition – a repetition of the Same though not recognised (remembered) as such – and its being enacted within the continuity of destiny, even if that destiny is in the first instance immediately personal, what can be taken as being repeated is the articulation of tradition understood as the already given. Tradition is destiny if it is accepted in its own terms. And yet as has been seen tradition is constituted by a continual repression. Again in the place of norms tradition in appearing as continuity and as destiny must at the same time be taken as pathological. Indeed it is possible to argue that it is tradition's pathology that allows occurrences happening outside of tradition's propriety, occurrences established, in part, as will be suggested by the working through and the related centrality of abeyance and vigilance.

Translating repeating

In his discussion of Freud's paper in 'Rewriting Modernity' Jean-François Lyotard defines 'working through' in what could be described as Kantian terms (the Kant of the *Third Critique*).[63] He formulates its specificity by plotting and then presenting its difference from 'remembering'.

> Differentiating itself from remembering, 'working through' could be defined as a work without end (*fin*) and therefore without will; without end in the sense that is not guided by the concept of a goal (*un but*), but not without finality (*finalité*).

(39)

The finality here can be taken as translating Kant's 'purposiveness'. 'Working through' therefore is not straightforwardly teleological. Indeed it is the absence of the teleological that leads Lyotard to privilege the absence of the end (understood in the twofold sense of purpose and point of finish) over the specificity of 'working through'. He summarises the Freudian enterprise in such a way that, because of what he takes to be Freud's apparent commitment to the emancipatory, and therefore of its having to run the risk of repeating the situation from which it intended to inspire 'emancipation', another possibility is presented as having to be found. The emancipatory Freudian undertaking is described by Lyotard as wanting to deconstruct the rhetoric of the unconscious, the preorganised set of signifiers which constitute the neurotic or psychotic device and what organises the life of the subject as destiny.

(40)

What is identified here as a deconstructive move may, within Lyotard's terms, only replay and thus repeat what it intended to deconstruct. Consequently, contrary to Freud's project, Lyotard, having connected what he describes as 'rewriting' to 'working through', goes on to suggest that what is in fact proper to each is not the 'recognition of the given, it is the capacity to let things happen (*advenir*) as they present themselves'(41). And yet *pace* Lyotard it is clear that the two possibilities are not really mutually exclusive. 'Working through' is never just a recognition and the 'capacity to let things happen' must play an integral role in the presentation, if not in the actual work of 'working through'. Furthermore the necessary presence of both 'recognition' and 'working through' will in the end check the establishing of any immediate link between the process of 'working through' and the sublime.[64]

It can be argued that the force of 'working through' once it has been translated from the simply personal – a translation taking place in, amongst other things, the generalisation of 'destiny' (*Schicksal*) – is that it gives rise to the possibility of an occurrence outside of predication (the chance effect) while at the same time locating that possibility in the necessity of there being a relation to the given, even if it is a relation that is to be established. (The dilemma within the Hegelian set up was that because this relation had to have already existed, it precluded or intended to preclude the possibility of chance. Chance's happening.) Recognition is the establishing. Both are necessary if recognition is possible; a point that is in fact already acknowledged by Lyotard in his earlier description, in the same text, of the complexity of a 'secret', a description that attests to, if not affirms, the primordiality of relation.

A secret cannot be a true secret if no one knows that it is a secret.

(36)

There must be a twofold movement: recognition and working through. What cannot be destroyed is the site of repetition – the place of 'acting out' – it must be worked through. Consequently working through is neither an emancipatory nor a non-emancipatory activity. This accounts for why Freud uses terms such as 'reconciliation' and 'tolerance' and juxtaposes 'overcoming' and 'continuing'. However, this terminology attests to more than a simple reconciliation. Tolerance and reconciliation, given a certain translation, are the results of having worked through the resistances and thus of having recognised the compulsion to repeat as a type of remembering. (It is thus a remembering that differs from the one that it takes for itself.) In taking over the compulsion as a compulsion it is no longer just compulsive. It has in a sense been given a history. Again what is being marked out here is the site of abeyance. There is no coming to tolerate the intolerable but a reconciliation to the irreconcilable. It is of course a reconciliation that demands an overcoming which displaces that which had been dominant hitherto. The intolerable is no longer there as itself. 'Working through' depends upon the temporal structure identified in the interpolation. The importance within the process is the growing awareness of what before had not figured in consciousness, a reworking of the present engendering new presentations. What is essential therefore is to try and develop this complex site and with it the temporality of the subsequent.

Again, with the subsequent, what it brings with it, is its own eventual translation from the field of the strictly psychoanalytic. The point of this particular translation is not to diminish the importance of psychoanalysis as such but rather to link it, as a mode of thinking, to other possible modes of thinking in which similar concerns can be said to figure. In each what is essential is a possible after-life; after-life as 'survivre', 'nachleben', life initially given within theology.[65] However, within the theological the Messianic impulse will mean that any notion of redemption will have to be based on the destruction of the given and the elimination of remembering. The apocalyptic is essentially theological. (With theology the present is given by, and the future is only possible because of the assumed reality of, crucifixion.) Distancing the theological and its sacrifice will demand that the after-life has to be thought as a form of repetition. Furthermore the after-life will necessitate that its realisation is the consequence of work – of working through the given – and that the given is such that it allows itself to be reworked such that the reworking is no longer a simple repetition of the self-same. One of the major complicating factors is that what are given within the tradition – given as part of it – are sites of interpretation which are taken up and articulated within the self-same, the repetition of the Same, and yet which will sanction their own iterative reworking. The latter is a possibility realised once the site is given the quality of an event and the particular interpretation reformulated as the pragma. It is this position that must be worked toward.

In its presentation in the *Project for a Scientific Psychology*[66] the process of *Nachträglichkeit* refers to the reworking of a repressed memory that becomes, as a consequence, traumatic. What had been repressed is worked on by a second occurrence such that the memory of the repressed is then made present. Its contents therefore are presented again for the first time as significant. The important point here is that what is described by Freud in the *Project* in relation to Emma is the active presence of mental functioning. In other words his concern is with interiority and its description. The analyst and the analyst's own presence as interpreter or translator do not figure. What seems to mark the presence of *Nachträglichkeit* in the *Project* is then a type of passivity; passivity in the strict sense that the text's concern is to show the way in which the relationship between the unconscious and conscious mind functions and the way in which memory – memory within the psychoanalytic – can be said to operate. (Clearly the source of the reworking lies in taking over and living out the consequences of the shopkeepers' laughter.) What is occurring subsequently is internal to the mind itself. There is, however, another possibility whose locus will not be restricted to a description of mental functioning as such but an inaugurated site – the instantiation of a state of affairs – that will involve the external activity of the interpreter and thus the presence of an other who will always be more than a simple addition. The move away from the simplicity of addition will also mean that presence has to be rethought. (Even if the 'interpreter' were to be the self in question it would have to be the case that the self would have already been divided.) The presence of the interpreter – an active presence marking the position's alterity while at the same time implicating that position as itself comprising part of the interpretive site – delimits a complex whose internality and thus complexity is both temporal and ontological. Moreover it is once again a site enacting the logic of the a part/apart.

What can be taken from the operation of *Nachträglichkeit* in the *Project* is a structural possibility; namely that the significance of a given occurrence comes to the fore and is thus acquired through a subsequent action in which the reiteration, the repetition, gives the occurrence – within memory – again for the first time. It is this structural possibility that figures within the 'interpolation' in 'Remembering, Repeating and Working-Through'. There what was essential was that the initial 'experience', the happening, did not register in consciousness and thus could neither have been forgotten (since there was no-thing to forget) nor understood. The registration of the memory, the taking over of the occurrence as 'understood', occurs retrospectively. This should be taken as another description of what is involved in the process of 'working through'. While on the most literal reading 'working through' involves a way of working with resistances in the analytic secession, in the larger context it can be understood as a way of taking up and responding to the given, and thus both with what is presented as the work of 'destiny', the fateful pre-existent continuity, and with that which arises within it. Again, in context 'working through' deals with the consequences of that which occurs originally, though again, subsequently, and in involving the necessary mediating presence of the analyst (interpreter) repositions the operation of *Nachträglichkeit*. The analyst's presence and actions become the second occurrence and have its effect. 'Working through' has the same temporal structure therefore as *Nachträglichkeit*. The translation of one to a larger context will involve the other's translation and thus recontextualisation of the processes they mark out.

What occurs subsequently occurs in relation to a complex set up in which passivity has given place to activity. In other words instead of primarily being concerned with a passive description of mental functioning – passive yet incorporating both subject and object – the presence of the analyst occasions the process of subsequent understanding and interpretation. The latter's taking place – in its taking place – has then to do with the recognition that destiny, its fateful heritage, is already given in a way such that its necessity is always able to be displaced. What are worked through therefore are the obstacles and resistances to that recognition. Again what is involved here is not emancipation if that is construed as enacting Cartesian destruction. It is rather a type of negotiation that presupposes the ineliminable presence of conflict, where the latter is understood as the necessarily irresolvable. This accounts in part for why continuity – the repetition of the self-same –

involves the effective presence of repression. The presence of the irresolvable has to be thought within the movement proper to displacing and thus in terms of abeyance. Again what will be essential to pursue is the translation of working through given that it can be assumed to bring the temporal and ontological considerations of the subsequent with it. In other words it cannot help but bring with it and thus into consideration the structuring force of *Nachträglichkeit* because, as has already been suggested, it provides working through with its temporal structure; with it a site is itself located that is always worked through and thus is maintained, of necessity, to be worked through.

Repeating – the open ended

The way of taking these considerations a step further, to carry on, and thus attempt to realise the translation of 'working through' and *Nachträglichkeit*, will be given by returning to the question of the name. What has already emerged from Freud's development of 'working through' is the impossibility of equating naming and being. However, this point has to be developed with care. The actual context needs to be clarified. In the paper Freud reproaches the analyst with having forgotten that naming the resistance will not result in its 'immediate cessation' (*unmittelbare Aufhören*). The resistance, the identification of what it is, its being what it is, is not provided by the name. While it bears a name it is both its name and more than its name. What this means is that the 'immediate' must give way to the mediate and as such 'cessation' as a desired goal will itself cede its place to the complex interplay of 'overcoming' and 'continuing'. The continuity involves 'defiance' and thus it must also involve vigilance. However, this is not all. It is not as though the material, the names, within the resistances and thus also within that which was compulsively repeated have to be removed, left to one side and guarded in order to preclude their possible reintroduction. If this were the case then all that would have been undertaken was a mirroring of the structure of repression. It is rather that the force of 'working through' and thus with it of 'construction', of re-using, re-utilising and thus repeating – again and anew – what is given, allows for the complex move which results in the reiteration of an-other narrative bearing and thus repeating aspects of what had been given; a narrative that will have overcome by continuing; a twofold movement held by the logic of a part/apart. (In more general terms – the terms given by translation's continuity – what must be recognised is that it is precisely this logic that is not able to figure within destruction and sacrifice. The complicating factor – a complication turning on the event – what cannot figure and thus cannot be thought, is exactly that which can play a constitutive role in the actual formulation of such philosophical positions. Here what turns on the event will in the end be that which affirms its presence.)

Despite their apparent differences all the latter moves are only possible precisely because of the impossibility of conflating naming and being; one being the other. And yet the impossibility does not hinder the fact that the name names and in naming designates a specific moment which in never being able to be commensurate with the named allows, nonetheless, for the name's repetition beyond itself. (Even in leaving any consideration of its necessity to one side it remains the case that the anoriginal complexity of any 'itself' should still be remembered.) The repetition of the name beyond its being presented, enacted, at a given point in time (a point bearing a date), and within precise confines, works to distance both the Cartesian and the Platonic conception of naming and in so doing reintroduces what what identified earlier as conflict naming. It should be added that the Platonic and the Cartesian while not taken as complete and therefore as necessarily self-completing unities can, nonetheless, be understood as bringing with them the two founding possibilities for the name; the name's tradition.

In the first place there is the name as that which designates the 'essential being' (οὐσία) of the named, the Platonic, and in the second the name as naming arbitrarily though absolutely the named, the Cartesian. As both of these positions were inter-articulated with their own construal of the epistemological they can be taken as marking out a dominant philosophical terrain; dominant possibilities present as the appearance of difference. Both the radicality and of course the liminality of conflict naming are in part established by conflict naming's relation to dominance – in its still being naming, still allowing and maintaining reference – as well as by the possibility that it is the repressed within it that in some sense sustains dominance's own repetition; sustaining its

founding moment in what amounts to their retroactive foundering, the retroactive indicating the place and consequence of
interpretation.

Accepting the primordiality of conflict opens up naming by
having to incorporate it. What this means here is twofold (twofold
exactly because one fold holds and folds on the other). In the first
instance it means that what the name names is the conflict to
appropriate the name – appropriation being the attempt to establish an identity between naming and being. In regard to the
opening question 'what is philosophy?', when rearticulated in
terms of this aspect of the primordiality of conflict, conflict
naming, what emerges is that the answer to the question is that
'philosophy' names the conflict to appropriate the name philosophy. What follows from such an answer is not an emptying of
the word (name) 'philosophy' but its being rewritten and therefore reincorporated into a different construal of tradition, a
construal allowing for both dominance and marginality but nonetheless one in which the ineliminable presence of conflict figures.
Its figuring demands its repression, an act which once achieved
will always show its result. The conflict to appropriate the name is
unending and yet the name is always appropriated and therefore
inevitably taken over. What this necessity entails is that the
difference between the name as taken over and the unending
conflict over the name needs to be articulated in terms of two
fundamentally different modes of being. In other words what is
involved here is ontological difference. Ontology is continually
taking the place of semantics by providing it with a place.
Ontological difference here alludes to Leibniz's formulation of the
monad, by in part repeating elements of what was taken, at an
earlier interval, to be at work within it; a difference therefore that
not only demands the presence of an ineliminable spacing and
thus relation within the name but which, in being anoriginally
present, is constitutive of the name itself, relation being that which
sustains the monad by marking the spacing that holds 'perception' and 'appetition' apart. The monad is itself in their being
held apart – spaced – while at the same time comprising a part of
it. (Again the complex 'itself', the 'itself' as anoriginally complex.)
What constitutes the name while apart within it, form, of necessity,
a part of it. The opening of spacing resists representation but
demands a continual though pragma-tic presentation. These considerations will bear upon since they bear that which emerges as

the other aspect of the fold; the fold in the twofold.

The second part of this twofold is that the presence of conflict has to entail that what the name names is precisely that which is judged to be the name, to be named. It should be added immediately that even if it is judged to be the name it can never overcome the constitutive ontological difference and thus be made absolutely commensurate with the name itself. What is allowed therefore to being commensurate is inevitably pragma-tic and therefore provisional and as a consequence has its own specific ontologico-temporal dimension. It is precisely in ontological and temporal terms that the name as the site of primordial conflict and the name as the pragma are held apart while at the same time comprising the name when taken in its totality (again, a totality constituted by the ineliminable presence of spacing). The pragma-tic, when understood as a specific instantiation within the generality of conflict, is always the result of an act of judgement. It follows that the temporality of judgement is defined by the presence of this act; an act presents it. (The assumption of the possible commensurability between naming and being is, once again, a residue of classical epistemology.) Conflict must itself be taken as already implicated – *qua* its name – in the process that it is taken to name. The name within conflict naming, within, that is, the affirmation of its being subject to a repetition in which it occurs again though anew – equally anew though again – is the name as event. As an event the name is the site of an irreducible plurality in which the pragma will always maintain its difference – its ontological difference – from the name. Complexity pertains here because difference will be maintained by the pragma holding in part the name; holding it by its being held as a name. In other words the pragma will be a name, it will name.

Translating, the pragma may be an interpretation, even a translation. However, the pragma will always be secondary and in addition, despite a given singularity, will allow for its own reworking and thus its own repetition. The presence of an intended singularity can never escape the inscription and thus the trace of that which marks out the pragma as secondary and with it affirms the possibility of the pragma's own repetition beyond the self-same, a repetition that draws the pragma into the event by drawing it, perhaps redrawing it, as an event. The secondary can only ever be provisional and therefore never completely secondary since what constitutes the primary is itself without determination

outside of a particular ontological description. The actual structure of representation is no longer apposite. Repetition will cause
another construal of presentation to be adopted, and in being
adopted the dominant problem of how presentation figures within
a dominating ontology of becoming – in sum the ontology of
conflict naming – is displaced and its positive and negative
determination held in abeyance. Another possibility is opened
up with the distancing of the repetition of the Platonic construal of
the interplay of presentation and becoming.[67]

Of the many problems that still endure one of the most significant can be identified in the following question: how does the
process of *Nachträglichkeit* – even the process as a structural
possibility – incorporate, or how can it be incorporated into, the
complex frame of naming? The work of *Nachträglichkeit*, its translation, has remained continually present in the preceding; here
what is involved is a different move, perhaps another translation,
in which the site of that work needs to be taken up as at work.
Answering the question of its relation to naming necessitates
opening with a contrast. Beginning therefore with the repetition of
the Same.

One of the intriguing consequences of Cartesian destruction
was that judgement was constrained to be an act which in general
terms could neither alter nor change. Given the coextensivity that
marked the structure of representation and therefore also Classical
epistemology all that judgement could be taken to involve was the
possibility of a repetition of the Same. The self-same in being
repeated became the act of judgement. Judgement therefore is
sustained by the name and therefore in judging repeats necessarily the name. In each instance, at every moment, the name
remains the same. Repetition is the name's reiteration as itself. It is
as though – maintaining the translation – repetition has become
the compulsion to repeat; the compulsion to maintain the self-
same in the latter's being taken over as destiny. The continuity of
what is repeated in its being repeated works to preclude any
interruption. There is no option. It has to be precluded since the
moment any interruption, a repetition other than that of the self-
same, is sanctioned, the name – the Cartesian name structured by
and within representation and which is exemplified by Descartes'
'thing' and repeated in contemporary theories of reference –
would have become, and become it of necessity, sundered. Conflict naming would therefore have intruded; an intrusion which

would have done no more than realise – actualise – that which was anoriginally present and where the realisation amounted to a form of repetition.

Judgement within conflict naming becomes a calculation, a negotiation, that in being provisional will always have to be differentiated from the possibility of the completion necessitated and thus envisaged by representation. What is opened up thereby is the site in which judgement comes to enact the political by maintaining it as an opening. It enacts the political by being it. (The political in question is the political thought philosophically.) Here the commensurability between naming and being has given way to a different identity, namely between acting and being. It goes without saying that acting demands – by enacting – its own complexity. Judgement is therefore being reworked; it is in its being reworked. The name repeated, in being reiterated, is reworked. The interplay of repetition and work is itself sanctioned by the ontology of the name. Repetition and work act out the event; act out its enactment. What judgement now allows is a reiteration, a repetition of conflict but not in terms of conflict's intended elimination but as the site of the necessity for negotiation – the response to the impossibility of finality and synthesis – and further judgements, the latter incorporating the consequences of holding to a specific designation, a specific answer to the question of what the name names. One consequence of the necessary openness of the site of judgement is that it becomes the only possible site in which justice will be able to figure. One name that such a site can take on and thus bear is community; another name for the site of the political's instantiation. It is at the point that what was described at an earlier stage as the politics of epistemology come to be linked to both the politics of naming and the politics of judgement. In all of these cases what has to be rethought is the political, a rethinking that is conditioned by the site. It will be a thinking that accords with centrality of ontology; ontology as anoriginally differential.

In contrast to repetition as the compulsion to repeat, provisionally the interplay of destiny and the self-same, there is another repetition. With it, with this other, repetition is inevitably interarticulated with that construal of the ontological which is itself the consequence of an iterative reworking, and thus of another repetition. It becomes therefore a consequence of that which it, itself, makes possible; a possibility and a realisation that affirms the anoriginal status of this 'itself' – and with it perhaps of any anoriginal itself – as an event. Any move back to *Nachträglichkeit*, a move that will occasion it and thus in which it is sanctioned – it, the process that it is – must position the ontological within and as part of the complex set up that it allows to be acted out. Within such a possibility is the event, the anoriginally plural event whose plurality is sustained by the ontological; ontology within its own repetition. With it, and in each instance accepting the reluctance to provide its details, both ontology and repetition as comprising that which can be designated by it come to demand their own consideration. It follows that they should be considered as it. In sum what endures is a complex site maintained by the interrelationship between ontology and *Nachträglichkeit*. The relationship is not a 'between' but is rather an already present interarticulation. Repetition, reworking and working through, that which presents the possibility of the subsequent, the after-life, take place and are thus only possible because of the mode of being proper to that which lives on, has an after-life, is repeated, etc. What is being marked out in the allusion to possibility is the event, its mode of being and thus the ontology of the event. The necessity imposed by the event, its being, is found in the impossibility of escaping the questions of the form: What is 'it' that lives on, has an after-life, etc.? How is 'it' able to be repeated such that the repetition of the self-same is interrupted? Part of the answer to this question will be that it allows for 'its' rearticulation within the logic of the again and the anew. Questions, however, will remain. What cannot be overcome is that 'it' is.

Opening up the event means that the question that must be taken up – a question marking out a possible though nonetheless still provisional conclusion – concerns how ontology works by working within this complex set up. More emphatically the question is, how does ontology figure? Any response to such questions needs to begin by trying to identify and thus to present with greater clarity precisely what it is that is being sought. What is it here that is figuring? Recognising the difficulty of the task will necessitate a certain caution. Any beginning will have to accept the tracking back and forth of translation, accepting it as the movement from the specificity of a particular structure of thought to another site, one with another and differing specificity. What is involved here is a movement of differing directions that resists polarity and with it the specular oscillation between universal and particular but which, nonetheless, brings the importance of differing moments and instantiations into play. The attempted generalising move will always be held back by its having to inaugurate a translation and thus another repetition. The intended finality of the universal will always be checked by repetition.

Continuing by taking up that which has already in part been set out means that a start will already have been made. It will have begun with the recognition that what within the clinical frame was designated as the 'compulsion to repeat' opens up the possibility of working through its own repetition. And to the extent that it is a repetition marking the abeyance of the self-same then it would involve a repetition articulated within and thus articulating the logic of the again and the anew. What characterises the compulsion is that what is repeated is 'acted out' as though it were not being repeated. The content is not repeated from memory. This compulsion therefore enacts a continuity comprising the repetition of the self-same (the latter always explicable as the Same). As such what can be taken to figure here – figuring with translation – is the repetition of tradition, not just the analysand's 'destiny' but tradition as the repetition of the Same (a continuity in which the new shows as no more than an occurrence noting the temporality of fashion). Returning to the clinical 'the compulsion to repeat' is a repetition that is maintained by repression and thus what maintains it will in the end allow it to be interrupted and therefore become a site of intervention and discontinuity. The compulsion to repeat while allowing for 'working through' resists by refusing to itself and thus for itself the status of an event. It is a status that is affirmed retroactively in the process of iterative reworking. At every moment therefore the present is charged with the possibility of its own interruption. What maintains the possibility is the event. *Nachträglichkeit* – iterative reworking – is the name for the temporality of interpretation where what is given to be interpreted has the status of an event. Interpretation, that interpretation charged with the possibility of redemption – naming and named by working through – involves an acceptance of the gift of tradition, tradition as the already given, that results in an interruption of mere giving and thus an interruption *of* the continuity of giving by occasioning an interruption *in* the repetition of the self-same. Iterative reworking gives a present that affirms a necessary discontinuity with what is presented. And yet that discontinuity in being the affirmation of irreducibility brings with it the necessity of both abeyance and vigilance; as such it is a discontinuity that sanctions overcoming because it allows for continuing. Continuing and overcoming, as has been indicated, enact the logic of again and anew. Deploying a formulation already used what is enacted is a going on that no longer just goes on. As always these are possibilities that on the one hand demand the abeyance of the logic of identity, while on the other they highlight the necessity of a remembering that is always charged with vigilance.

Finally, the event marks the primacy of a necessary irresolvability. And yet the difficulty with this term and it is a difficulty that pertains equally to terms such as irreducibility is their negative characterisation. (Negation, in this sense, seems to harbour the possibility of its own counter positing.) With the event it is not as though resolvability is an option. Equally it is not as though reducibility can be envisaged. If both are thought within the frame of finality – the frame of an inevitable teleology – then neither can account for what is taking place. The given place of language – its being given in place – lends itself to its own reworking; a move which if it is successful means that what is given, given in being reworked, is the event. The event can never be commensurate with itself since the 'itself' will already have been a plural possibility. A plurality whose presence while repressed within, though functionally also for, the repetition of the self-same, is nonetheless affirmed within conflict naming, within the monad and within the possibility of an iterative reworking (remembering that each of these sites demands complexity in that each will 'itself' be subject to, or forced to enact, what 'it' has set up). Affirmation will be linked to the necessity for the abeyance of the polarity marking the logic of identity. Henceforth identity will always be secondary. In being secondary, in being pragma-tic, it will have, when what is involved is a judgement, complete priority. What it can never have is absolute finality, the end as completion. Priority and finality are given by the anoriginal presence of a differential ontology.

The name, in naming the conflict to take over the name, while at the same time allowing for the specific act of naming, the pragma, necessitates the presence of a spacing that constitutes the name while at the same time demanding of the constituent parts a difference that is explicable in ontologico-temporal terms, i.e. the mode of being and the temporality proper to the pragma differ from the mode of being and the temporality proper to conflict naming, the name and thus the event. This difference occurring at the same time works, as has already been indicated, to reinforce the ontologico-temporal nature of this difference. It is a difference that is maintained as the name, held within it. In being maintained and held, and with this difference sanctioning the name's repetition, reworking and redemption, the name has become the event. What has been opened up thereby is the possibility of another thinking that will always demand an account for its being open ended.

Notes

These notes as well as conveying necessary textual references are also intended to allow other forms of deliberation to take place and the presentation of summary statements to be given. The place and date of publication of texts (books and articles) used are found in the bibliography. The latter also contains works which, while not referred to as such in the body of the work, played an important role while it was being written.

1 These preliminary comments envisage a further volume to be entitled *The Politics of Judgement*. The latter work will involve an attempt to work through the interrelationship between judgement, politics, tragedy and community. The pivotal figures in this endeavour will be Kant, Hegel and Heraclitus. What will be central is another construal of the relationship between the event and judgement. The most significant attempts to rethink the nature of judgement have involved an important engagement with Kant. See in particular Caygill (1989) and Lyotard (1991).

2 The ubiquity of the beginning problem should not be accepted at face value. Central to the argument being presented here is that what must be given equal consideration is what makes it a problem. The intriguing consequence of asking this question is that it places the problem within its own history. As such its contextualisation robs it of its feigned urgency while at the same time works to open up the problem of the beginning. What is also raised is the question of how these 'conditions' are to be understood, and therefore what must be addressed is what arises if what is entailed by these conditions is the retention, if not the inescapability, of a quasi-transcendental presence. Gasché (1986) has addressed the problem of the resilience of the transcendental and the role in plays it Derrida's work.

3 References to Hegel's *Logic* will be to the English translation by W. Wallace (Hegel 1978) followed by the German text (Hegel 1970). All German references to Hegel will be to this edition, in the case of the *Logic* to Band 8 and Band 2 for the *Difference Essay*.

4 G.W.F. Hegel. *The Difference Between Fichte's and Schelling's System of Philosophy* (Hegel 1977). All references to the English translation will be to this edition. Reference to the German will be to the edition cited above. All references will appear in the body of the text. This allusion

to the *Difference Essay* indicates in part why, within the frame of this present undertaking, Hegel's critique of singularity is of such importance. The position that will be argued at a later stage is that while Hegel recognises the impossibility of singularity he misconstrues what it is that singularity would be.

5 The problem of the *'eigentümlich'*, the problem named by it, is the interplay of singularity and chance. The problematic status derives from the fact that what is involved in Hegel's formulation is in the end neither singular nor the subject of chance (the chance subject). What is brought out therefore is the philosophical difficulty of presenting chance. It is only by being able to think the possibility of an occurrence outside of prediction that the avant-garde becomes philosophically possible.

6 The relationship between working through and what Freud designates by the term *'Durcharbeiten'* (working through) will be broached in a later part of the work. What will need to be traced are the consequences of taking the interplay of *'Nachträglichkeit'* (translated and thus provisionally understood as 'iterative reworking') and *'Durcharbeiten'* as marking out the possibility of a reformulation (perhaps a rethinking) of repetition.

7 This passage can be taken as a direct reference to the work of Walter Benjamin. While the 'same' is not being presented – here as there – his formulation of the locus of truth in *One Way Street* Benjamin (1979), as that which is to be uprooted from its place in historical continuity is of central significance.

> Truth wants to be startled abruptly, at one stroke from her self-immersion, whether by uproar, music or cries of help.
>
> (95)

The difference here with Walter Benjamin is that the radical possibilities within repetition – those which emerge when repetition is subject to the process that it itself names – remain largely unthought in his work.

8 As has already been indicated *Nachträglichkeit* will play – and is playing – a fundamental role here. What will be suggested is that it sanctions a reformulation of the temporality of interpretation. For additional studies of this term within the context of psychoanalysis (in the work of Freud and Laplanche) see Benjamin (1992a, 1992b) and more generally Forrester (1990: ch. 8). It is of course the work of Jean Laplanche that has brought *Nachträglichkeit* and thus the problem of time in psychoanalysis to the fore. Seen in particular Laplanche (1970, 1988).

9 What is introduced here is the necessity to take up the ontology of the object. It is precisely this task which will be undertaken in terms of developing an ontology of the event. The event emerges as a founding plurality whose constitution structures, while being structured by, irreducibility. The specificity of this complex irreducibility resists any rapid generalisation and therefore calls for another form of philosophical description.

10 Intentional logic needs to be understood as the attempt by the work to enact the project that it has set for itself. The impossibility of an absolute realisation of this project – the bringing to presence of a one-to-one relation between pro-ject and pro-jection, a homological mimesis – is an important area of philosophical inquiry. It is not, however, on its own sufficient for philosophical thinking. There will always be more than this simple negativity; a negativity characterised in mimetic terms since what is involved is a breakdown of the one-to-one.

11 Tradition, while presenting itself as homogeneous, and thus as a unified continuity, will always contain that which allows that homogeneity to be sundered. (Tradition's pathology is indicated thereby.) And yet the importance of the presentation of the homogeneous should not be denied. It is in terms of such a presentation that it becomes possible to describe dominance and thus the inclusion of power within tradition, as well as its functionning as the pre-given, as the gift that is already given. As will be seen it is precisely because of this set up that 'working through' becomes the conditioned response to tradition's self-given identity. What is brought out more generally in any consideration of tradition is the necessity to take up as a philosophical problem the temporality of history. For important advances in this direction see Ermarth (1992), Kiesel (1985), Koselleck (1985) and especially Osborne (1992).

12 While identifying the limits of Bergson his importance lies in the centrality he places on 'becoming'. For a sympathetic reading of Bergson that emphasises, that opens up this aspect of his work see Deleuze (1968). The limit to it however is to be located in the centrality of the image – the necessity to maintain two distinct forms of memory and with it two registers of time where the distinction between them is epistemological in so far as it is posed in terms both of access to what can be known and the types of knowledge possible in each case. For Bergson access to the reality of things is via an intuition which then leads to an analyse. In his own terms this is expressed as

> a placing of oneself (*on s'installe*) . . . by an act of intuition in the concrete flow of duration (*dans l'écoulement concret de la durée*).
> (Bergson 1987:210)

Moving from intuition to analyses involves a translation from one scheme to the next, a translation effected via symbols and images. Even accepting all the attendant problems of the image let alone the viability of self-installing into and then out of duration there is another problem, this time pertaining to the actual formulation of 'duration'. At an earlier point in 'Introduction à la métaphysique', 'duration' (*la durée*) is presented in the following terms:

> Yet there is no state of soul (*d'état d'âme*) that is so simple which does not change at every instant, there is no consciousness without memory, no continuation of a state without addition, at the present feeling (*au sentiment présent*), of the memory (*souvenir*) of passed moment. It is that of which duration consists. The interior duration

is the continuous life of a memory which prolongs the past into the present. . . . Without this survival of the past in the present there will not be duration but only instantiation (*l'instantanéité*).

(200–1)

Absent from this passage is the possibility that addition, the presence of the past in the present could involve a transformation, in the latter case of both elements and in the former of an addition which was itself the work of repetition. In this instance the presence of the past in the present has no effect on the present as such. It is rather that it includes the past, its being 'prolonged' in it. The present therefore is not so much the site of work but a site to be worked over. While this distinction is not absolute the argument advanced throughout this text is that the present is always a worked site and it is precisely this which allows it to be a site to be worked over. Again this will depend upon anoriginal complexity. What this will mean is that presentation will emerge as the pragma, itself a presentation whose complexity is found in its always bearing the mark of the anoriginal. (In regard to the anoriginal see note 14.) In the end what cannot be thought by Bergson is the pragma.

13 The relationship between redemption and repetition is complex in that redemption is a form of repetition. A work can be said to have been redeemed once its place within the continuity of tradition is broken up such that the potential after-life (*nachleben*) inherent in the work is realised. Its realisation will be the work's repetition occurring again for the first time. Here redemption takes up the work of Walter Benjamin, though equally it differentiates itself from that work in that the capacity of the work to have an after-life has to be understood as fundamental to the ontology of the object of interpretation, i.e. the mode of being proper to such a work. The object is an event to the extent that its potential and thus its after-life is being realised. Central to thinking the realisation of a work's after-life will be repetition; a redeemed conception of repetition . Detailing the nature of the object of interpretation – presenting its ontology – opens up a further philosophical task. See Benjamin (1993) for a detailed presentation of this aspect of Walter Benjamin's work.

14 Despite the difficulty of any attempt at a summary that eschews any direct reference to its work, the anoriginal must be given a more precise location. It is not surprising that a significant part of contemporary European philosophy is concerned with the attempt to think an origin that is neither singular nor origin as *arché*. Here this distancing is undertaken in terms of the anoriginal. While the term may lack immediate novelty, that which it is assumed to identify is an ontological complex that cannot be represented because there is no one thing to represent. Fundamental to the formulation of this complex is the presentation of naming in the *Pensées* and the inherent complexity of the monad (even as it is presented by Leibniz in the *Monadology*). The anoriginal is included in the attempt to think original difference as ontological difference.

15 Again this is to indicate that what is taking place is and will remain a

working through. The question that endures, however, is how the ontology of the event is such that it both occasions and sanctions this particular activity. This question must be assumed to be being answered throughout the body of this text. In sum of course it is the work of the anoriginal.

16 The link between affirmation and the avant-garde is discussed in detail in Benjamin (1991). See in particular chapters 1 and 12.

17 The importance of experimentation forms an integral part of Jean-François Lyotard's writings on art and the practice of philosophy. It is clear that these writings have exercised a great deal of influence on this work. The major point of disagreement concerns the place attributed here to the ontological.

18 Nor it must be added is there the complacent acceptance of tradition. Such a complacency would amount to the unfettered presence of the repetition of the 'Same' (another form of this 'Same' is historicism's continuity). There needs to be a different thinking. A possible way towards this end is provided by Nietzsche. In *Ecce Homo* Nietzsche (1969) describes 'The doctrine (*Die Lehre*) of eternal recurrence' as the

unconditional and infinitely repeated circular course of all things (*aller Dinge*).

(273)

The question that immediately arises from this passage is how 'things' are to be understood. What things are these? These are difficult questions since any answer will depend, in the first instance, on the consequences of Nietzsche's critique, advanced in the first part of *The Will to Power* (Nietzsche 1968) of what can be called, though perhaps too loosely, oppositional thinking. For example, value and valueless, theism and atheism do not give the borders of thinking. Nihilism becomes the name for that procedure which is caught in this specular oscillation. Overcoming the position of the 'scholar' means that what needs to be rethought is rethinking. What this will mean here is that the thought that takes place 'beyond', the approach to value that involves a 'transvaluation', is neither destruction nor utopian since it will in the end depend upon a different temporal scheme and with that scheme a different ontology of the name.

19 One of the most significant works comprising part of this rethinking of memory is D.F. Krell's (1990) *Of Memory, Reminiscence, and Writing*. In addition for an important reminder of the ineliminable presence of the political in any discussion of memory see Comay (1990).

20 The importance of the *Difference Essay* (Hegel 1977) is that not only is it the place where 'need' is first formulated as that which provides philosophy with its source, Hegel uses it in order to define his relation to contemporary philosophy. It is of course a definition that works to incorporate that philosophy – philosophy in its diversity – into the larger project of Reason by rethinking and thus reformulating the nature of philosophical diversity. As a text therefore it occupies a pivotal role in the history of difference.

21 For detailed and clearly varied discussions of some of the different

ways of construing the relationship between Hegel and Heidegger see Gillespie (1984), Haar (1985) and Janicaud (1991). What is essential for the position being argued here is that both are philosophers of the absolute (Spirit, Being), with the important consequence that it is the absolute which determines the history of philosophy as the history of philosophy. What figures within it as part of that history depends upon the specific form and conception of the absolute.

22 All references to the work of Descartes are to the Alquié edition (1988). In the case of the *Meditations* the edition established by G. Heffernan (Descartes 1990) has also been consulted. The translations by J.Cottingham *et al.* (Descartes 1985) have been of great assistance and at times have been adopted.

23 In the letter Descartes argues that the Pyrrhonians 'had concluded nothing certain' (II, 14) from their use of doubt but that it was nonetheless possible to make use of it as a philosophical strategy for arriving at certainty.

24 The importance of Fichte's position – as presented in the 'Fundamental Principles' of the *Wissenschaftslehre* – lies in the way in which the positing of X is identical to the being of X and that the possibility of thinking the negation of X (-X) is also given. What is constructed therefore is a logic of identity and negation that will determine the bounds of the possible. As will be suggested in regard to naming, the naming of X can never be identical with X and as such positing is not identical to being. The relationship will always involve greater complexity. The reason why this is the case is due to the ontology of X when X takes on the form of an event.

25 Curley (1978: 53).

26 Wilson (1978: 64–5).

27 There is a prevailing tendency to try and find not just links but actual points of contact between Augustine and Descartes. While there may be certain terminological and argumentative consistencies the projects had radically different aims. In regard to the presence of the epistemological, however, Descartes was concerned to establish the supremacy of science while Augustine was primarily concerned with wisdom (*sapientia*). Indeed he argues in the *De Trinitate* that it is *sapientia* that secures the certainty of *scientia*. The relationship between these two epistemological terms – wisdom and science – is expressed by Gilson (1960) in the following precise way.

> Wisdom needs science in order to achieve its own purpose. Knowledge of the eternal must control and direct the temporal, but it cannot bring its actions to bear upon the temporal unless it knows how that is done. . . . When science is subordinated to wisdom in this way and becomes its tool, it remains distinct from wisdom but now it is good, legitimate, necessary.
>
> (121)

28 The presence of mimesis – present for example in Descartes' suggestion in the *Discourse on Method* that his readers should 'imitate' him – opens up a vast area of inquiry. Mimesis will return with ritual

in that ritual can be understood as the simply mimetic. Sacrifice and destruction can therefore be provisionally understood as part of an attempt to interrupt within the mimetic, causing its repetition (mimesis as a form of repetition) to come to an end. Consequently the philosophical strategies of both Descartes and Heidegger can be taken as attempts to end the mimetic via destruction and sacrifice. (Parenthetically Descartes' own stated evocation of the mimetic in the *Discourse* becomes doubly interesting.) The impossibility of this task does not entail the inevitability of the mimetic but rather demands its being rethought.

29 Arnauld and Nicole (1970: 66).

30 The importance of the dominance of method in the work of both Descartes and Locke has been argued with great precision by Schouls (1980). A different and in the end more consequential work that offers a radical reformulation of, amongst other things, seventeenth- and eighteenth-century thought is Foucault (1966). The importance of Foucault is that his analysis indicates the way in which representation was the dominant structuring force within what he calls the 'classical episteme'. The limit lies in the inability to think the possibility of the disruption of that dominanace as occurring either at the time or subsequently in the work of that period being reworked.

31 Gueroult (1983: 84).

32 While its detail cannot be presented here it is possible to note the demise of the coextensivity at work within the Classical conception of sign, even though it still endures in any positing of a one-to-one relationship either between cause and expression or between signifier and signified. (Philosophical concern with reference, even that concern when reference reaches the point of its own impossibility, Quine's *Word and Object*, remain Classical.) One moment of its demise – the possible end of the Classical sign – is inherent in the move made within psychoanalysis away from the structure of signification proper to hypnosis and towards taking the sign as necessarily overdetermined. Another example concerns the discussion of taste in Huysmans's *A Rebours*. When in contradistinction to the Zolarian universe constituted of *'faits vrais'*, there exists Huysman's counter world in which it is impossible to establish the exact divide between artifice and nature, the project of writing nature, of writing it up, will have vanished. As a pivotal moment in the overcoming of the Classical and the affirmation of complexity Huysman's counter to Zola must be accorded almost the same status as Freud's divergence from Breuer. In both cases from out of the one-to-one there emerges the necessity of the originally overdetermined. The emergence of semantic complexity will of course demand recourse to the ontological in order to account for the perdurance of the breakdown of the 'Classical sign' and recovery of an existent polysemy.

33 *La Logique ou l'art de penser* though known as the *Port Royal Logic* was written by Arnauld and Nicole and went through a number of major rewritings between 1660 and 1683. The edition used here is the fifth edition published in 1683. All references are to the 1970 Flammarion

republishing. While it cannot be argued for here it remains the case
that the significance of this work for an understanding of contemporary Cartesianism is almost inestimable.

34 Kristeva (1981: 159).

35 All references to Pascal which are given in the body of the text are to
the edition established by Lafuma (Pascal 1963).

36 Marin (1975), Léveillé-Mourin (1978) and de Man (1981) are all
concerned with the way in which the problematic of representation
figures in the writings of Pascal.

37 While the theological is central to Pascal's undertaking for a work that
seeks to focus almost exclusively on Pascal as a writer of theology see
Miel (1969). There is an aspect of the *Pensées* that is rarely discussed
under the heading of theology, namely the references throughout the
text to Jews and Judaism. Even Lionel Cohn (1963) in his admirable
and scholarly study 'Pascal et le judaïsme' does not take up what is
reiterated within Pascal's presentation. It is not simply that, for
example, 273 reiterates the necessity for Christianity of its being
refused by the Jews (for an analysis of this necessary inclusion that
excludes in terms of what is called the logic of the synagogue see
Benjamin (1991: ch. 5))

it is their refusal that is the foundation (*le fondement*) of our belief.

It is also the case that along with Augustine and thus calling on a
configuration established by the Christian Bible, Pascal presents the
Jews as blind, blind of necessity. Pascal is concerned with blind Jews,
perhaps even with blinding them. And yet of course maintaining this
figure of the Jew will necessitate recourse to the reciprocity between
sight and truth and in the end the problematic of representation
whose centrality, it will be argued in this interval, is being actively
displaced. The relationship between representation, sight and truth
and their place in the history of philosophical anti-Semitism will need
to be taken up. The tradition of truth as perception proliferating
within different forms cannot escape its own incorporation of power
by the allusion to either objectivity or history.

38 Marin (1975: 119). Whatever reservations are expressed here concerning Marin's work it must be said that *La Critique du discours*
remains the most important study of Pascal published thus far. It
endures as an indispensable point of reference for any work on either
Pascal or the *Port Royal Logic*.

39 All page references to Hegel are given in the body of the text; the page
number to the English edition precedes the German.

40 Schmidt (1988: 79).

41 There is an obvious though nonetheless important distinction between chance and necessity, the latter marking out the place of
prediction. What is involved is the complex process of movement. For
Hegel chance is presented as that which falls outside of relation and
yet that falling is only an appearance. Beyond appearance there is an
already present relation. The movement here therefore is from the
already existent to its becoming present. Allowing chance a chance

will be to allow for the possibility that the movement could take place in a different direction. Here chance would be an occurrence that moved into relation. It is possible to escape the confines of constraint and yet a constraint need not give the relation as already existing. (For constraint see Benjamin (1992c).) The coming into relation rehearses in another form the chance effect and in so doing is itself already implicated in a philosophical thinking of the avant-garde.

42 In other words what is involved here is not Hegel's actual discussion of time as it appears in the second part of the *Encyclopedia* but the implicit temporality at work in the structuring of the positions being presented here; the time in the formulation.

43 One of the most articulate formulations of a theory of the remainder is found in the work of Jean-Jacques Lecercle. See in particular Lecercle (1991: 61–95).

44 One obvious example of such a self-referential unity is the Platonic form. It enters into relation via the process of 'participation'. The consequence and hence the function of the form's participation is providing the particular with its identity. It can have no identity outside of that which is provided by the 'presence' (παρουσία) in it of the form. It is for example the participation in it of the form of Beauty that makes a particular vase beautiful. This point is made with great precision by Plato in the *Phaedo* 100c 4–6.

> whatever else is beautiful except for Beauty itself (αὐτὸ τὸ καλόη) is beautiful for no other reason than because it partakes (μετεχει) of that Beauty.

The question that arises here, and it is a question that could in terms of the structure it seeks to elucidate be correctly described as dominating the dialogues, is, what is Beauty? The task of answering this question does not lie in providing instance or examples but Beauty itself; Beauty understood as a self-referential unity.

45 While it is a task whose difficulty means that all that can be done here is allude to the issues, it remains the case that Novalis's stated position in the *Fichte-Studien* (Novalis 1978) that philosophy is 'originally a feeling' (*ist ursprünglich ein Gefühl*) (18) needs to be taken as a proposition that already works to distance the logic of identity.

46 Leibniz (1875–90). All references are to this edition and are cited in the text by volume number followed by page number.

47 There will always be a problem of philosophical vocabulary. The recognition of the problem prompts different responses. Here rather than seek the false clarity of definitions the way suggested by Nietzsche amongst others will be adopted. It is simply to recognise that there is no other language than the one philosophy already has. As such what is essential is the redemption of certain terms and ways of phrasing. A redemption that lends itself to the further description of invention. While this is a semantic point, its importance is that it can function as a *mise-en-abyme* for the work itself in so far as this semantic possibility can only be realised by the retention of the effective presence of a certain ontology of the name, an ontology that construes

the name as an event, the name as the site of conflict naming. Names allow for their own reworking and consequently invention and experimentation in recognising the hold of constraint but in displacing its dominance hold open by working through the philosophical.

48 The problem of contemporary philosophy's relation to Platonism was identified by Nietzsche in the description of his own philosophy as an 'inverted Platonism'. The problem is how the inverting or overturning is to be understood. Equally what is also raised is the possibility of retrieving that which was initially articulated within Platonism and thus lost to it. Becoming, as will be argued throughout, is not the other side of Being. However, the response cannot be destruction in either the Cartesian or the Heideggerian sense. Abeyance becomes another destructive possibility; a possibility thought within repetition.

49 The difficulty of *Monadology* 14 is clear. 'Perception' is formulated as a representation. (The problem is attempting to distinguish between the activity and and passivity of perception.)

> The passing state (*L'état passager*) which envelops and *represents* a multitude in unity or in the simple substance is nothing other than perception.

(my emphasis)

50 Raising even in an allusion Heraclitus' formulation of the 'always flowing' (ῥέοη ἀεί) is to raise a fundamental philosophical problem. In sum what is involved is how the relationship between being and becoming is to be understood. Within the Heraclitean context the problem hinges on how the 'always' (ἀεί) is to be interpreted. Any answer to this question must begin with the problem of how to understand the difference between the Platonic ἀεί (e.g. *Cratylus* 439d 5) and the Heraclitean one. A way in to taking up the specificity of the problem in Heraclitus would be to take up the description of fire in Fragment 30 as that which is ἀείζωον (ever-living). Within the fragment fire while 'ever-living' involves both 'kinderling' and 'going out'. In other words it allows for differing presentations, and thus change within the 'always'. Consequently in contradistinction to the Platonic construal in which the 'always' demands the continuity of self-identity, Heraclitus allows for another formulation of identity. While it cannot be explored here the key to it is provided by the claim that everything takes place 'in relation to conflict' (κατ' ἔριν). The primordiality and centrality of conflict opens up the necessity to think the relation between 'justice' and ontology (cf. Fragment 80). In part this will be the theme of *The Politics of Judgement*.

51 A preliminary version of the following engagement with Heidegger and a tentative elaboration of the logic of sacrifice was presented at 'L'ethique du don: Rencontre en hommage à Jacques Derrida', a conference held at the Abbaye Royaumont in December 1990. Comments made by participants at that encounter are gratefully acknowledged.

52 The treatment of the gift and of sacrifice throughout this section is intended to engage with the work of Adorno, Derrida and Bataille.

Derrida's recent *Donner le temps* (Derrida 1991) is essential for any attempt to take up the gift in a systematic way. Within this current undertaking some formulations – indeed the attempt to challenge the possibility of a pure giving – are intended to take up Derrida's own specific formulations.

53   Here rather than offering a synoptic reading of Heidegger, one text has in the main been made to bear the proper name. And thus rather than Heidegger being the question what is being questioned is the strategy of what has been termed thinking *'without'* as it is present in *Time and Being*. This is the Heidegger in question. Page references to Heidegger's works are given in the body of the text. The details of the editions used are in the bibliography. In the case of *Time and Being* the first page reference is to the English edition and the second is to the German. Because of the importance that is often attached to location of works within Heidegger's oeuvre the first publication dates have been included in the text. For a different discussion of sacrifice in Heidegger's work, a discussion that concentrates on Heidegger's own use of the term, see Sallis (1990: ch. 6). What has been undertaken here is the attempt to elucidate an implicit logic of sacrifice which, clearly, is never named as such.

54   The most remarkable philosophical treatment of sacrifice to date is 'L'insacrifiable' by Jean-Luc Nancy (1990). It is hoped that a return can be made to this text if only to try and untangle why its attempted rescue of Heidegger is in the end unsuccessful. Part of the reason will be the necessity for Heidegger's project of sacrifice. The unstated presence of destruction demands the implicit necessity of sacrifice. In *Time and Being* one cannot be thought without the other.

55   Part of the analysis of the impossibility of thinking 'without' derives from taking up – and it is a taking that may have dealt harshly with what was taken – the force of Derrida's analysis of *'sans dette'* in 'Pas' (Derrida 1986a). The possibility of being *'sans dette'* cannot escape the necessity of *'s'en dette'*. This aspect of Derrida's 'Pas' can be taken as indicating why trying to do without will always be inextricably connected – even in the formulation of the project – to a doing with. It is not that the analysis here has been taken further, it has only been taken in a different direction.

56   For the most part the term *Ereignis* has been left untranslated. It is unclear what is gained from adopting the rendering 'event of appropriation'. Throughout this section *Ereignis* has of course been translated time and again. For a more conventional reading of *Time and Being* and in particular the *Ereignis* see White (1985: ch. 5).

57   The term 'epochal present' is intended to provide a way of taking up the conception of the present within the formulation of the philosophical task. The intended way is philosophical. Hegel's presentation of the contemporary both forms and informs his conception of the philosophical task. Heidegger's construal of the present as 'indifferent to the question of Being' plays a structuring role in the task given to thinking. There are of course many other examples. In each instance what is involved is a construal of the present that determines the

philosophical task. The present in these instances is not to be taken as simply historical because of this functioning reciprocity. In order to identify it here the term 'epochal present' has been used. As such it may provide a way in to taking up the present as a philosophical problem.

58 The development of reconciliation in this text has been greatly influenced by Comay (1990). A more detailed attempt to trace some of the consequences of a reconciliation to irreconcilablity is found in Benjamin (1991: ch. 8; 1993).

59 This is more complex than it appears because what is still opened up as a possibility is that what is marked out – designated – is also potentially secularised and in being secularised is able to open up the future.

60 While the presentations of the language of sight in Descartes and Heidegger are not straightforwardly physiological and are intended to be figurative they raise, nonetheless, the history of the complex interplay between sight, truth, blindness and error/sin. These implications cannot be avoided. Nor moreover can the obvious mapping onto the structuring of Christianity and with it Christian anti-Semitism of this complex construal.

61 The problem posed by the literal and figural is in part to do with its self-presentation as an either/or. What needs to be remembered is not only their identity-sustaining symbiosis but that it entails that the displacing of one necessarily involves the displacing of the other. This position has been argued for in Benjamin (1989: ch. 1).

62 Freud (1975a: vol. 12). The German text is found in Freud (1975b). All page references will be given in the text; the English page number is followed by the German.

63 Lyotard (1988b). All page references are in the text. In relation to Lyotard's work it should be remembered that he has deployed and made use of the process of *Nachträglichkeit* in Lyotard (1988a). Again the difference is the status attributed to ontology and therefore to the event.

64 What is involved here is the attempt to differentiate the temporal structure of the sublime from claims made about the overall importance of sublimity. This position has been argued for in greater detail in Benjamin (1991: ch. 7).

65 Both these terms '*survivre*' and '*nachleben*' raise the question of how what it is that survives or has an after-life facilitates this state of affairs. While the term '*nachleben*' relates to the work of Walter Benjamin, 'living on' is a theme that has been explicitly taken up by Jacques Derrida. See Derrida (1986b). Neither Walter Benjamin nor Derrida are concerned with the above mentioned question.

66 For an important and influential interpretation of the *Project* see Laplanche (1970). The English text is in Freud (1975a: vol. 1). The German text is in Freud (1950).

67 Again the point being made in this instance takes up the themes already introduced in note 50. A way of undertaking the distancing of the Platonic would be to trace the implications and assumptions behind the presentation of Heraclitean positions in the *Theaetetus*. Here the role played by Theodorus is central.

Bibliography

Adorno, T. and Horkheimer, M. (1986) *Dialectic of Enlightenment*, trans. J. Cumming, Verso Books, London.

Arnauld, A. and Nicole, P. (1970) *La Logique ou l'art de penser*, Flammarion, Paris.

Bataille, G. (1967) *La Part maudite*, Les Editions de Minuit, Paris.

Benjamin, A. (1989) *Translation and the Nature of Philosophy*, Routledge, London.

Benjamin, A. (1991) *Art, Mimesis and the Avant-Garde*, Routledge, London.

Benjamin, A. (1992a) 'Translating Origins: Psychoanalysis and Philosophy', in L. Venuti (ed.) *Rethinking Translation*, Routledge, London.

Benjamin, A. (1992b) 'The Unconscious: Structuring as a Translation', in J. Fletcher and M. Stanton (eds) *Jean Laplanche: Seduction, Translation, Drives*, ICA, London.

Benjamin, A. (1992c) 'Architecture et contrainte', *Chimeres* 17.

Benjamin, A. (1993) 'Time and Task: Benjamin and Heidegger Showing the Present', in A. Benjamin and P. Osborne (eds) *Walter Benjamin's Philosophy (Destruction and Experience)*, Routledge, London.

Benjamin, W. (1979) *One Way Street*, Verso Books, London.

Bergson, H. (1987) *La Pensée et le mouvant*, Presses Universitaires de France, Paris.

Burkert, W. (1983) *Homo Necans*, trans. P. Bing, University of California Press, Berkeley.

Caygill, H. (1989) *Art of Judgement*, Blackwell, Oxford.

Cohn, L. (1963) 'Pascal et le judaïsme', *Chroniques de Port-Royal* 11-14.

Comay, R. (1990) 'Redeeming Revenge: Nietzsche, Benjamin, Heidegger, and the Politics of Memory', in C. Koelb (ed.) *Nietzsche as Postmodernist*, State University of New York Press, Albany.

Critchley, S. (1992). 'The Problem of Closure in Derrida' (Part Two), *Journal of the British Society for Phenomenology* 23 (2).

Curley, E. (1978) *Descartes Against the Skeptics*, Blackwell, Oxford.

Deleuze, G. (1968) *Le Bergonisme*, Presses Universitaires de France, Paris.

Derrida, J. (1986a) 'Pas', in his *Parages*, Galilée, Paris.

Derrida, J. (1986b) 'Survivre', in his *Parages*, Galilée, Paris.

Derrida, J. (1991) *Donner le temps*, Galilée, Paris.

Descartes, R. (1985) *The Philosophical Writings of Descartes*, vols 1 and 2, ed. and trans. J. Cottingham *et al.*, Cambridge University Press, Cambridge.

Descartes, R. (1988) *Oeuvres philosophiques*, vols 1–111, ed. de F. Alquié, Garnier, Paris.

Descartes, R. (1990) *Meditationes de primas Philosophia/Meditations on First Philosophy. A Bilingual Edition*, ed. and trans. G. Heffernan, University of Notre Dame Press, Notre Dame.

Descombes, V. (1991) 'The Principle of Determination', *Thesis Eleven* 29.

Ermarth, E. (1992) *Sequel to History*, Princeton University Press, Princeton.

Forrester, J. (1990) *The Seductions of Psychoanalysis*, Cambridge University Press, Cambridge.

Foucault, M. (1966) *Les Mots et les choses*, Gallimard, Paris.

Freud, S. (1950) *Aus den Anfängen der Psychoanalyse*, Imago, London.

Freud, S. (1975a) *The Standard Edition of the Complete Psychological Works*, Hogarth Press, London.

Freud, S. (1975b) *Schriften zur Behandlungstechnik*, S. Fischer Verlag, Frankfurt.

Gasché, R. (1986) *The Taint of the Mirror*, Harvard University Press, Cambridge.

Gillespie, M. (1984) *Hegel, Heidegger and the Ground of History*, University of Chicago Press, Chicago.

Gilson, E. (1960) *The Christian Philosophy of St Augustine*, trans. L.E.M. Lynch, Random House, New York, and Gollancz, London (1961).

Gueroult, M. (1983) *Dianómatique*, vol.1, Aubier Montaigne, Paris.

Haar, M. (1985) *Le Chant de la terre*, L'Herne, Paris.

Hegel, G. (1970) *Werke in 20 Bänden*, ed. E. Moldenhauer and K. Michel, Suhrkamp, Frankfurt.

Hegel, G. (1977) *The Difference Between Fichte's and Schelling's System of Philosophy*, ed. H. Harris and W. Cerf, State University of New York Press, Albany.

Hegel, G. (1978) *Logic*, trans. W. Wallace, Oxford University Press, Oxford.

Heidegger, M. (1958) *The Question of Being*, trans. W. Kluback and J. Wilde, Twayne, New York.

Heidegger, M. (1972) *Zur Sache des Denkens*, Niemeyer, Tübingen

Heidegger, M. (1988) *On Time and Being*, trans. J. Stambaugh, Harper, New York.

Janicaud, D. (1991) *A nouveau la philosophie*, Albin Michel, Paris.

Kiesel, T. (1985) 'The Happening of Tradition: The Hermeneutics of Gadamer and Heidegger', in R.Hollinger (ed.) *Hermeneutics and Praxis*, University of Notre Dame Press, Notre Dame.

Koselleck, R. (1985) *Futures Past*, trans. K. Tribe, MIT Press, Cambridge.

Krell, D. (1990) *Of Memory, Reminiscence, and Writing*, Indiana University Press, Bloomington.

Kristeva, J. (1981) *Le Langage, cet inconnu*, Editions du Seuil, Paris.

Laplanche, J. (1970) *Vie et mort en psychanalyse*, Flammarion, Paris.

Laplanche, J. (1988) 'Temporalité et traduction: Pour une remise au travail de la philosophie du temps', *Psychanalyse à l'université* 53.

Lecercle, J. J. (1991) *The Violence of Language*, Routledge, London.

Leibniz, G. (1875-90) *Die Philosophischen Schriften*, ed. C. Gerhardt, Berlin.

Léveillé-Mourin, G. (1978) *Le Langage chrétien, antichrétien de la transcendance: Pascal-Nietzsche*, Vrin, Paris.

Lyotard, J. F. (1988a) *Heidegger et 'les juifs'*, Galilée, Paris.

Lyotard, J. F. (1988b) 'Réécrire la modernité', in his *L'Inhumain*, Galilée, Paris.

Lyotard, J. F. (1991) *Leçons sur l'analytique du sublime*, Galilée, Paris.

de Man, P. (1981) 'Pascal's Allegory of Persuasion', in S. Greenblat (ed.) *Allegory and Representation*, Johns Hopkins University Press, Baltimore.

Marin, L. (1975) *La Critique du discours*, Les éditions de minuit, Paris.

Miel, J. (1969) *Pascal and Theology*, Johns Hopkins University Press, Baltimore.

Nancy, J. L. (1990) 'L'insacrifiable', in his *Une pensée finie*, Galilée, Paris.

Nietzsche, F. (1968) *The Will to Power*, trans. W. Kaufman and R. Hollingdale, Vintage Books, New York.

Nietzsche, F. (1969) *Ecce Homo*, trans. W. Kaufman, Vintage Books, New York.

Novalis (1978) *Werke,* vol. 2. Carl Hanser Verlag, Germany.

Osborne, P. (1992) 'Modernity is a Qualitative, not a Chronological Category', *New Left Review* 192 (March/April).

Pascal, B. (1963) *Oeuvres complètes*, ed. L. Lafuma, Editions du Seuil, Paris.

Rajchman, J. (1990) *Philosophical Events: Essays of the Eighties*, Columbia University Press, New York.

Sallis, J. (1990) *Echoes. After Heidegger*, Indiana University Press, Bloomington.

Schmidt, D. (1988) *The Ubiquity of the Finite*, MIT Press, Cambridge.

Schouls, P. (1980) *The Imposition of Method*, Oxford University Press, Oxford.

White, D. (1985) *Logic and Ontology in Heidegger*, Ohio State University Press, Columbus.

Wilson, M. (1978) *Descartes*, Routledge, London.

Index

actative 97
Adorno, T. 202
ad-venture 7, 30
after-life 180, 189, 196
alterity 19, 57, 133
anew 16, 19, 20, 25, 26, 41, 43, 148, 189, 190, 191
anoriginal 6, 10, 24, 28, 59, 61, 63, 75, 76, 78, 79, 92, 108, 110, 112, 118, 122, 124, 128, 129, 196
Aristotle 115
Arnauld and Nicole 56, 62, 199
association 5
Augustine 198, 200; *De Trinitate* 198

Bataille, G. 202
beginning 1, 2, 3, 6, 30, 31, 83, 99, 129, 193
Benjamin, W. 23, 194, 196, 204; *One Way Street* 194
Bergson, H. 22, 195
body 33, 35, 36, 40, 46–8, 52
Breuer, J. 169, 173, 199

Caygill, H. 193
chance 5, 87, 89, 90, 93, 96–8, 101, 102, 105, 109, 159, 194, 200, 201
Clarke 114
Cohn, L. 200
Comay, R. 197, 204
communication 13
community 13, 188, 193
complexity 10, 21, 22, 24, 26, 28, 29, 32, 57, 61, 75, 78, 79, 83, 116, 127, 186, 191, 196

conflict 10, 61, 64, 65, 69, 72, 81, 82, 91, 112, 182, 185, 186, 188
conflict naming 61–82, 110, 112, 118, 184–92, 202
contemporary 1, 45, 205
continuity 12, 13, 14, 16, 27, 41, 51, 61, 78, 84, 87, 88, 184
Curley, E.M. *Descartes Against the Skeptics* 38–42, 198

dating 17
deconstruction 17
Deleuze, G. 195
Derrida, J. 193; *Donner le temps* 202; *Pas* 203
Descartes 4, 21, 30, 34–60, 73, 76, 77, 83, 84, 110, 111, 123, 136, 138, 144, 204; *Discourse on Method* 35, 38, 54, 56, 198, 199; *Meditations* 34–42, 198; *Passions of the Soul* 36, 48, 50; *Principles of Philosophy* 35, 39, 56; *La Récherche de la vérité* 76–7
destruction 1, 4, 20, 33, 37, 38, 40, 42, 44–6, 50–3, 58, 60, 61, 63, 67, 74, 76, 80, 119, 134–6, 144, 148, 156, 165, 176, 182, 184, 187, 197, 199, 202, 203
difference 7, 20, 23–6, 29, 34, 43, 70, 86, 92, 96, 109
diremption 5, 6, 28, 31, 34, 85, 92, 94–6, 100, 106–8, 111, 118, 126
disassociation 5, 11
distance 9, 34, 63, 65–6, 68, 72–3, 75, 81, 115

distancing 2, 4, 14, 63, 67, 70, 75, 76, 11, 196
dualism 46

epistemology 2, 36–42, 63, 67, 112
Ereignis 140, 141, 149–56, 160, 162, 203
Ermarth, E. 195
eternal recurrence 197
eternity 163–4
event 1, 2, 6, 7, 14–21, 24–7, 29, 30, 33, 47, 53, 59–61, 73, 82, 93, 94, 102, 108, 109, 111, 122, 125, 126, 130, 157, 186, 189–94, 196, 197, 202

Fichte 86, 198; *The Science of Knowledge* 36
forgetting 10, 20, 29, 33, 50, 52, 58, 61, 137, 144, 151, 154, 156, 165, 166
Foucault, M. 199
foundationalism 2, 4
Freud, S. 26, 178, 180, 183, 194, 199, 204; *Constructions in Analysis* 172, 173; *Project for a Scientific Psychology* 172, 181; *Remembering, Repeating and Working Through* 169–71, 174–7

Gasché, R. 193
Gassendi 43
gift 10, 11, 26, 27, 38, 42, 45, 51, 109, 129–33, 136–8, 190, 195, 202, 203
Gillespie, M. 198
Gilson, E. 198
Gueroult, M. 60, 199

Haar, M. 198
harmony 6–8, 86
Hegel 5–9, 21, 32, 33, 60, 83–11, 134, 179, 193, 194, 197, 200, 203; *Aesthetics* 111; *Difference Essay* 7, 31, 34, 84, 85, 90, 101, 194, 197; *Encyclopedia* 201; *The Philosophy of Nature* 94; *The Philosophy of Right* 111; *Shorter Logic* 6, 34, 84, 96–101, 115

Heidegger 4, 11, 32, 38, 60, 123, 135–65, 198, 199, 204; *Being and Time* 135, 139; *On the Essence of Truth* 141; *The Question of Being* 135, 136, 138, 166; *Time and Being* 134, 136, 140, 142–52, 155, 158, 162, 166, 203; *What is Philosophy?* 135
Heraclitus 193, 202
history 13, 15, 16, 22, 25, 30, 31, 34, 41, 84, 105, 195,
homology 6, 8, 12, 29, 73
Huysmans, J.K.: *A Rebours* 199
hypnosis 169–70

identity 3, 5, 7, 13, 19, 20, 23–5, 31, 33, 47, 56, 86, 89, 112, 117, 191, 198, 201, 202
inauguration 4, 53, 58
intentionality 23
interpretation 14, 16–19, 23–5, 58, 70, 83, 126, 127, 185, 194
irreducibility 14, 15, 18, 21, 24, 26, 61, 131, 190, 194

Janicaud, D. 198
Judaism 200
judgement 1, 2, 12, 15, 54–60, 63, 66, 68, 78, 81, 82, 91, 110, 112, 113, 140, 186, 188, 193
Jünger 136
justice 188, 202

Kant 193; *Third Critique* 178
Kenny, A. 39, 42
Kiesel, T. 195
Koselleck, R. 195
Krell, D. 197
Kristeva, J. 62, 200

Laplanche J. 194, 204
Lecercle, J.J. 201
Leibniz, G.W. 15, 60, 61, 113–28, 185, 201; *Monadology* 115, 118, 119, 122, 124, 196, 202; *New Essays on Human Understanding* 117
Léveillé-Mourin, G. 200
Locke, J. 56, 199

Lyotard, J.F 193, 197, 204;
  Rewriting Modernity 178–9

de Man, P. 200
Marin, L. 200; *La critique du
  discours* 68–71, 74, 80
memory 29, 30, 33, 46, 49–51, 76,
  137, 144, 157, 170, 181
Miel, J. 200
mimesis 195, 198, 199
modernity 45, 60
monad 15, 61, 113, 114, 116, 118,
  119, 120–2, 125, 128, 185, 191,
  196

Nachträglichkeit 16, 24, 26, 58, 169,
  172, 173, 181–3, 187, 189, 190,
  194, 204
name 9, 10, 18, 21, 33, 59–83, 111,
  127, 183–8, 192, 197, 202
naming 9, 10, 21, 28, 31–3, 43, 53,
  58, 60–83, 105, 107, 110–12, 127,
  145, 176, 184, 185, 196, 198
Nancy, J.L. 203
need 83–6, 91, 92, 95–100, 106,
  107, 197
new, the 11–28, 119
Newton, I. 113, 114
Nietzsche, F. 201, 202; *Ecce
  Homo* 197; *The Will to Power* 197
Novalis: *Fichte-Studien* 111, 201

ontological difference 15, 24, 122,
  142, 185, 186, 196
ontological plurality 123–6
ontologico-temporal 18, 78, 81, 93,
  115, 119, 158, 161, 186, 191, 192
ontology 2, 4, 11, 14–19, 23, 24,
  26, 29, 36, 45, 53, 55, 58–62, 67,
  73–7, 81, 122, 126, 130, 159, 162,
  196
Osborne P. 195

paradox 19–25, 120, 168
Pascal, B. 60, 64–82, 124; *De
  l'esprit géometrique* 64;
  Pensées 64, 65, 196, 200
Plato: *Cratylus* 202; *Phaedo* 201;
  Theaetetus 204

plurality 18, 24, 29, 63, 73, 74, 76,
  78, 81, 92, 93, 97, 108–12, 115,
  121, 123
poetry 166–7
pragma 20, 24, 25, 27, 59, 71, 72,
  82, 88, 108–13, 112, 130, 149,
  163, 176, 181, 186, 191, 196
pragma-tic 185–6
presentation 4–9, 12–14, 28–9, 33,
  34, 59, 62, 63, 65, 71, 75, 76,
  80–2, 88, 108, 111, 187, 202

question 31, 32
Quine: *Word and Object* 199

recognition 4, 7, 19, 31, 179
reconciliation 175, 180, 204
redemption 4, 23, 53, 58, 192, 196,
  201
refusal 10, 11, 42, 45
Reinhold 7, 86, 87, 104
relation 1, 5, 11–28, 52–4, 63, 67,
  69, 72, 92, 93, 108–12, 115, 118,
  127, 159, 165, 200, 201
relativism 67, 68, 81
remembering 50–2, 60, 170–80
renewal 2, 16, 18
repetition 1, 2, 11, 12, 14, 16,
  19–28, 30, 37, 42–6, 49, 52–63,
  72–4, 77, 78, 81, 83, 88, 91,
  126–30, 165, 166, 168, 174, 180,
  186, 189, 190, 192, 194, 196, 199,
  202
representation 2, 8, 29, 36, 40, 41,
  47, 54–81, 91, 111, 112, 127, 200
responsibility 78, 175
reworking 1–4, 11–17, 22–6, 28,
  30, 33, 52, 53, 57, 61, 63, 68, 71,
  83, 88, 109, 110, 112, 116, 126,
  129, 148, 165, 181, 186, 188–92,
  202
ritual 138, 143, 144, 147, 148, 154,
  156, 198, 199

sacrifice 133, 136–48, 154, 156,
  165–8, 175, 180, 184, 199, 202,
  203
Sallis, J. 203
Same, the 1, 18, 19, 22, 27, 29, 42,

45, 56, 57, 60, 70–3, 78, 82, 109,
121, 138, 166, 169, 181, 190, 197
Schelling, F.W.J 86
signature 17, 18
signification 62, 65, 67, 71, 81, 142
singular 7, 12, 15, 16, 18, 20–2, 28,
31, 44, 63, 96, 100, 107, 155
singularity 11, 12, 15–21, 28, 32,
44, 59, 76, 78, 82, 84, 94–6,
107–10, 134, 148, 154, 159, 165,
194
Socrates 36, 37
space 113–19, 125
spacing 12, 15, 34, 59, 66, 73, 75,
81, 92–5, 108, 110, 111,
116–21, 126, 127, 185
spatiality 15, 93, 117

task 2, 6, 9, 23, 30, 85, 158, 159,
160, 165, 203
temporality 7, 11, 13–17, 21, 26,
38, 45, 53, 57, 74, 87, 89, 93, 110,

114, 118, 194
time 7, 12–23, 34, 40, 60, 63, 65–8,
72, 74, 77, 81, 87–9, 93, 104, 109,
110, 114–22, 157, 159, 163, 164
trace 12
tradition 1, 10–30, 33, 38, 42, 43,
45, 46, 61, 72, 109, 110, 127, 178,
195, 197
tragedy 193
translation 165, 177, 179, 180,
182–90, 195

White, D. 203
Wilson, M.D.: *Descartes* 39, 42, 198
work 1, 2, 8, 10, 12, 13, 15, 21–7,
30, 33, 60, 78, 116, 126, 165, 166,
168, 188
working through 170, 173, 175,
177–83, 189, 190, 194, 195, 197

Zola, E. 199